The Novel as Family Romance

Rembrandt, *Adam and Eve*

The Novel as Family Romance

LANGUAGE, GENDER, AND AUTHORITY

FROM FIELDING TO JOYCE

Christine van Boheemen

Cornell University Press

ITHACA AND LONDON

Cornell University Press gratefully acknowledges
a grant from the Andrew W. Mellon Foundation
that aided in bringing this book to publication.

First published 1987 by Cornell University Press.

International Standard Book Number 0-8014-1928-X
Library of Congress Catalog Card Number 87-47553
Printed in the United States of America
*Librarians: Library of Congress cataloging information
appears on the last page of the book.*

*The paper in this book is acid-free and meets the guidelines for
permanence and durability of the Committee on Production Guidelines
for Book Longevity of the Council on Library Resources.*

For Saskia, Melchert, and Paul

Contents

Preface

In this book I examine the English novel over the last three centuries, with primary focus on Fielding's *Tom Jones,* Dickens's *Bleak House,* and Joyce's *Ulysses.* The term "family romance" suggests the two major perspectives that are at work here.

Originally Freud's label for a person's neurotic fantasy about his or her origins in which parentage was in some way elevated or improved upon, "family romance" has gained general currency among literary and critical theorists. Their use of it is founded on the realization that Freud's insight into the constructed nature of the stories his patients told is not limited to fantasy, but applies in some degree to all stories that designate identity in terms of a relation to origin—be the origin literary, philosophical, sociological, religious, or historical. I am suggesting, in the first place, then, that in this book I view the genre as typically presenting a story about the transcendent importance of humanity's relation to origins.

I am also pointing to this work's participation in the tradition of psychoanalytic literary criticism. My readings demonstrate the influence of Derrida, Lacan, and Foucault, from whom, for all their differences, I have learned a way of thinking—a way of looking at phenomena, ideas, and structures which grasps these in terms of relations and functions, rather than in terms of predetermined identities and essences. Thus this book discusses the function of the novel as a confirming mirror of subjectivity and analyzes how that function is produced and maintained by the systematic interrelationship of contemporary ideas about origin, identity, gender, and language.

Though the book was written in 1984–1985, its intellectual debts are much older. John McNamara of the University of Houston introduced me to French structuralism in 1973. Rice University's English Department proved astonishingly hospitable to a foreign female graduate student—married and the mother of two. In the summers of 1978 and 1981 the schools of Criticism and Theory at the University of California at Irvine and at Northwestern University provided me with an opportunity to learn from Geoffrey Hartman, Fredric Jameson, Joseph Riddel, and Hayden White.

I am grateful to many friends and colleagues—including Mieke Bal, Joris Duytschaever, Geert Lernout, Anneke and Jan van Luxemburg, Fritz Senn, Robin Smith, and Willem Weststeijn—who helped me to articulate my ideas, read parts of the manuscript, or assisted in the search for bibliographical references.

The Netherlands Institute for Advanced Study in the Humanities and Social Sciences at Wassenaar provided a congenial place to revise the manuscript in 1985–1986. Special thanks are owed to its library staff, which worked untiringly to locate books and periodicals that usually proved unavailable in the Netherlands.

I am grateful to the Faculty of Letters of the University of Leiden for making it possible for me to attend conventions and symposia of the International James Joyce Foundation, where I have had the opportunity to test—often to defend—the ideas in this book in informal discussions. The support and friendship of foundation members have been most valuable, and I especially profited from a difference of opinion with Christine Froula, which we have continued to debate over the years.

Acknowledgment is also due to the Forum on Psychiatry and the Humanities of the Washington School of Psychiatry and to Yale University Press for permission to draw on my " 'The Universe Makes an Indifferent Parent': *Bleak House* and the Victorian Family Romance," published in *Interpreting Lacan,* ed. Joseph H. Smith and William Kerrigan, Psychiatry and the Humanities 6 (New Haven: Yale Univ. Press, 1983), pp. 225–59. It appears in

slightly modified form as Chapter 5 of this book. Thanks also to
the Porter Institute for Poetics and Semiotics in Tel Aviv for permission to use, in abbreviated and modified form, "The Semiotics
of Plot: Towards a Typology of Fictions," which appeared in
Poetics Today 3, 4 (1982), 89–97.

CHRISTINE VAN BOHEEMEN

Wassenaar

The Novel as Family Romance

Introduction

This book on the English novel, engendered by Continental European theory, was conceived where it is published, in the United States, and born in the Netherlands. The increasing sophistication of the intellectual exchange between Europe and the United States not only makes an intercontinental project of this kind possible, it also alerts us to the possible presence of culture-related interpretive axioms and biases that may serve to safeguard interpretive traditions. To clarify the intellectual perspective from which this contribution to Anglo-American scholarship on the English novel arose, as well as its limits and limitations, I think it wise to begin my discussion with an account of critical method and theoretical perspective. Because my intellectual stance is itself the product of the shifting configuration of the structure of subjectivity which will be the focus of my analysis, this introductory account necessarily becomes a compressed summary of the content of the book.

Let me begin by pointing to an aspect of the complex problem implicit in my argument: the interrelationship of authority and gender. In the "Circe" chapter of *Ulysses,* meek Leopold Bloom, shaking a girl by her shoulders, commands: "Speak, you! Are you struck dumb? You are the link between nations and generations. Speak, woman, sacred lifegiver!" (xv, 4647–49).[1] "Circe" may be called the "unconscious" of *Ulysses.* Let us, for the moment, go

[1]James Joyce, *Ulysses: A Critical and Synoptic Edition,* ed. Hans W. Gabler (New York: Garland, 1984). My citations use roman numerals for each separate episode of the novel and arabic numerals for the line number(s).

I

along with this characterization and assume that Bloom's words inadvertently reveal the underlying attitude toward authority of both the speaker and the text in which Bloom is made to act. Woman is called "sacred lifegiver," berated for her refusal to speak, and commanded to do so because as "the link between nations and generations" she holds the secret to the mystery of death—hence eternal life. Here the idea of woman as image of nature and as means of passage of the flesh of masculine identity— traditional in Western texts—has changed to take on a transcendent, mythic power, that of giving life. It is a notion in marked contrast to the orthodox Christian view, which reserved absolute origination and authority to the masculine principle, God the Father. Rather than the spiritual principle, the mind, or the divine word of God, which institutes the alpha and omega of history, Leopold Bloom's words project as the be-all and end-all material nature and biological reproduction in the figure of woman; and the desire of both Bloom and *Ulysses* is to make this woman speak, to hear the voice of origin.

This brief fragment from *Ulysses* raises a cluster of extremely important questions that are central not only to Western literature, philosophy, and theology but equally to all forms of social and intellectual organization. How can the conceptualization of origin, traditionally personified as masculine, become feminine? What does the change signify with regard to the history of authority and legitimation, the notion of subjectivity? Has the idea of woman's otherness become the emblem of Modernity?[2] Why the necessity

[2]One of the current preoccupations of literary theory is the identification of the difference(s) between modernism and postmodernism (or poststructuralism) as epochs in literary history and as styles of writing and thought. Many different definitions exist, often using the difference between *Ulysses* and *Finnegans Wake* as the boundary marker. Whether such differentiation is inspired by a genuine need for critical insight or is just academic theorizing, the net result is often either confusing or reductive of a complex and multifaceted phenomenon. In this book I shall use the terms *Modern, postmodern,* and *poststructuralist* without a circumscribed dictionary meaning, since I believe that the view and evaluation of a text and a period are not objective but determined by the perspective from which we speak. Thus Joyce's *Ulysses* may be regarded as modern or postmodern depending on our readerly strategies. Even Flaubert and Sterne are mentioned in connection with postmodernism. I shall use the term *Modern(ity)* to indicate that inclusive tradition of thought and writing which critically evaluates the specularity of Western metaphysics.

for the metaphor of gender? Moreover, what are the implications for women writing and speaking in a Modern epoch?

I might have found an explanation in recent psychoanalytic theory. The injunction "Speak, woman, sacred lifegiver" could be taken as the expression of womb envy—the repressed masculine rage at exclusion from the mysterious process of gestation. Psychoanalysis, however, offers a static and universalizing explanation that does not account for historical change. It fails to help us understand the how and why of Joyce's denotation of origin and authority as feminine otherness, which may be regarded as representative of Modern writing and thought in general.[3] Nor does it help us disentangle the Gordian knot of the mutual determination governing the production of notions of origin, authority, and gender. Because I am a European trained in a philological tradition, my attempt to make sense of this complexity inevitably leads me to the past, not to valorize it as more authentic because supposedly closer to a moment of origin but to use it as point of contrast and comparison from which to define and understand the relationship between authority (or subjectivity) and gender in the present. In fact, my procedure is differentially contrastive: I read, and implicitly compare, past and present strategies of authorization. Thus my reading of Fielding's designs derives from the differences in his conceptualization of authority from Dickens's in *Bleak House* and Joyce's in *Ulysses*—the novels selected for discussion.

What this book offers, then, is best seen as an odyssey, a circular quest encountering different ways of understanding and projecting authority, which first takes us to the rationalist constitution of a transcendent subject in *Tom Jones* but which has no firm, objective, external point from which to take our bearings. My readers will note that I refer briefly to Descartes's projection of subjectivity in the *Discourse on Method* and to Hegel's *Logic* (just as I shall later point to Darwin's *Origin of Species* in connection with *Bleak House* and to Derrida and other twentieth-century thinkers when discussing *Ulysses,* but these excursions into other forms of discourse are not meant to ground my analysis in a "higher" form of discourse,

[3]The implication of the feminine in Modernity is demonstrated and documented at length by Alice A. Jardine, *Gynesis: Configurations of Woman and Modernity* (Ithaca: Cornell Univ. Press, 1985).

what Lyotard might call a *métarécit*. My pointers are not intended to suggest that I consider philosophy or science somehow more objective, a truer or more direct form of expression. My reason is simply one of economy. The texts I refer to are generally known, and their familiarity allows me to make a generalizing point without having to include a long analysis.

This strategy raises a question, however. Why do I limit my discussion to literature if, as my argument implies, the structure of subjectivity in a literary work is not just the effect of individual choice but expressive of the discursive formation of an epoch? My choice here, like the choice to limit the readings to works from one literary tradition, was not inspired merely by a need to give shape and cohesion, however arbitrary, to my project. I realize that my decision to limit my discussion to literary texts may be perceived as an attempt to preserve the self-identity and superior status of the "literary," at a time when the boundaries between disciplines and forms of discourse are almost everywhere being taken down. As my argument itself shows, I do not see the novel as a privileged form of discourse; that·I nevertheless privilege it in this argument is owing to my theoretical, Lacanian perspective on the function of the genre. Lacan's theory of the mirror stage motivates my interest in a form of discourse which defines itself as the realistic reflection of the contemporary world. Its "rise" in the seventeenth and early eighteenth centuries suggests that the genre is itself product and embodiment of rationalist conceptualizations of transcendent subjectivity and that the form of its subsequent "flowering" and supposed "death" may relate to a changing notion of that subject. For an analysis of the mutual determination of subjectivity and gender, the fact that the genre has always been related to the feminine also seems auspicious. But as I said, my primary consideration is its mimetic nature. The generic form of the novel—its combination of imitative realism with rhetorical emplotment—offers a unique opportunity to study the relationship between subjectivity and gender as a self-consciously deliberate and therefore "representative" *Darstellung*. The novel personifies and stages its own conceptualizations of ultimate origin and identity. Indeed, the textual organization of the fiction, its "plot" in the widest sense, enacts the contemporary cultural blueprint, the logic of signification.

Each novel reproduces the contemporary conceptualization of the constitution of subjectivity in the act of projecting a semantically unified world. My suggestion is that the function of the genre is (or was) to provide humanity with an instrument, a mirror, in which to see itself reflected as transcendent subject—a superior and detached agent controlling and ordering its world and the medium that creates that world: language. Just as the individual human subject, according to Lacan, resorts to the totalizing image of his or her body in the mirror as a gestalt in order to gain a sense of bodily unity and mastery, so, I would argue, Western rationalism finds its belief in transcendent subjectivity confirmed in and supported by the contemporary reflection of the novel; and it is its mimetic function (which redoubles the self-reflection inherent in all forms of discourse while personifying, hence genderizing, difference) that makes the relationship between signification and gender clearer than it is in other forms of discourse.

Since the novel's dramatization of its own authorial premises is best studied in family romances—fictions that project the relationship to origin as the journey of a return home—I have chosen to discuss the semantic structure of three circular quests that seem representative of eighteenth-, nineteenth-, and twentieth-century notions of subjectivity on the grounds of contemporary acclaim as well as their central place in the canon of English literature. The discussion of more novels would not significantly alter my conclusions. It therefore seems preferable to concentrate on the thorough analysis of a few works rather than to aim at a wide-ranging but diffuse argument. Instead of reading these three family romances as embodiments of the perennial theme of a return to origin, I will try to bring out the complex interrelationship between textual organization, the configuration of subjectivity, and the conceptualization of origin in order to demonstrate that the idea of subjectivity correlates with the formal (semantic and structural) organization of the fiction itself.

Thus, close textual analysis of *Tom Jones* shows that the bastard Tom becomes worthy of an inheritance and a prestigious place in the social hierarchy through a process of splitting or reduplication and simultaneous hierarchical valorization (as a rejection of the "other") which informs both the theme and the structure of the fiction. The oppositional logic upon which Tom's subjectivity depends, as does the story projecting it, reminds me of Descartes's exemplary strategy for attaining subjectivity in the *Discourse on Method*. In a very general context, Fielding's way of constituting subjectivity might be regarded as structurally similar to the Christian splitting of body and soul, Jung's transcendence of the "shadow" in the process of individuation, and the Freudian transcendence of the Oedipus complex. Perhaps Fielding's novel may be taken as projecting, almost archetypally, the oppositional, binary logic that supported the notion of a transcendent subject in Western culture from its rationalist constitution until the advent of Modernity.

A hundred years later the unquestioned self-evidence of Fielding's authority is lost. Dickens's narrative strategy in *Bleak House* addresses the threatened erosion of meaning by a symbolic fog that undermines identity, origin, and subjectivity, as well as narrative authority. Dickens's *Darstellung* of Esther Summerson's quest for subjectivity suggests that revision and rewriting salvage subjectivity in redefining it. Dickens's pen sketches a new order, a new clarity—hence meaning—dissolving the fog that obscures origin.

Joyce, however, celebrates what Dickens fears. *Ulysses* proves a deliberate attack on the foundation of oppositional thought, the logical principle of the excluded middle, and hence on the idea of transcendent subjectivity. Joyce proposes a differential, semiotic logic that allocates authority to the collective cultural discourse rather than to the individual author. Thus the family romance of *Ulysses* fails to bring the time-honored marks of fictional subjectivity: marriage, inheritance, love, or even the slaying of a rival suitor. Open-ended and indeterminate in many respects, *Ulysses* tries to escape the dichotomous ordering of Western metaphysics.

What these readings demonstrate is that the constitution of transcendent subjectivity rests upon a narcissistic strategy of excluding otherness in order to self-reflect the same.[4] More specifically, the

---

[4]The work of Julia Kristeva, *Desire in Language: A Semiotic Approach to Literature and Art,* ed. Leon S. Roudiez (New York: Columbia Univ. Press, 1980), and Luce Irigaray, *Speculum of the Other Woman* (Ithaca: Cornell Univ. Press, 1985), but especially, *This Sex Which Is Not One* (Ithaca: Cornell Univ. Press, 1985), made this clear to me.

otherness to be excluded and repressed proves to be embodied as and denoted feminine—duplicitous, obscuring of transcendent origin, material, and threateningly natural.[5] Thus, *Tom Jones* and *Bleak House* articulate the progress toward selfhood and maturity of their protagonists (both male and female) as the transcendent rejection of the qualities of the mother as symbol of otherness. In thus eliminating the threat of supplementarity, which questions patriarchal self-identity, the plots argue, demonstrate, and reconfirm the notion that meaning depends on the relationship to a singular principle of origin, which in Western discourse is conceived of as the father.

What makes the study of the inscription and function of the mother in narrative strategy especially interesting, as Michel Foucault has implied, is the correlation of the attitude to the "other" as medium for self-transcendence with the attitude to another medium, language. The shifting practice of the inscription of otherness is also a change in style of authority because woman's duplicity (the possible lie about paternity) seems identified with the mediating nature, the sign function of language which allows the possibility of the lie. Thus the thoroughness with which otherness is repressed relates to the author's conceptualization of his or her own predicative authority. Whereas *Tom Jones* playfully demonstrates almost absolute patriarchal control and authority (language is regarded as index, and fiction understood as iconic), the structure and theme of *Bleak House* acknowledge the threatening presence of otherness and aim at eradicating it. To that end a new revisionary version of patriarchal authority, centered upon the detection of truth rather than its proclamation, is drafted to clear the fog obscuring origin and meaning. *Ulysses,* finally, would seem to perversely turn the structure and meaning of what we might call the plot of patriarchy inside out. It flaunts its "feminine" indeterminacy and celebrates flux and open-endedness. However, Joyce's Modern foregrounding of language, like his staging of Molly Bloom, should not be seen as overturning the plot of patriarchy. *Ulysses,* too, proves to hinge on a strategy of doubling which is

---

[5]See on this Hélène Cixous, "Sorties," in *La jeune née* (Paris: 10/18, 1975), pp. 115–245.

meant to safeguard patriarchy, however paradoxically, in designating not material reproduction but textual productivity as origin. If Western literature has traditionally seen the feminine as
emblematic of nature and biological origin, Modern thought from
Joyce to Derrida rests upon a double dispossession or repression of
"femininity" and the appropriation of otherness as style.

Thus the semiotic perspective of this book suggests that the move
toward open-endedness and self-consciousness in twentieth-century writing should be understood dialectically, as a return of the
repressed rather than as a new, regressive, or newly narcissistic self-
involvement presaging the death of the novel or the end of Western
civilization. Western reliance on media to establish and confirm
subjective self-identity paradoxically lends the medium (whether
woman or language) an aura of presence.[6] What we are witnessing
in Modern fiction and thought may not be just a denial of mimetic
representation, truth, or meaning but the most recent and most
sophisticated attempt of Western thought to come to terms with an
ever more present, ever more disembodied otherness.

It should be clear that my study is influenced not only by Lacan.
The progressive movement of my argument from the early modern period to postmodern contemporaneity might suggest that this
book is meant to be a history of the conceptualization of the transcendent subject. But as my focus on the organization of information and the structural constitution of forms of subjectivity indicates, readers should not expect a listing of facts. My attention is
focused on the structuration of what Lacan would have called the
symbolic order, and Claude Lévi-Strauss the organization of
culture. Therefore, not only because I have chosen to focus exclusively on the genre of the novel but because I am interested in
bringing out a logic, principles of ordering, my study offers no
account of contemporary political events, technological changes,
developments in economic and monetary policy or the family,
which are all cognate to the structural principles I point to in the
novel. Each or all of these, and many more, might have been the

[6]Jean-Joseph Goux, in *Economie et symbolique* (Paris: Seuil, 1973), and *Les iconoclastes* (Paris: Seuil, 1978), takes this point of view—without questioning the necessity of the myth of gender as the basis for signification.

object of an analysis of the organization of symbolic order. I ignore them here—though I am aware of how intricately interwoven the web of culture is—again, not because I wish to privilege literature. Perhaps my endeavor is best understood in the context of Foucault's *The Order of Things: An Archaeology of the Human Sciences*. Though I take the opposite tack, selecting but one instance from the wide range of discursive formations, my focus is similar to Foucault's. His concern is with the articulations, modes of thought, unconscious assumptions that first founded and then foundered the concept of Man. He argues that an important change in the organization of thought occurred after the Renaissance and before the Age of Reason. "This involved an immense reorganization of culture, a reorganization of which the Classical age was the first and perhaps the most important stage, since it was responsible for the new arrangement in which we are still caught."[7] It was also the age of the discovery of the presence of language. Though my study is fully different in focus and expression, my debt to Foucault rests in our shared aim to recount the fate of the mutual determination of the notion of language and the structure of subjectivity since the end of the seventeenth century and, beyond that, the continued implication of the structure of subjectivity with gender.

Here we arrive at the question of the feminist method of this study. My readings demonstrate how profoundly the idea of gender is interwoven with that of signification, with important consequences to the focus of this book. I have not tried to present a gender-neutral discussion of the formal developments of fiction, nor do I make a liberal feminist argument that attempts to redress the repressive exclusion of women. If I had tried to write the first, the basis of my argument, the relationship between gender and signification, would have had to be ignored. On the other hand, since the novel, more than any other genre, displays the authority of women, I might have selected my examples from female authors to celebrate the important contribution women have made to the development and prestige of the genre. Books by women might have demonstrated the function of gender connotations in

[7](New York: Random House, 1973), p. 43.

patriarchy's constitution of self-transcendent subjectivity equally well. As the discussion of *Jane Eyre* in a later chapter will show, however, I would have had to "deconstruct" the articulate feminist content of such works. To have done so might have heightened the force of my point about the intertwining of gender and signification in our culture, but because it might also have been misconstrued as an attack on feminist aims, I have decided to focus on works by male authors.

That I felt it necessary to eschew women writers suggests that feminism itself is in transition from an oppositional to a differential logic. While my decision betrays a rather suspect adherence to an oppositional logic, the study as a whole is, I hope, inspired by the vision of a new political project: the analysis and articulation of the many and profound ways in which connotations of gender are used for the purpose of signification. These days Mr. Deasy's cliche in *Ulysses* "A woman brought sin into the world" (II, 390) is easily recognized as an expression of ideology rather than fact, but this recognition does not mean that we have grown fully aware of the extent to which gender (the cultural connotation of sexual difference) is still used as a vehicle for comprehension and a rationale for meaning. As Mary Ellmann argues in *Thinking about Women,* the habit of resorting to cliches of gender to make sense of our world is very deeply ingrained and apparently inescapable.[8] A Modern feminism, aware of the dichotomous and ultimately self-defeating effect of an oppositional logic (which leads to separatism rather than inclusion), points to the implication of gender and signification in the hope that the conflation will eventually lose its seemingly natural self-evidence. Since we live and write in a patriarchal culture, the notion of a gender-free or even truly dialogic—rather than oppositional and hierarchical—signifying system is no more than an imaginary ideal at present. Realizing that all writing that makes sense is implicated, even if antagonistically, in the dominant structure of sense making, one can, nevertheless, keep pointing to the implication of gender in signification in the hope and trust that the knot will ultimately disintegrate.

Most immediately pressing, it seems to me, is the need to indi-

[8](New York: Harcourt Brace Jovanovich, 1968), pp. 2–26.

cate the highly sophisticated but no less profound reliance of Modern writing itself (from Joyce and Freud through Derrida, Deleuze, and Lacan) on connotations of gender in its argumentation. We should beware lest the socially determined function of woman as mediator of desire in combination with the idea of woman as vessel of ideality solidifies into the hypostasis of an absolute, metaphysical otherness that transcends human intellection and experience. As Lacan (who himself resorts to the connotations of woman's otherness for rhetorical purposes and who seems to identify language and the symbolic order with an ultimately masculine phallus) points out in his discussion of Joyce: "The whole need of mankind is to have an 'Other' of the 'Other.' That 'Other' is generally called God, but psychoanalysis reveals that it is simply Woman."[9] As my reading of Joyce will argue, we should watch out for an idolatry of woman as "other" as the possible myth of Modernity.[10] Simultaneously, we should realize the limits of the usefulness of Lacanian theory. While it provides an excellent heuristic tool with which to bring out relationships between attitudes to language and ideas of gender, especially in Fielding and Dickens, its acceptance of this relationship as status quo and its identification of the phallus with masculine gender ("imaginary" in its own terms) mark the point where the theory itself becomes part of its own diagnosis.[11]

No doubt, to the feminist eager to change the social oppression of women, my interest in analyzing discursive practice may seem conservative—though not if we realize that writing is not opposed to politics but is itself a form of action. The question is once again one of logic and determination of origin. An oppositional logic distinguishing between an ens reale (what is independent of the mind) and an ens rationis (what is dependent upon the mind) will denote the ens reale—politics, society, history—as autonomous in origin. A Modern semiotic perspective, however, no longer feels

[9] "Le sinthome: Bouts-de-réel," Le séminaire de Jacques Lacan, text established by J. A. Miller, Ornicar 9 (1982), 39, translation mine.

[10] See also Kristeva, p. 158.

[11] See Anthony Wilden, System and Structure: Essays in Communication and Exchange, 2d ed. (London: Tavistock, 1980), chaps. 10 and 17, for a critique of the imaginary epistemological premises of Lacan's theory.

the force of this opposition and may assign priority to signification over either the ontologically real or the subjectively mental. Such a view is not without consequences for our polical stance. If we hold, to use Umberto Eco's words, that "as subjects, we are what the shape of the world produced by signs makes us become,"[12] we may wish to try and change the structure of sign production, since signification and history are mutually determined. This book about the "plot" of the novel was written from that perspective.

[12]*Semiotics and the Philosophy of Language* (Bloomington: Indiana Univ. Press, 1984), p. 45.

I

The Fiction of Identity/

The Identity of Fiction

Le Paradis est toujours à refaire.
—André Gide, "Le traité du Narcisse"

The novel is the form of mature virility.
—Georg Lukács, *The Theory of the Novel*

Human beings are social creatures, and stories are an intrinsic part of our communal existence. From earliest childhood we are exposed to narrative. The child listens, at first perhaps without comprehension, later with delight. As soon as we gain command of language, we begin to tell stories ourselves. Inventing, narrating, we understand and explain who and what we are. In imposing a narrative pattern upon our experience and ideas, we create the meaning and significance of our lives and ourselves. In giving shape and form we determine sequence, allocate polarities, institute hierarchy, and thus reproduce the predetermined semantic blueprint of our culture.

We may cherish the feeling that our stories are the product of our unique individuality and that they reflect our personal interests and experience. Of course they do, but the forms we use, the structures by which we create order and meaning—the logical or conceptual operations that organize experience—are inherited. The significance of our stories derives from their relation to the models of signification operative in our society—causality, centrism, linearity, and teleology—which are our inescapable unconscious heritage.

More broadly, even before we are born, we are situated in a web

13

of stories pertaining to our gender, our parents' expectations, our social role. Individuals are born into a collective discourse comprising prohibitions, commands, roles, value judgments, exempla, fairy tales, and so on, which are absorbed through parents, school, the media, and other social institutions. I suggest that narrative provides an unconscious pattern of cultural conditioning, a grammar of structuration, about which we reflect as little as about the grammar of our mother tongue. Though it usually remains unconscious, its importance is tremendous. From infancy, the world and the "self" are mediated through the formal and semantic patterns this grammar of structuration imposes. Our lives enact these patterns, and our identity is molded and defined by the slots, channels, and grids the collective discourse allows.

The interaction between narrative and the constitution of self-identity has often been pointed out, especially in recent years.[1] The most convincingly simple demonstration I know, however, is found in Joyce's fiction. As Hugh Kenner points out, Joyce "early grew convinced that people shape their environment with the help of stories they know, and trap themselves into playing parts in those stories."[2] All of Joyce's fiction centers upon the importance of narrative, but the interaction between self, world, and story is most clearly staged in the opening pages of *A Portrait of the Artist as a Young Man*. A fragment of narrative is Stephen Dedalus's first recorded impression: "Once upon a time and a very good time it was there was a moocow coming down along the road and this moocow that was coming down along the road met a nicens little boy named baby tuckoo." The fairy tale that marks this earliest moment of self-consciousness is important because it displays Stephen's articulation of himself as individual subject. Stephen inserts himself into the preexistent story by means of psychological identification: "*His* father told *him* that story: *his* father looked at *him* through a glass: *he* had a hairy face. *He* was baby tuckoo."[3] Ste-

[1]See, for example, Peter Brooks, *Reading for the Plot: Design and Intention in Narrative* (New York: Knopf, 1984); Roland Barthes, "Introduction à l'analyse structurale des récits," in *Poétique du récit* (Paris: Seuil, 1977), pp. 7–58.

[2]"Circe," in *James Joyce's "Ulysses,"* ed. Clive Hart and David Hayman (Berkeley: Univ. of California Press, 1974), p. 342.

[3](London: Granada, 1977), p. 7, my emphasis.

phen's self-identity is formed and confirmed by projection into the slot the story provides. Without the medium of story, sensation would not have crystallized into subjectivity. Thus the human subject "inscribes" himself or herself in culture through language.

What Joyce demonstrates here is an aspect of our being in the world of which we generally tend to remain unconscious. Perhaps it wounds our narcissistic illusion of control to realize that our sense of subjectivity relies on the presence of a medium: without signifier there would be no subject. Recent psychoanalytic and Modern discourse articulates, however, what in Joyce's text necessarily remains implicit. In the words of Jacques Lacan, "Man speaks, then, but it is because the symbol has made him man" or, more directly, " 'That he sustains as subject' means that language allows him to regard himself as the scene-shifter, or even the director of the entire imaginary capture of which he would otherwise be nothing more than the living marionette."[4] Since we seem to believe that our relationship to the medium is one of perfect mastery rather than dialogic interdependence, we also fail to inquire how and to what extent not merely the idea of subjectivity but its conceptual configuration depends on identification with the structural patterning of language and culture. I am thinking of the "secondary modeling," to use Jury Lotman's term, of customs, models, and roles.[5] Again, my example derives from Joyce's novel. In the first sentence Stephen is not merely provided with the opportunity of establishing his subjectivity by inserting himself into the narrative. As a "he" (inflected "him" and "his"), Stephen immediately participates in a structure of hierarchical differences relating to gender and generation. As baby tuckoo he is part of a family, the most elementary form of social structure. More specifically, the realization of his own identity coincides with the acknowledgment of the differences from but basic similarity to the father. This, in turn, positions the child in relationship to his medium, language. It is the father who tells the story. He is the source of language, authority, and order. He controls and provides the medium for the projection of self-identity. Being a "he" like the

[4]*Ecrits: A Selection*, trans. Alan Sheridan (New York: Norton, 1977), pp. 64, 272.
[5]*Die Struktur literarischer Texte* (Munich: Wilhelm Fink, 1972), p. 39.

father who tells the story, means that "he" will become a speaking subject, an "author" himself. Learning to invent and narrate, he reproduces the father's authority and his unquestioning command over the medium; as long as the son wishes to identify with the image of the father, the mediating function of language need never be acknowledged.

A Portrait is, we know, a fiction describing the attempted escape from the cloying web Irish culture has woven to entrap the self. Stephen learns to fear the collective discourse of his culture as an agent constricting his freedom of speech and thought, and he decides to go into exile to become a free and original author, an artist. The irony is that this act of escape is simultaneously the confirmation of what, at an unconscious level, may well be the most fundamental aspect of the primal lesson. In rejecting his own father as a role model and replacing him with the mythic artificer Daedalus, he may be rejecting the claims of kith and kin, but he preserves the basic structure of identification and differentiation of the primal scene of subjectivity, which now reveals itself as the blueprint of patriarchy. Stephen's identity as artist (no less than his potential for becoming a speaking subject) depends on the identification with a father figure, even if that figure is only known as narrative and, through narrative, as an abstract idea. The transmission of the story from father to son establishes more than the sexual identification of the child. It simultaneously generates, proves, and transmits the authority of the father as the origin of meaning and identity, and it valorizes the transmission of cultural identity in language over the biological reproduction of the species. Joyce depicts the mother's role in the advent of culture as subservient; she plays the accompaniment for Stephen's dance. Betty Byrne, offering sweet lemon platt, is a temptation to be passed by.

This brief reference to Joyce's first novel is not meant as an exhaustive analysis, but it helps me to establish a number of interrelated points. First, the self cannot make itself present as self-conscious subject except through language. Second, the language by means of which the self positions itself as self-conscious subject is language that has already undergone a secondary semantic modeling, so that the subject forms itself through identification with a structure of differences. Finally, identification with the story of the father means irremediable alienation from the mother, from a sense of full, symbiotic presence. What we have reached here is a paradox. Without language, there is no subjectivity, no culture, but subjectivity and self-consciousness imply a transcendent alienation from nature, a forgetful repression. We might say that the advent of consciousness, entailing the inescapable lack of full presence, reenacts the biblical Fall in each individual life.

If language is the mark of human alienation from nature, it also provides a palliative, however illusive the relief. Pierre Macherey has argued that the critical question is not "What is literature?" but "What necessity does it embody?"[6] The novel, more than other forms of narrative, it seems to me, functions psychologically to cover up the scars left by separation from nature. In *Beyond the Pleasure Principle,* Freud begins to demonstrate my meaning. He reports a game played by a one-and-half-year-old boy. Throwing away a small object, a bobbin, he utters sounds resembling the word *fort* (German for "gone"); its recovery is marked with *da* ("present"). To Freud the game the little boy kept repeating seemed a symbolic strategy for mastering the trauma of separation from the mother, staging both departure and return in language and gesture. Aided by the play with the bobbin, what D. W. Winnicott calls a "transitional object,"[7] which stands for the physical presence of the mother, the child masters his anxiety, sublimating it into a preoccupation with mimetic rhythm and verbal play.

The scene bears, of course, radically different interpretations. Lacan regards the occurrence described by Freud as the moment of entry into language and the mark of detachment from the mother. John Irwin sees the scene as an act of symbolic revenge.[8] What seems important to me is that the medium for coping with the anxiety of separation and detachment is not just language per se but language patterned as ritual play, poetry almost. Just as the bobbin can function as transitional object for the little boy because

[6]*Pour une théorie de la production littéraire* (Paris: Maspéro, 1966), p. 179.

[7]*Playing and Reality* (Harmondsworth, Eng.: Penguin, 1980).

[8]Lacan, *Ecrits,* pp. 101–3; Irwin, *Doubling and Incest/Repetition and Revenge: A Speculative Reading of Faulkner* (Baltimore: Johns Hopkins Univ. Press, 1975).

its concrete material presence substitutes for the tangibility of the mother while its small size allows him full control, so the patterning of sound and meaning alleviates the self-alienation caused by separation from the mother. It cleverly turns language—the mark of detachment—into its own object.

"His Majesty the Ego," Freud pointed out, is the "hero alike of every day-dream and of every story."[9] In other terms, we might argue that one of the important functions of patterned language is to heal or dress the wound of human alienation from self-presence, inflicted by the realization of dependence on an "other." The play with language allows the little boy to forget his loss and to redirect the focus of attention. Lacan's reading in particular supports this suggestion, emphasizing that the repetitiveness of the game "destroys" the reality of the object and creates a substitute "reality" that is imaginary: "His action thus negatives the field of forces of desire in order to become its own object to itself."[10] The utterance originally intended as substitute thus becomes its own goal and satisfaction. It produces its own alternative reality.

Lacan has made another, comparable point in his formulation of the mirror stage. In order to gain a sense of bodily unity and mastery, of self-coherence, the individual human subject uses the image of his or her body in the mirror as a projective gestalt. The child's idea of himself or herself as "self" is mediated by this totalizing reflection in the medium. I suggest that the genre of the novel, its psychological function, its synthetic combination of fact and fiction, as well as its role in contemporary culture, are best understood by analogy with these ideas of Lacan. Through its aesthetically patterned language, the genre provides the transitional substitute for an undifferentiated participation in nature, almost making up for the loss of symbiosis with the mother in the projection of its own cultural reality. As realistic narrative providing a totalizing representation, a fully rounded life story of an individual subject in contemporary history, the novel gives mankind the imago of a distinct, self-present subjectivity.

From this point of view it is not surprising that such themes as

9"Creative Writers and Day-Dreaming," *Standard Edition*, vol. IX, p. 150.
10*Ecrits*, p. 103.

orphanhood, homelessness, *Bildung,* or the quest for identity should be typical for the genre. Edward Said pointed out that "the primordial discovery of the novel is that of self—and *primordial* is intended here in a privileged way: the primordial as preeminent, as the prior, as the first validating condition for intelligibility."[11] In addition to understanding the self as the discovery of fiction, my psychoanalytic perspective recognizes that the medium allows us to project and constitute selfhood and self-identity in the very act of telling, listening, and reading. The preoccupation with life stories may be related to the cultural change from a theological to a humanist world view during which the genre was created, but as realistic narrative, the novel is also, simultaneously, the medium that preeminently (more than philosophy, science, history, or latitudinarian theology) constituted and validated the idea of the transcendent subjectivity of human beings. Fictional narrative embodies contemporary history and thought, but it also remains the expression of how an epoch imagines the human subject, as well as the elaboration of its own psychological function, its *Wirkung* as transitional object.

In psychoanalytical terms the impulse of the novel, and the content of most fictions, might be understood as the reflection of a primal fantasy. "In their very content, in their theme (primal scene, castration, seduction)," write Jean Laplanche and J.-B. Pontalis, "primal fantasies also give an indication of the retroactive hypothesis [upon which they are founded]: They relate themselves to origins. Like myths, they pretend to lend a local habitation, a name, and a 'solution' to what presents itself as an enigma to the child; they dramatize as moments of coming-into-being, as origins of the story, what to the subject appears as a reality of the kind which demands explanation, a theory."[12] What makes the novel as form of discourse relating origin and identity unique, however, is its attempt to deny the ineluctable otherness, the presence of absence, the ontological gap that necessitates discourse. Mimetic fiction, in presenting itself not as a mediated, provisional image but

---

[11]*Beginnings: Intention and Method* (New York: Basic Books, 1975), p. 141.

[12]"Fantasmes originaires, fantasmes des origines, origine du fantasme," *Les Temps Modernes* (April 1964), 1854–55.

as a true reflection, short-circuits the presence of otherness, the lack of full being which inspires and marks human communication in language. The novel represses, or tries to repress, the absence of the mother.

More emphatically, the convention of realism—which, as we shall see, tautologically mirrors contemporary assumptions about truth, identity, and causality—narcissistically allows humanity to ignore the presence of otherness outside and inside the self. Realism, excluding the different, confirms expectations and affirms self-identity, in turn, allowing readers to forget they are dealing with a medium: humanity can take itself for its mirror image.[13] In its most extreme form, the specular illusion may lead to an idolatry or fetishism that attributes to the image reflected in the medium a deeper truth, a brighter vitality, and a greater intensity than to reality itself. D. H. Lawrence's insistence that the novel is the Bright Book of Life, its vitality trembling on the ether, reminds me, oddly and obliquely, of Winnicott's criteria for the transitional object: "It must seem to the infant to give warmth, or to move, or to have texture, or to do something that seems to show it has vitality or reality on its own."[14] My aim here is not to erode the moral importance of fiction, nor do I wish to question the validity of its humanist project. On the contrary, I want to shift and broaden it to include the recognition of the informative presence of the "other" in our definition of humanity. In order to do so, I shall argue that the history and development of the genre illustrate the dependence on an "other" for the constitution of the speaking subject.

Earlier, I discussed the relationship between the novel and the constitution of the subject in general terms. The question remains to be asked, How does the rhetorical patterning of fiction contribute? The most important formal feature of narrative which invites the projection of transcendent subjectivity is its projection of a semantically unified world. The novel "seeks, by giving form, to uncover and construct the concealed totality of life," Georg Lukács

---

[13]See Elizabeth Ermarth, "Realism, Perspective and the Novel," *Critical Inquiry* 7 (1981), 499–521. See also Stephen Heath, *The Nouveau Roman: A Study in the Practice of Writing* (London: Elek Books, 1972).

[14]Winnicott, p. 6.

wrote at the beginning of this century.[15] More recently, Frank
Kermode asserted that "men, like poets, rush 'into the middest,' *in
medias res,* when they are born; they also die *in mediis rebus,* and to
make sense of their span they need fictive concords with origins
and ends, such as give meaning to lives and poems."[16] Though
they speak from totally different perspectives on the social and
moral function of fiction, these critics agree about the significance
of its formal intention, which they see as the projection of a unified
pattern of order transcending the contingency of human experience. The most useful description of this unifying effect is found in
Coleridge's often-quoted letter to Joseph Cottle of 1815:

> The common end of all *narrative,* nay, of *all* Poems is to convert a
> *series* into a *Whole:* to make those events, which in real or imagined
> History move on in a *strait* line, assume to our Understandings a
> *circular* motion—the snake with it's Tail in its mouth. Hence indeed
> the almost flattering and yet appropriate Term, Poesy—i.e. poi-
> esis—*making.* Doubtless, to his eye, which alone comprehends all
> Past and all Future in one eternal Present, what to our short sight
> appears strait is but part of the great Cycle—just as the calm Sea to us
> *appears* level, tho' it indeed [be] only a part of a *globe.*[17]

To Coleridge the circularity of the work of art, deriving from the
semantic unification of all the information given within it, is an
image of the Divine Mind and its unifying perception of the grand
design of the cosmos. In fact, as J. Hillis Miller notes in *Fiction and
Repetition,* the order of the work of art provides Coleridge with an
image and idea from which to derive by analogy the confirmation

[15] *The Theory of the Novel: A Historico-Philosophical Essay on the Forms of Great
Epic Literature,* trans. Anna Bostock (1920; rpt. Cambridge, Mass.: MIT Press,
1975).
[16] *The Sense of an Ending: Studies in the Theory of Fiction* (1966; rpt. New York:
Oxford Univ. Press, 1973), p. 7.
[17] In *Unpublished Letters of Samuel Taylor Coleridge: Including Certain Letters Re-
published from Original Sources,* ed. Earl Leslie Griggs (New Haven: Yale Univ.
Press, 1933), vol. II, p. 128. I quote from J. Hillis Miller, *Fiction and Repetition*
(Cambridge, Mass.: Harvard Univ. Press, 1982), p. 24. The passage is also cited
by Mark Taylor in *Journeys to Selfhood: Hegel and Kierkegaard* (Berkeley: Univ. of
California Press, 1980); and M. H. Abrams, *Natural Supernaturalism: Tradition and
Revolution in Romantic Literature* (New York: Norton, 1973).

of the existence of God: "What the Globe is in Geography, *miniaturing* in order to *manifest* the Truth, such is a Poem to that Image of God, which we were created with, and which still seeks Unity or Revelation of the *One* in and by the *Many*."[18] Thus the unity reflected by the design is hypostatized as supernatural in origin as well as end. Instead of concluding with Coleridge that narrative unity is the reflection of the Father, however, we may argue the reverse, that the notion of Divine Providence is the absolute projection of the effect of narrative arrangement.

What is the connection between Coleridge's celebration of formal unity and my argument about subjectivity and the novel? It seems to me that the form and content of the novel—typically a history of an individual human life and its relation to origin—invite the projection of the idea of the subject as a transcendent entity or instance above, behind, or within the handiwork of the fiction. The prototypical movement of plot works to unify beginning and end. Thus it creates a magic suggestion of wholeness, atoneness, which invites the projection of a transcendent design of the self, just as the image of the circular snake signified Divine Providence to Coleridge.

As our analysis of *Bleak House* will argue, this basic unifying intention of plot is foregrounded in the detective story. The point of its narrative action, its telos, is the revelation of the hidden, unifying causal event that produced the mystery and contingency of the situation at the beginning of the fiction. Thus the narrative act relates beginning to origin and end. The detective story, however, is only the intensified form of all historical or epigenetic models of explanation, which lead us back to origin and sketch a trajectory from the moment of origin to the present.[19] That the epigenetic plot presenting the relation of the individual to origin should have been so popular in the novel has to do with the valorization of the idea of origin in our culture. Origin is the key principle, the condition of meaning and signification. Once we

---

[18]Coleridge, quoted in Miller, *Fiction and Repetition*, p. 24.
[19]See Brooks, *Reading for the Plot*; Viktor Sklovskij, "The Mystery Novel: Dickens' *Little Dorrit*," in *Readings in Russian Poetics: Formalist and Structuralist Views*, ed. Ladislaw Matejka and Krystyna Pomorska (Ann Arbor: Michigan Slavic Publications, 1978). pp. 220–27.

know the origin of a person or a phenomenon, we know its mean-ing and identity. "Origin is the source of the nature in which the being of an entity is present," Heidegger explains.[20] In Western thought, origin—having and knowing the relation to the transcen-dent beginning—conveys essence, presence, and authority. Thus the circularity of plot, the structural relationship of beginning and ending (the beginning always implicitly anticipating the ending), is a formal device reflecting the central meaning-making structure of our culture: it relates entities to a single origin and cause. Hence it not only makes meaning, as required by Western thought, it also appeals to the profoundest human psychological need to be "one."[21]

As my introductory paragraphs pointed out, we "can't go home again." There is no road that will take us back to Paradise; the belief in presence upon which our idea of the subjective self rests must inevitably remain unconfirmed. Moreover, the structure of return to origin, the circularity of the epigenetic plot which figures presence to us, itself rests upon rhetorical manipulation that viti-ates the logic of linear, historical thought. The best-known dem-onstration of this dependence is Cynthia Chase's analysis of *Daniel Deronda,* which I shall briefly summarize here because we shall later note a similar organization in *Tom Jones* and *Bleak House.*[22] Although Eliot's novel begins with the presentation of a proud young woman, it soon appears that not she but the mysterious young man who rescues her from debt is the protagonist of the fiction. This good and gallant man, the foster child of an aristo-cratic family, is ignorant of his birth and too polite to ask his guardian about it. As the story progresses, Deronda's noble char-acter shines brighter and brighter, his good deeds culminating in

[20]"The Origin of the Work of Art," in *Poetry, Language, Thought* (New York: Harper, 1971), p. 57.

[21]On the desire to be "one" again as the most profound drive constituting human beings as human, see Anthony Wilden, "Lacan and the Discourse of the Other," in Jacques Lacan, *The Language of the Self: The Function of Language in Psychoanalysis,* trans. Wilden (New York: Dell, 1968), pp. 190–91.

[22]"The Decomposition of the Elephants: Double-Reading *Daniel Deronda,*" *PMLA* 93 (1978), pp. 215–28. Jonathan Culler, in *The Pursuit of Signs: Semiotics, Literature, Deconstruction* (Ithaca: Cornell Univ. Press, 1981), pp. 176–78, provides a summary discussion of Chase's conclusions.

the rescue of a Jewish girl. Helping her to find her lost relatives, he enters Jewish circles. To the experienced reader of romance it does not come as a surprise that Deronda himself eventually proves of Jewish descent.

The design of the novel, its relation of origin to end, brings about a reversal in the identity of the protagonist from non-Jewish to Jewish, from foster child to son, but in this transfiguration the intrigue exploits an odd ambivalence. The common denominator of both "identities" is Deronda's goodness. Initially, Deronda is exceptional because of his moral stature. Later on, this quality is "explained" and confirmed by the nature of his origin. In Eliot's ideology—at least in this fiction—being Jewish equals being good. For the fiction to progress toward the revelation of Deronda's Jewishness, it was necessary that he show exemplary goodness from the beginning. What is presented as effect (he proves Jewish) is truly cause (he was good all along). The design of the novel, then, its unity, hinges on a hysteron proteron and works by exploiting the possibilities provided by the double temporal level of narrative—the original time of action (and mystification) need not coincide with the time of narration (and discovery).

Important here is the reminder that our ideas about origin and our myths of return are self-styled and "imaginary," in the sense that they are projected by our imagination. Their explanatory force rests upon the mediating presence of language and consciousness itself. Since the generic task of the novel is to portray the history of individual lives, accounting for and sketching human subjectivity by relating it to origin, the genre itself may be considered a version of what is usually taken as a specific instance of the form: the family romance, which, Freud says, "serves as the fulfilment of wishes and as a correction of actual life."[23] If narrative mediates origin, suggesting it without making it absolutely

---

[23]"Family Romances," *Standard Edition,* vol. IX, pp. 238–39. Freud points to a typical daydream of the adolescent, which helps "in the task of getting free from the parents of whom he now has a low opinion"; such daydreams "replace them by others, who, as a rule, are of higher social standing." In other words, the family romance is a self-styled fantasy about origin. It should be noted that I am not using the term family romance pejoratively, as symptom of illness.

present, the origin presented is always an imagined one—already formed or contained in narrative, whether cultural or personal. Just as the family romance of the individual is his personal construction of identity, the generic function of the novel may well be to serve as the family romance of Western culture.

Each of the three novels selected for discussion here presents a homecoming, a story of return to origin, a circular quest like Homer's *Odyssey,* or perhaps I should say a *Divine Comedy* spanning beginning and end, Genesis and Apocalypse. At any rate, these fictions project the metaphor of man's ontological condition of alienation from presence or origin as a metonymy, a linear progress, a journey to selfhood. I have deliberately chosen these novels because in structure and theme they stage the intention and function of the genre of the novel itself: in tying origin to end they try to breach and remedy the painful paradox of human consciousness, its awareness of alienation and the discontinuity of human existence. One might call *Tom Jones, Bleak House,* and *Ulysses* exemplary fictions.

Though I have already suggested that the unifying design of narrative rests upon the exploitation of the doubleness of its temporal scheme, the inevitable recurrence of division and reduplication in the very process of establishing circular unity is demonstrated more clearly in Claude Lévi-Strauss's analysis of the structure of myth, which will be my model in analyzing *Tom Jones.* The unifying effect of mythic plot, Lévi-Strauss suggests, rests upon a peculiar propensity of "primitive thought" which contradicts the primary Aristotelian axiom of the excluded middle. Mythic plot first projects an irreconcilable contradiction (embodied in the form of animals, gods, or abstract forces); then the "resolution" of this opposition is brought about through a slow process of redefinition, replacing aspects of the semantic charge of a pole of the opposition until eventually the two opposing poles are no longer contradictory and can be united. In Lévi-Strauss's own words: "We need only assume that two opposite terms with no intermediary always tend to be replaced by two equivalent terms which admit of a third one as mediator; then one of the polar terms and the mediator become replaced by a new triad, and so on."[24] The Oedipus myth, for instance, presents the progressive mediation of a contradiction concerning origin. It addresses the problem: born from one or born from two.

What Lévi-Strauss designates as the central problem of the Oedipus myth, this book will pose as the unconscious motive of the unifying intention of fictional plot and its reliance on closure to create meaning. Thus one advantage of Lévi-Strauss's analysis of myth is that it allows us to see the novel in structural relation to other genres of narrative addressing the problem of human identity: the story given in Genesis, for instance, and also Freud's more recent reformulation of the Oedipus myth.[25] Second, it alerts us to the paradox that language, or the peculiar metonymic logic of narrative, offers the imaginary transcendence of the inevitable dualism and divisiveness of the human condition, of which it is itself the natural sign. Just as the paradox of the Fortunate Fall turns the most lamentable event of human history into an occasion for joy—since it was the reason for the coming of Christ the Redeemer—so the teleological rhythm of plot presents a vicarious restitution in language. Narrative is the implicit glorification of the power of language to evoke presence, which is used as a remedy against awareness of alienation or the Fall.

Another implication of Lévi-Strauss's example is that, although narratives violate the principle of noncontradiction of traditional logic, the suggestion of unity and singularity inevitably rests upon the practice of differentiation. The final effect may justify the means—the sense of the ending may make the listener forget the

[24]"The Structural Study of Myth," in Lévi-Strauss, *Structural Anthropology,* trans. Claire Jacobson and Brooke Grundfest-Schoepf (Harmondsworth, Eng.: Penguin, 1972), p. 224. For an extended analysis of Lévi-Strauss's notation of myth, see Elli Köngäs Maranda and Pierre Maranda, "Strukturelle Modelle in der Folklore," in *Literaturwissenschaft und Linguistik,* ed. Jens Ihwe (Frankfurt: Athenäum Fischer Taschenbuch, 1973), vol. II, pp. 127–215.

[25]Edmund Leach, *Genesis as Myth and Other Essays* (London: Jonathan Cape, 1969), pp. 18–21, demonstrates the structural similarity between Genesis and Oedipus. Lévi-Strauss himself argues the structural connection between the Greek Oedipus myth and Freud's reformulation. On the structural similarity between myth and the novel, see Jury M. Lotman, "The Origin of Plot in the Light of Typology," *Poetics Today* 1, 1/2 (1979), 161–85; and Christine van Boheemen, "The Semiotics of Plot: Towards a Typology of Fictions," *Poetics Today* 3, 4 (1982), 89–87.

repetitive reenactment of splitting and reduplication which is its precondition—yet the unity of closure rests upon differentiation. Lévi-Strauss forces us to recognize, again, the imaginary nature of the unity and transcendence produced by narrative. The unity of closure is itself the product of a process of splitting and doubling, of discrimination, even when it presents itself as a magical *coniunctio oppositorum*. Fielding's *Tom Jones* will show us in detail how plot must first institute doubleness, in the form of paired characters, and then remove one of the two from the scene of action to resolve the intrigue. The final at-oneness of Tom, Allworthy, and Sophia rests upon the excommunication of Blifil and the qualities he stands for. René Girard claimed that "the conditions favourable to thought coincide with the death of the surrogate victim."[26] Though I question the historical projection underlying his theory, my argument follows his in suggesting that the unity and presence brought about by language and design rest upon the repression of the presence of difference; and just as in the human psyche repressed material is not lost but remains present as symptom, the novel contains the representation of its own "other" within itself.

In short, the family romance of the novel, in addition to being the trajectory toward unitary origin, is also an instrument for establishing difference. In its progress toward unity it creates polarities and hierarchical oppositions, inevitably repeating the functioning of language and consciousness. In order to suggest the unity that allows the reader's projection of subjectivity, however, doubleness and difference are swept under the carpet of unifying design. What we note here is the inescapable paradox of all attempts at ultimate explanation. Difference, if undone or overcome by narrative reasoning, will return elsewhere.[27] Close reading will

---

[26] *Violence and the Sacred,* trans. Patrick Gregory (Baltimore: Johns Hopkins Univ. Press, 1977), p. 234.

[27] Leach, *Genesis as Myth,* bases the central myth of Western culture on the process of differentiation. "Religion everywhere is preoccupied with the first, the antinomy of life and death. Religion seeks to deny the binary link between the two worlds; it does this by creating the mystical idea of 'another world,' a land of the dead where life is perpetual. The attributes of this other world are necessarily those which are not of this world; imperfection here is balanced by perfection there. But this logical ordering of ideas has disconcerting consequences—God comes to belong to the other world. The central 'problem' of religion is then to re-establish

demonstrate discontinuities, breaks, reduplications, and aporias in the most unified work of verbal art.

What we shall note in our readings of *Tom Jones* and *Bleak House,* then, is that the plot I have called family romance constitutes the speaking subject dialectically, even if the dependence on dialectic is suppressed. Tom's journey to selfhood depends upon the splitting of the "self" into "natural" and "rational" halves. His "natural" self—instinctive appetite—is transcended when he embraces prudence (Sophia) and renounces the multiple attractions of fickle fortune. While nature is thus excluded from the constitution of Tom as subject worthy of inheriting Paradise Hall, the idea of nature necessarily remains present in the fiction as the "other." Without the representation of the contrastive idea of nature, Tom's prudence would be lacking in meaning. Its significance derives from the contrast. Though the presence of otherness must be denied and excluded if true subjectivity is ever to be constituted, otherness is nevertheless the necessary prerequisite of subjectivity in the plot.

My concern with unity and differentiation in narrative arises from the determination of Western culture—and especially, perhaps, rationalist humanism—that singular, *unitary* origin is the source of signification and meaning. "The Absolute is identical with itself," Hegel declares.[28] Essence and presence derive from the relationship to a single point of origin. In bringing about the unity of ending, narrative enacts the signifying strategy underlying Western metaphysics. Its progressive transcendence of the presence of the "other" permits the ego to affirm its identity with itself as "I am that I am" in a doubly self-reflexive formulation that denies the informative presence of otherness.[29] More specifically, I am concerned that the novel—humanity's ideal image of itself—has intensified the Western cultural practice of personifying this strategy of signification—designating single origin as God the Fa-

---

some kind of bridge between man and God. This pattern is built into the structure of every mythical system" (pp. 9–10).

[28] *Hegel's Logic,* trans. William Wallace (Oxford: Clarendon Press, 1975), p. 166.

[29] For a more sociologically oriented approach to the constitution of the subject, see Rosalind Coward and John Ellis, *Language and Materialism: Developments in Semiology and the Theory of the Subject* (London: Routledge, 1977).

ther and the "other," if mentioned at all, as the mother (to whom Satan, evil, and Eve are closely allied). The idea of the mother—matter as original presence—is not and cannot be acknowledged, for in the patriarchal culture we live in, origin and meaning are necessarily designated as spiritual, *geistlich*. The central focus of thought is the metaphor of the father, and only when we can adopt a fully dialogic understanding of both/and will this double bind be transcended.

Surveying the history of discourse, we might draft a list of polarities operative in human conceptualization, in which the left-hand term is implicitly or explicitly coded masculine and central, whereas the term in the right-hand column is its contrastive "other," usually personified as feminine:

Culture	Nature
Mind	Body
Intellect	Feeling
Logos	Chaos
Form	Matter
Truth	Lie
Presence	Absence
Spirit	Matter
Identity	Difference
Sky	Earth
Time	Space
Life	Death
Light	Darkness

The list could, no doubt, be extended, but these examples suffice to demonstrate how pervasively we order reality by means of these gender-coded dichotomies. These oppositions are fundamental in that they are the very tools of conceptualization. In one and the same act of understanding we privilege the paternal signifier by ranking it above its maternal partner, if we do not exclude the maternal altogether.[30]

---

[30]See, for example, Genevieve Lloyd, *The Man of Reason: "Male" and "Female" in Western Philosophy* (London: Methuen, 1984); Jacques Derrida, *La dissémination* (Paris: Seuil, 1972), esp. p. 86; Cixous, *La jeune née*.

Our thinking is inevitably patriarchal or logocentric, then. Patriarchy is the received structure of reason, truth, and meaning—in short, of culture as we understand it. Its "plot" is the exclusion of the presence of the "other." The novel as family romance, reductively personifying the complexity of experience as the contrastive pair of father and mother, is both the intensified reflection of the implication of gender in signification and the prime object for studying its history and functioning, especially with regard to the constitution of the subject.[31] In the following chapters I shall try to demonstrate that the idea of an "other," personified as mother, is the hidden center of the theme and structure of *Tom Jones, Bleak House,* and *Ulysses,* lending internal coherence to these texts. The protagonists' achievement of subjectivity, as well as the representation of the process, depends on the progressive exclusion of the heterogeneity of the feminine. Since the presence of the "other" as the supportive scaffold for meaning and identity is suppressed or covered up, my readings must necessarily focus on symptomatic peculiarities, knots and twists in the narrative strand, significant omissions that betray the informative absence of the "other." The purpose of my readings will be to demonstrate that the name-of-the-father (Lacan's term for the abstract power of patriarchy) depends on the informative presence of the mother; she is its indispensable medium. It is not my intention to supplant the designation of the father as ultimate origin by a myth of the mother; all I hope to do, and can do, is ask attention for the repressed process of the production of meaning and point to its inscription in terms of difference in gender. Nor do I claim to be speaking about actual, historical relations between the sexes. The novel is humanity's

---

[31]Gilles Deleuze and Félix Guattari, in *Anti-Oedipus: Capitalism and Schizophrenia,* trans. R. Hurley et al. (New York: Viking Press, 1977), argue that the family, with its triangular organization of similarities and differences, has become the most fundamental signifying structure of Western thought, and their book denounces that situation. They object to the repetitive determinism of reducing experience to the cookie-cutter pattern of the triangular Oedipal situation: "In the aggregate of destination, in the end, there is no longer anyone but daddy, mommy, and me, the despotic sign inherited by daddy, the residual territoriality assumed by mommy, and the divided, split, castrated ego" (p. 265). Joyce calls it the "sameold gamebold adomic structure" in *Finnegans Wake* (New York: Viking, 1974), p. 615.6. Subsequent references to *FW* will be by page and line number in the text.

own imaginary reflection of its world. My study does not touch upon social practice per se; it bears primarily on the ways different epochs have used gender difference as a means of self-conceptualization. I wish to uncover the blueprint of discourse, signification, and thought and to demonstrate its reliance on sexual difference; understanding of this reliance may help us recognize similar strategies of inscription in journalism, advertising, small talk, history, sociology, anthropology, and other fields of study.

I have related the unifying intention of plot to Freud's structure of the family romance because that structure constitutes origin. In order to argue the "plot" of patriarchy, its ulterior design, I should like to return to Freud. In *Moses and Monotheism* he noted with regard to the question of origin, "Maternity is proved by the evidence of the senses while paternity is a hypothesis, based on an inference and premise."[32] Whereas the role of the mother in originating the child is natural, biological, and self-evident, the father's participation needs the proof of language, of story. Without the woman's oral designation of the father, paternity remains indeterminate. Patriarchy, as a complex interrelationship of language, law, inscription, and the designation of the relationship to the father as single source of origin, name, and identity, would seem an idealist "plot" to "sublate the natural or physiological evidence of motherhood into a prospective historical or psychological continuity," as Gayatri Spivak writes.[33] Culture, language, and, more pointedly, the plot of family romance are, according to Humphrey Morris, patriarchy's "originary substitute for an originary missing connection. The problem of establishing authoritative metalanguage *is* the problem of establishing paternity."[34] It follows, then, that woman is not a being in her own right, a subject. If patriarchy presents the father, thus culture, language, or *Geist,* as the locus of origin and meaning—denying the importance of material reproduction and the body—woman's role must be secondary. She

---

[32]Trans. Katherine Jones (New York: Vintage Books, 1967), pp. 145–46.

[33]"Displacement and the Discourse of Woman," in *Displacement: Derrida and After,* ed. Mark Krupnick (Bloomington: Indiana Univ. Press, 1983), p. 190.

[34]"The Need to Connect: Representations of Freud's Psychical Apparatus," in *The Literary Freud: Mechanisms of Defense and the Poetic Will,* ed. Joseph Smith, Psychiatry and the Humanities 4 (New Haven: Yale Univ. Press, 1980), p. 343.

reproduces only the flesh, which is no more than the medium for cultural inscription. She is the house of passage in which father and son meet, the means of exchanging patriarchal power.

In addition to its importance in understanding the history of our culture, the notion of patriarchy as the transumption of nature and matter has significance for the novel. The plot of the family romance, redoubling the strategy, is its distilled essence. Its structural designation of origin, reducing the multiplicity of character, event, and situation to a unitary conclusion, reenacts the repression of nature. Moreover, as an act of language use, narrative itself sketches the movement toward the position from which narrative can occur. It *is* the trajectory toward subjectivity. Thus the study of the process of family romance is at once an analysis of narrative authority. The journey to selfhood positions the protagonist as author, and the embodiment of this trajectory is in turn the reflection of how the epoch imagines this process. "The mental attitude of the novel is *virile maturity*," Lukács claimed.[35] His words are not the expression of cheap male chauvinism; they point to an essential aspect of the genre which is usually overlooked because the novel has always had a close tie with the feminine.[36] Its history lists more female authors than that of other genres; it often portrays the life and history of female protagonists. This high visibility of the feminine, however, does not contradict my argument. With, perhaps, such rare exceptions as Moll Flanders and Sister Carrie, the depiction of woman in fiction has always staged her assimilation to the patriarchal structure, if not her tragic fate should she fail to conform. A typical precondition for woman's assumption of a place in society is the rejection or denial of her autonomy, whether with regard to sexual reproduction or to her use of language. The final effect of the fiction is the reconfirmation of the supremacy of the symbolic order in which woman cannot be given autonomous subjectivity. Her speech and authority derive from patriarchy, as each narrative enactment confirms. In short, the law of the genre—the ineluctable modality to which it conforms, which it im-

---

[35] *The Theory of the Novel,* p. 88, my emphasis.

[36] See Michael Danahy, "Le roman est-il chose femelle?" *Poétique* 25 (1976), 85–106.

poses, and to which it lends reality—is the supremacy of the father. The novel is the instrument of patriarchy, giving presence to its predominance in the act of utterance.

Since my point may arouse considerable resistance, it may be necessary to pause briefly and examine the double bind of the female writer more closely by analyzing the narrative strategy of what feminist critics from Virginia Woolf to Gilbert and Gubar have considered an exemplary feminist novel. Charlotte Brontë's *"Jane Eyre* parodies both the nightmare confessional mode of the gothic genre and the moral didacticism of Bunyan's *Pilgrim's Progress* to tell its distinctively female story of enclosure and escape, with a 'morbidly vivid' escape dream acted out by an apparently 'gothic' lunatic who functions as the more sedate heroine's double." Thus writes Sandra Gilbert in *The Madwoman in the Attic,* about this "distinctively female *Bildungsroman,"* which, she says, presents a "basic female enclosure-escape story."[37] *Jane Eyre* would seem to be the living proof that there is an alternative female aesthetic that escapes patriarchal determination.

It is true that *Jane Eyre* makes a strong claim for women's rights to intellectual and economic independence, threatening revolution if women remain confined to passive inactivity. Jane protests: "Women are supposed to be very calm generally: but women feel just as men feel; they need exercise for their faculties, and a field for their efforts as much as their brothers do; they suffer from too rigid a restraint, too absolute a stagnation, precisely as men would suffer; and it is narrow-minded in their more privileged fellow-creatures to say that they ought to confine themselves to making puddings and knitting stockings, to playing on the piano and embroidering bags."[38] Even more convincing than Jane's articulated rebellion is the success of her quest. She gets it all: independence, a loving family, an aristocratic husband who adores her, children, and, most significant, power. Her marriage is a partnership in

[37]Sandra M. Gilbert and Susan Gubar, *The Madwoman in the Attic: The Woman Writer and the Nineteenth-Century Literary Imagination* (New Haven: Yale Univ. Press, 1979), p. 314. See also Patricia Meyer Spacks, *The Female Imagination* (London: Allen and Unwin, 1976), pp. 58–66.

[38]Charlotte Brontë, *Jane Eyre,* ed. Q. D. Leavis (1847; rpt. Harmondsworth, Eng.: Penguin, 1976), p. 141, cited hereafter in the text.

which Jane seems the dominant member. In Gilbert's words: Cinderella and the prince become democratic equals. That this notion is, and certainly was, politically subversive needs no proof. Matthew Arnold's comments on Brontë's "hunger, rebellion, and rage" have become legendary. Thus read *mimetically,* as the representation of a woman's quest for subjectivity, *Jane Eyre* adds to the masculine tradition of the quest for subjectivity a specifically feminine element in its coverage of activities, problems, and feelings that are intrinsically related to women's experience. Women have made, and do make, a real contribution to the genre in theme and subject. As Gilbert and Gubar argue, they have also enlarged the possibilities of the novel as form by adapting traditionally non-realist modes and styles (gothic, romance) to the expression of woman's sense of her own otherness.

But the novel can also be viewed from a different readerly perspective. Instead of studying it mimetically or even psychologically, as the dramatization of women's unexpressed and inexpressible rage, I should like to focus on its strategies of articulation. What allows the narrative to make its feminist point?

Like *Tom Jones, Jane Eyre* presents the quest for subjectivity as the orphan's search for a permanent home. "Poor obscure, plain, and little" (p. 281), Jane lacks even the good-natured charm that is Tom's claim to attention and power. Thus she misses the one quality that in a patriarchal determination of her identity lends woman power (and a home and a place in the social structure). Jane's anger not only derives from envy and spite; it also recognizes the injustice that the accidental circumstance of beauty and not character or intelligence should have been designated woman's "identity." Her aunt Reed barely tolerates her, since her intelligence and anger make her different, a "discord" in Gateshead Hall. Locked into the red room in punishment for her rebellion and rage at being "other," Jane confronts the reality of her position: in the mirror she finds reflected not an autonomous self but her otherness—the fact that as woman she has no autonomy, no identity independent of patriarchal determination at all. Otherness is her essence: "All looked colder and darker in that visionary hollow than in reality: and the strange little figure there gazing at me with a white face and arms specking the gloom, and glittering eyes of fear moving where all else was still, had the effect of a real spirit: I thought it like one of the tiny phantoms, half fairy, half imp" (p. 46).

Jane's quest for autonomy, then, will necessarily be an ambivalent adaptation to patriarchal notions; she finds support in patriarchy's own valorization of mind over body and exploits her intellect (connoted masculine) to gain economic independence. She begins by outsmarting her aunt Reed by invoking the name and memory of her deceased uncle, thus turning the ghostlike, symbolic power of patriarchy against its actual power. If Jane is determined "other," she, in turn, interprets patriarchy as a spiritual rather than a physical force. Throughout her life she will rely on an ideal, romantic, and revisionary notion of patriarchy to guide her steps until she marries Rochester, who is himself the embodiment of that idea.

In order for this to happen, Jane's quest must first pass a gallery of female portraits surveying contemporary options: Christian meekness and submission (Helen Burns), self-effacing gentility (Mrs. Fairfax), cold disdain (Miss Temple), "French" sensuous vanity (Adèle and her mother), or upper-class imperiousness (Blanche Ingram), to end with sisterly affection (dependent for its perpetuation on money bequeathed by an uncle). Whatever Jane does, she will have to accept dependence on patriarchal determination. Though she does not accept St. John Rivers's offer to accompany him as helpmeet in his missionary work, she is severely tempted, because his appeal, while denying the importance of love and affection, is made in the name of an abstract spiritual principle. Through the miraculous intervention of nature, however, she is united to Rochester.

My point in providing this plot summary is to enforce awareness that what happens in the story also happens at the level of articulation: Jane's reunion with Rochester, the seeming triumph of feminine desire, is brought about at the expense of the exclusion of the otherness of Rochester's legal wife: a man-eating monster, a vampire, "intemperate" and "unchaste," worse than any harlot, a "clothed hyena," with "virile force" (resembling in stature and type of beauty Jane's rival Blanche Ingram). We may well echo the question of the text: "What crime was this, that lived incarnate in

this sequestered mansion, and could neither be expelled nor sub-
dued by its owner?—what mystery, that broke out, now in fire
and now in blood, at the deadest hours of night? What creature
was it, that, masked in an ordinary woman's face and shape, uttered the voice, now of a mocking demon, and anon of a carrion-
seeking bird of prey?" (pp. 239–40). The answer is, of course, a
woman, an excluded woman—woman as patriarchy connotes and
fears her. If we interpret the figure of Bertha Mason as just the
expression of Jane's subconscious rage—as Gilbert does—we miss
the point. Bertha Mason must die for Jane to get what she wants.
Her death makes Jane's happiness possible. The monstrous figure
of Bertha Mason is both Jane's and Brontë's scapegoat. Her exclusion eradicates female otherness and safeguards patriarchy. But in
resorting to this strategy of exclusion, Brontë—as we shall see
more clearly after the discussion of *Tom Jones*—employs the time-
honored rhetorical strategy of the exclusion of the feminine, which
patriarchy uses to protect the coherence of self, society, and text.
Indeed, the author "unsexes" both herself and her protagonist.
Bertha Mason's insanity is only the more extreme form of Jane's
rage, her exclusion, her unearthly eeriness, the impression she
gives of "scheming plots underhand" (p. 58), not to forget the
archetypal connotation of liar. It is St. John himself who calls
Jane's speech "violent, unfeminine, and untrue." Thus Bertha's
sacrifice is also the exclusion of Jane's own otherness, her final
assimilation to patriarchy's conception of woman's identity.

   A curious phenomenon in the narrative strategy of the text confirms my reading. The novel is presented as a first-person retro-
spective account of Jane's life, but it concludes by appropriating
Jane's narrative voice. Instead of lending her autonomous authority, the conclusion wholly dispossesses her of her power to speak,
allowing her only to echo St. John's words: " 'My master,' he
says, 'has forewarned me. Daily He announces more distinctly,
'Surely I come quickly!' and hourly I more eagerly respond,
'Amen; even so, come, Lord Jesus!' " (p. 477). Thus Jane's voice
fuses with St. John's address to and celebration of his Lord and
Master. From a rhetorical perspective, *Jane Eyre* is not so much a
celebration of female autonomy as the repetition of Jane's ambivalent strategy of fighting under the banner of a Christian revi-

sion of patriarchy, more propitious to women than the feudal variety because it valorizes spirit over body.

Whereas woman cannot be the "subject" of the novel, then, she is its text, just as she was already patriarchy's text before the novel arose. In her analysis of Eve's education in Milton's *Paradise Lost,* Christine Froula focuses on the fact that Eve is required to renounce the pleasurable recognition of herself as beautiful provided by the mirroring surface of the water, to identify with the less amenable masculine shape of Adam, who, I hardly need say, was made in the Father's image. The evidence of sense impression must be renounced and transcended in favor of the abstract, intangible idea. The undoing of feminine self-sufficiency is "the genesis of Genesis," Froula argues.[39] Indeed, Milton's depiction of the *Bildung* of Eve is emblematic of the "plot" of patriarchy. It requires dematerialization, disembodiment, the triumph of abstract spirit over tangible matter. Its resonance harks back in history to Moses' denouncement of idols and graven images and points forward to Freud's affirmative reinterpretation in *Moses and Monotheism,* which glorifies Mosaic law as the victory of thought over sense impression, civilization over nature, patriarchy over matriarchy.

Milton is important to this study for several reasons. In addition to his emphasis on the importance of the abstract idea, which will later aid in understanding the dialectic of the inscription of gender in the history of the novel, his work embodies the rationalist humanist inspiration of Christian epic,[40] which formed the model for Fielding's *Joseph Andrews.* Most important, however, Milton's depiction of the education of Eve demonstrates that woman—as medium of patriarchal self-presence—becomes patriarchy's focus of attention, desire, and voyeuristic drive. Her otherness, her exclusion from culture (which patriarchal discourse inscribes as "castration"), her nakedness, and later in history, her sexuality, become the fascinating mystery inviting inscription. Woman—in her otherness—becomes patriarchy's prime object of representation.

[39]"When Eve Reads Milton: Undoing the Canonical Economy," *Critical Inquiry* 10 (1983), 317.

[40]See Dennis R. Danielson, "*Imago Dei,* 'Filial Freedom,' and Miltonic Theodicy," *ELH* 47 (1980), 670–82.

The triumphant Roman emperor entered the city in a procession that displayed the vanquished to the populace as proof of his victory. It would be an exaggeration to use this relationship as metaphor for the condition of woman's presence in the patriarchal text, but Milton's inscription of Eve, and the Rembrandt etching that illustrates this book, point to the function of the image in the composition of the text as a whole: Eve's otherness confirms Adam's masculine transcendence; she *is* his subjectivity.

In Rembrandt's etching (antedating *Paradise Lost* by some twenty years) Eve, vividly naked, is placed at the center; the viewer's eyes are made to focus on her belly and her sex. The circle of her navel, the point marking the link between generations but also the abyss at the heart of presence, is the central point of her figure and of the picture. It unites the two like an upholsterer's button. A diagonal line moves the beholder's eye from the apple in Eve's hand (the formal copy and symbol of the circular navel) to Adam's uplifted hand. Interestingly, however, this hand is not held up to receive the apple. It is the uplifted, admonishing finger representing patriarchy. The other hand, closer to the apple, seems to be warding off the seductive appeal of the fruit. Since the figure of Adam is placed higher than Eve, the message of the representation would seem to be Adam's rejective transcendence of Eve's naturalness and sexuality, but this message contradicts the story we know from the Bible. It was Adam's acceptance of the apple which betokened the Fall. Indeed, the composition of the representation as a whole seems to reflect a more overtly patriarchal rewriting of Genesis, hinging on the opposition between nature and culture. The figures are placed on a diagonal line that moves upward from right to left. Though Eve is placed in the middle, she stands significantly lower than Adam, and is associated with an elephant and a monstrous Satan in the shape of a winged crocodile hanging in a tree. The semantics of the picture would seem to suggest a progress from frightening, primeval nature (monstrous and, paradoxically, phallic), via Eve, to Adam's finger pointing to the invisible Maker.

More than anything, this brief analysis suggests that representation is itself a patriarchal undertaking and must necessarily issue from the patriarchal point of view, but in order to inscribe itself, patriarchy needs the figure and idea of woman as the "other" that confirms its self-presence. Whereas the inscription of woman as "other" remains the scaffolding for patriarchy, each century imagines that otherness differently. Consequently, the configuration of subjectivity changes too. As medium for patriarchal self-presence, the idea of the mother shares the fate of all less privileged poles in dialectical oppositions. The repressed eventually returns; slaves turn into masters. With regard to the inscription of the figure of woman in the novel, we note that, because of patriarchy's necessary dependence on her otherness, that otherness, understood as originary nature, unrestrained sexuality, duplicity, or multiplicity of meaning, has paradoxically gained privilege and prestige, especially in postmodernist texts.

To outline the shift in the inscription of woman and her role in the constitution of the subject, I should like to begin by quoting Max Horkheimer and Theodor Adorno's *Dialectic of Enlightenment,* which clearly identifies patriarchy with Western culture and its history: "For millennia men dreamed of acquiring absolute mastery over nature, of converting the cosmos into one immense hunting-ground. It was to this that the idea of man was geared in a male-dominated society. This was the significance of his reason, his proudest boast."[41] Defining reason as the contrast-effect of nature, Horkheimer and Adorno centrally situate the inscription of woman as nature in the history of Western culture. As we shall see later, however, in the history of the novel the dream of "absolute mastery over nature" patly applies to *Tom Jones.* Tacitly omitting the guilt of the mother who obscures the place of her son in society by covering up his origin, the fiction designates origin, identity, and home as deriving solely from the patriarchal structure. The seeming self-containment of Fielding's authorial attitude (dependent, as we shall find, on his understanding of the medium, language, as index of presence) seems to have lost its self-evidence by the mid–nineteenth century, however. In Dickens's *Bleak House,* paternal origin is obscured and subjectivity and meaning are threatened by the presence of the mother. The design of the fiction becomes an attempt to retrace the path to the father, clearing the

[41]Trans. J. Cumming (1944; rpt. New York: Seabury Press, 1972), p. 248.

fog obscuring origin and identity, which has been loosened by
Lady Dedlock's illicit genesis of Esther Summerson. A new conception of nature (whether regarded as the last intimation of original presence, as in romantic poetry, or understood as materialism
and science is not immediately relevant here) has come to threaten
patriarchy's self-presence as spirit, and Darwin's revisionary account, *The Origin of Species,* provides an analogue to Dickens's
style of authority. Finally, in Joyce, we note the emphatic celebration of the natural as originary power. In addition to the minute
attention given to the physical reality of Dublin, one notes the
depiction of bodily functions, which had always been excluded
from fictional representation. More specifically, Joyce focuses on
woman as *das ewig Weibliche,* making her the alpha and omega of
his fiction. Indeed, it might be argued that in Joyce the hierarchical
structure of patriarchy is overturned, that *Ulysses* and *Finnegans
Wake* stage the presence of the mother.[42]

That conclusion would be mistaken, however. What happened
in the centuries between Fielding and Joyce is not the acknowledgment of the "other" as subject and original presence. Rather, patriarchy's *other* medium, language, changed in connotation; the
reversal from absence to presence is not the breakdown of the
patriarchal project but its more sophisticated inscription. In *The
Order of Things,* Michel Foucault points to a shift from "representation" to "signification," destroying the "profound kinship of
language with the world" which existed just before the rise of the
novel.[43] Unlike the older era of representation, which took language as index of the real, the later episteme regards it as medium,
sign.[44] Foucault's suggestion is helpful in describing the break
between the two epistemes as a turn from grammar (as the reincarnation of paradigm) to philology (the tracing of origins) and from
natural history to biology—changes that articulate the difference
between *Bleak House* and *Tom Jones.* Most important, however,

[42]See Colin MacCabe, *James Joyce and the Revolution of the Word* (London: Macmillan, 1978).
[43](New York: Random House, 1973), p. 43.
[44]Roland Barthes relates this shift to the turn from a feudal society, where
monarchy is based on land, to an industrial economy, where there is no immediately tangible origin of wealth or power.

Foucault alerts us to the tie between the conceptualization of the idea of the mother and the attitude to language. Language, as medium of communication, is defined by its relation to indecidability. As Umberto Eco expresses it, "*Every time there is possibility of lying, there is a sign-function:* which is to signify (and then to communicate) something to which no real state of things corresponds. . . . The possibility of lying is the *proprium* of semiosis just as (for the Schoolmen) the possibility of laughing was the *proprium* of Man as *animal rationale.*"[45] This possible presence of the lie is what language has in common with woman (who can hide paternity), and just as an ideal patriarchy must repress the possibility of equivocation concerning patrilinear descent, it must fix the referential dispersion of words for absolute self-presence. Thus the history of the inscription of woman in patriarchy is tied to patriarchy's understanding of language and its style of narrative authority.

At first sight, this argument may seem only to confirm the demise of patriarchy. Joyce's style exploits the plurality of meaning, the gap between word and reality for the suggestive force of his own representation, just as he foregrounds the feminine. In fact, it is not wrong to think of Joyce as the precursor of *écriture féminine:* his style flaunts its subversive otherness, coded feminine.[46] The history of the novel would seem to have given increasing visibility to woman—from discourse *about* woman to that *by* woman to Joyce's discourse *as* woman. Fictional authority styles itself as woman—marking the suspension of, to use Derrida's words, "the decidable opposition between true and non-true."[47]

The point is, however, that Joyce's move is not the opening up to the originary presence of the "other" but the assimilation of those qualities coded "other" to what remains the constitutive instrument of patriarchy: discourse, text. The inscription of Molly

[45]*A Theory of Semiotics* (Bloomington: Indiana Univ. Press, 1976), pp. 58–59.
[46]Hélène Cixous, with whom the notion of *écriture féminine* is identified, may have been influenced by Joyce, with whose works she is intimately acquainted. *The Exile of James Joyce,* trans. Sally A. J. Purcell (London: John Calder, 1976), first published in French in 1968, offers a close reading of Joyce, without, however, touching on the thesis of my book.
[47]*Spurs: Nietzsche's Styles* (Chicago: Univ. of Chicago Press, 1979), p. 107.

Bloom—Joyce's creature and muse—remains the obsessed projection of patriarchal ideas of otherness. It still codes the "other" by means of sexual difference. Now, however, femininity is inscribed not as maternal generativity but as the (supposed) groundlessness of woman's experience of the sexual act. More than ever, she is man's idea of woman, patriarchy's text. As Derrida and Lacan proclaim, there is no truth of woman in herself, since "there is no truth in itself of the sexual difference in itself, of either man or woman in itself."[48] Her inscription then, even if it is the emphatic foregrounding rather than the repression of an idea of nature, is no more than the magic attempt to contain and defuse the threat of the presence of the "other." Instead of breaking down the patriarchal project, Modernity provides its most sophisticated expression. Sublating difference, marking everything "inscription," it subverts the reality and importance of body, flesh, and matter, which are "always already" denoted patriarchal text. Eve has finally become totally disembodied. Indeed, from a long historical perspective, Modernity's inscription of woman as undecidable otherness and its high charge of sexually colored idiom may not be very different from Rembrandt's use of Eve as text, and it accomplishes Milton's design to "spiritualize" Eve, eroding her substantiality; the idea of man necessarily follows.

I have no illusion that it is possible to step outside the sway of patriarchy. Its logic seems, at present, still incontrovertible. Like Archimedes, the female critic who wishes to object to the use of gender as metaphor and who desires a change in the contemporary inscription of woman as a primarily sexual creature rather than *animal rationale* (even if she realizes that the coding in terms of gender is not, and cannot be, intended to refer to actual women as historical beings) lacks a point from which to move the world of discourse.[49] Moreover, in writing, she inevitably makes herself the accomplice of the patriarchal project. If she cannot escape participation, however, she can choose her own subject matter and style. In the analyses that follow, to create awareness of the im-

[48]Ibid., p. 103.
[49]See Myra Jehlen, "Archimedes and the Paradox of Feminist Criticism," *Signs* 6 (1981), 575–601.

plication of connotations of gender in signification, I shall deliberately reemphasize difference, pointing again and again to the moments when the textual (hence patriarchal) requirement of single
origin and meaning perverts the logic of noncontradiction. Moreover, I shall use "historical" material for my argument, because
only the difference of the past can demonstrate that the inscriptions
of the "other" are variable, encouraging the recognition that the
images our culture so obsessively projects in advertising, movies,
fiction, and so forth, need not exhaust the possible. All inscriptions
and legitimations are human products, and the future need not be
like the present. If that future is to come about—however impossible it may be, at present, to *think* it—we must continue to investigate the complex configurations of woman, origin, and authority
in the discourses of our culture. As Derrida writes, "Their history
is history itself, a history which philosophy alone, inasmuch as it is
included therein, is unable to decode."[50]

[50]*Spurs*, p. 87.

2

The Novel as Foundling

a speech
Of the self that must sustain itself as speech
——Wallace Stevens, "The Well
Dressed Man with a Beard"

In our society literature is a luxury. Unlike scientific or philosophical discourse, fiction is not clothed in the prestigious aura of truth or necessity. The stories we tell about ourselves and our society may be taken as reflecting a deeper, psychological truth; yet they are valued differently from other forms of discourse since they do not provide tools by which humanity conquers its world—or so, at least, popular understanding would seem to hold. It is my intention here to show that the novel *is* a central text, much more central than our idolatry of fact and figure allows us to acknowledge. Discourse analysis has shown how the truths of philosophy or history rest upon rhetorical configurations. Are we not almost invited to demonstrate, then, that the rhetoric of the novel conveys an argument—more specifically, an argument about human identity and nature? The novel is neither a playful caprice of the imagination, divorced from any bearings in the "real," nor merely the mirror reflection of society. There is a process of mutual interaction and reconfirmation between text and history, and the image in the mirror constitutes and confirms the idea of human subjectivity in an interactional process.

This is a large and ambitious claim, which I shall try to prove in a reading of Fielding's *Tom Jones*. I have chosen this novel over other eighteenth-century fictions because Fielding's consciousness of the innovative nature of his endeavor makes it relatively easy to detect the set of assumptions and ideas which supported the birth

44

of this new "species." The main points of my reading of *Tom Jones*—which will follow in a later chapter—will rest upon a demonstration that the argument of the fiction reflects the structure of the constitution of a subjective self as internal division and the exclusion of otherness. The structure of this "journey to selfhood," to use Mark Taylor's words,[1] is shared by many narratives that explain human beings to themselves (whether Genesis, Descartes, Hegel, Kierkegaard, Freud, or Lacan). I must here anticipate that demonstration with an introductory exploration of the intertextual roots of the novel in Genesis and *The Odyssey* and with a tentative exploration of its relation to the contemporary philosophical and literary debate on the nature of man. It is a metalepsis demanded by my subject. The circularity of the epigenetic plot and the tautology of Fielding's argument mark any point of beginning as arbitrary. To establish the importance of Fielding's novel as a representative fiction and to place it in the contemporary history of ideas, therefore, I will begin this discussion with a bird's-eye view of some of the larger issues of context and structure involved in understanding the novel as the fiction of identity and will leave the analysis of the text to the next chapter.

The Search for the Name-of-the-Father

The full title of Fielding's novel, *The History of Tom Jones, a Foundling,* claims to present a history—a true account of factual events—about a child without ties to parents or place in society. Fiction is rife with protagonists whose parentage is unknown. The nineteenth-century novel in particular tends to present its protagonists as orphans, semiorphans, or foundlings. Esther Summerson, whose story we shall trace in a later chapter, is a case in point, a representative heroine who shares her homelessness with Jane Eyre, Oliver Twist, Daniel Deronda, Lucy Snowe, Jude Fawley, Henry Esmond, Heathcliff, and countless other fictional figures. The predominance of the orphan in the Victorian novel would seem to suggest that the theme of homelessness, the search for the

---

[1] *Journeys to Selfhood.*

father, had special symbolic resonance in that era, as indeed my reading of *Bleak House* will confirm. It should not be thought that the figure of the orphan, or its symbolic resonance, is limited to that period, however. Indeed, the image of the orphan, the foundling or bastard, may well be identified with the genre itself.[2] The English novel begins with a portrayal of alienation from the parents in the histories of Robinson Crusoe, Moll Flanders, Pamela, and Clarissa, even though these characters are not orphans in the strict sense of the word. The problematic awareness of a breach between the individual self and the matrix, a sense of alienation from full presence—"transcendental homelessness," as Lukács calls it—is one of the mainsprings of the eighteenth-century novel. Even Tristram Shandy's inability to begin the account of his birth ironically reverses the accepted theme.

This generic preoccupation with paternity is related to social changes, especially the rise of the middle class and the disruption of a traditional rural society, the revisionary unbinding of the structure of feudal society. These changes, the crumbling of the idea of what Lovejoy called the Great Chain of Being, may themselves be understood as correlated with changes in the manner of ordering and understanding the world which are reflected in developments in social organization.[3]

The novel's concern with parentage may be more than the direct expression of actual social conditions, then, though it is, of course, a necessary collateral. We might see it as an algebra, a symbolic language in which the problems of order and identity inherent in human self-consciousness can be articulated and redefined. The orphan and the other figures belonging to the family romance express actual historical circumstances, as well as providing "things to think with." Like the counters of an abacus, they are instruments in a process of reordering, of imagining more satisfying configurations of humanity's origin and place in the cosmos. Thus the predominance of the figure of the orphan in the genre of the novel suggests that fiction, rather than present brilliant but

[2]See, for example, Marthe Robert, *Roman des origines et origines du roman* (Paris: Bernard Grasset, 1972).

[3]For a discussion of the differences between a Renaissance and an eighteenth-century ("classical") categorization of reality, see Foucault, *The Order of Things*.

ultimately limited imitations of the social reality (much like Dr. Johnson's view of seventeenth-century Dutch painting), aims at making a statement about alienation from full presence, a statement that can be compared to the articulations, however differently embodied, of philosophy and religion. Each enactment of the family romance is an attempt to define human identity in relation to an original source. Each version of the motif is a revisionary conceptualization or restatement of the ontological problem of human separation from nature and ignorance of the All. In short, the story of the orphan allegorizes a possible relationship between being and existence. Whereas the problem of redefining man's identity may have been especially acute in the nineteenth century (for reasons we shall see later), the history of the novel begins as a redefinition of the articulation of the relationship between being and existence which had formed the basic cultural text of a preceding epoch as expressed in the biblical story of Genesis.

Fielding's history of a foundling is not just a story of the discovery of parentage; it offers a specific form of family romance. The account of Tom's adventures progresses toward an apocalyptic end that echoes the beginning, albeit with a difference. The narrative offers an account of Tom's discovery of his true home and parentage which leads him back to the place from which he was originally expelled. Thus the story presents a circular quest in which origin is related to end in a totalizing vision. The oppositional two (Allworthy and Tom) are fused into one, and "identity" is revealed as a temporarily obscured presence awaiting rediscovery. *Tom Jones* offers a secular version of the dialectic myth of return, earlier embodied in Homer's *Odyssey* and Milton's epic sequence *Paradise Lost* and *Paradise Regained,* which are intertextually present in the novel through overt allusion.[4]

---

[4]My suggestion of a mythic structure in realistic narrative may seem to mingle concepts that distinguish between genres and modes. Nevertheless, recognition of the intertextual roots of the genre, and of *Tom Jones* in particular, seems increasingly influential. Sheridan Baker, the editor of the Norton Critical Edition, *Tom Jones: An Authoritative Text* (New York: Norton, 1973), points out that the psychological effect of this fiction is its fulfillment of what may be the reader's "deepest psychic need, to find his identity, and with it the dream of recognition, riches, and the beautiful princess" (p. vii). For a discussion of *Tom Jones* and romance, see Henry Knight Miller, *Henry Fielding's "Tom Jones" and the Romance*

One peculiarity of the story rests in the scandalous fact that the protagonist is a bastard, a child born outside the patriarchal law that governs culture and understanding. As in Fielding's earlier novel *Joseph Andrews,* the rewards at the end of the quest—the discovery of a home, a bride, a fortune, and social position—are attendant on the discovery of the name-of-the-father. All benefits accruing to the protagonist, though perhaps not directly dependent on the revelation of birth, are related to the issues of law and the acknowledgment of patriarchal authority. The curious point about *Tom Jones* is that Fielding should have chosen to let Tom remain a bastard, even after his lineage has been discovered; this aspect of the story raised contemporary objections about its morality, especially from Richardson.[5] It would have been a relatively simple change in the story to reveal that Bridget had always been married to Tom's father.

Tom's bastardy, however, does add a special point to the symbolic resonance of the story. One of the implications of Tom's illegitimacy is that it transforms the circular quest from a search for an actual father (whether alive or dead) into the quest for the name-of-the-father, for a symbol in language representing the law of patriarchal transmission of power, property, and identity. It makes Tom's quest at once more specific and more abstract and universal. If the circular quest as a form of family romance allegorizes the relationship between being and existence (or God the Father and man), Fielding's emphasis on Tom's illegitimacy defines *being*

Tradition, ELS Monograph Series 6 (Victoria, B.C.: Univ. of Victoria Press, 1976); and J. Paul Hunter, *Occasional Form: Henry Fielding and the Chains of Circumstance* (Baltimore: Johns Hopkins Univ. Press, 1975). Their intertextual approach to the novel, on which my reading is also based, had its inception with Battestin's *The Moral Basis of Fielding's Art: A Study of "Joseph Andrews"* (Middletown, Conn.: Wesleyan Univ. Press, 1959).

    [5]Samuel Richardson to Mrs. Donellan, February 22, 1752, in *Novel and Romance, 1700–1800: A Documentary Record,* ed. Ioan Williams (London: Routledge and Kegan Paul, 1970), p. 174. Here Richardson points out that Fielding made "his hero . . . a natural child, because his own first wife was such." For the contemporary discussion about the point of Tom's illegitimacy, see F. T. Blanchard, *Fielding the Novelist: A Study in Historical Criticism* (1926; rpt. New York: Russell and Russell, 1966), pp. 38, 41, 63, 68. C. J. Rawson, *Henry Fielding and the Augustan Ideal under Stress* (London: Routledge, 1972), discusses the issue.

more closely as the abstract or symbolic principle of paternity—a spiritual rather than a physical power or presence.

Fielding's strategy acquires special interest in connection with Lacan's revision of Freudian psychoanalysis. Freud postulated the murder of an *ur-Vater* as the primal scene of culture. This murder is reenacted in the individual Oedipal desire to kill the father, a desire that must be repressed to bind the self to society. Lacan imagines this primal repression not as a historical, albeit archaic fact, but as the moment of advent of language. The *ur*-father is already a metaphor, a word or name rather than a physical presence. While Lacan keeps the Freudian personification of the father as agency and source of patriarchal law, consciousness, and culture, he disembodies and dematerializes it, as the "name-of-the-father." True power rests not with the father's greater physical strength but with the symbolic authority representative of an ulterior law governing consciousness, language, and society—together embodying the symbolic order.

By keeping his hero illegitimate Fielding presents his fiction as a quest for the name-of-the-father, a quest for the symbolic principle of patriarchy and of Western culture. Lacan's emphasis is helpful in establishing the representative nature of Fielding's story, as well as its continued relevance for us today. The trajectory that returns Tom to Paradise Hall—the move away from an unspeakable tie to the mother and to nature which marks his assumption of patriarchal power and responsibility—sketches the narrow path toward selfhood and identity which is important in post-Renaissance Western culture: Tom's journey to selfhood mirrors the journey outlined by (Protestant) Christian, Freudian, or Lacanian doctrine.

Since the narrative that presents this journey reenacts the transition from nature to culture (the prerequisite for accession to law, language, and narrative in its exclusion of the otherness of woman), we might read *Tom Jones* as a fiction that points the way to narrative authority: it leads the protagonist to the place and position from which he is entitled to speak. Thus *The History of Tom Jones, a Foundling* self-consciously enacts what we might well call the plot of plot. The relevance of our investigation of the structure of the fiction, then, extends beyond the individual case. It will crystallize the implicit and unconscious process, the "plot," by which our culture constitutes the subjective self.

The story of Tom is also the story of his accession to language and authority, so that the attribute "a foundling" could also be taken to bear on the genealogy of the fiction itself. The question about Tom's identity is also a query about the legitimacy and authority of the genre, and the process of discovery which is the plot of *Tom Jones* is simultaneously the justification of the art of "Invention,"[6] the kind of writing which attempts to sketch an image of human nature and identity, which is "novel" not only in form but in intention. The legitimacy of the new species of writing is closely related to the new vision of human identity and place in the world. The novel both reflects and constitutes a new, modern understanding of man. Fielding's concern to legitimize his procedure, to distinguish his invention from "idle Romances which are filled with Monsters" (IV, i), testifies to the importance he attached to the fiction, as does the argument in the Preface to *Joseph Andrews* that his seemingly illegitimate kind of writing was descended from an absent and lost parent, the comic Homeric epic *Margites*. Just as Tom is a bastard of genteel lineage, so the fiction into which this ambivalent figure is projected is redeemed from exclusion by virtue of its descent from a prestigious ancestor. Fielding's concern for this point testifies to the seriousness of his belief in the representative "Truth" of his fiction.[7]

There seems an identification in Fielding's mind between the formal expression and the nature of his fiction. His great fear is that his story will be classified with the frivolous novels and romances after French example, which Shaftesbury in his "Mis-

[6]Henry Fielding, *The History of Tom Jones, a Foundling*, 2 vols., ed. Martin Battestin and Fredson Bowers, The Wesleyan Edition of the Works of Henry Fielding (Oxford: Clarendon Press, 1974), IX, i. References to book and chapter appear hereafter in the text.

[7]See Homer Obed Brown's important essay "*Tom Jones:* The 'Bastard' of History," *Boundary 2*, 7, 2 (1979), 201–33, which makes a similar point and to which my reading of *Tom Jones* is deeply indebted. Fielding's "argument" for the truth of his fiction was not idiosyncratic. Lord Monboddo's *Of the Origin and Progress of Language* echoes Fielding's claims and points out that the new species of narrative is "a legitimate kind of poem." See E. M. W. Tillyard, *The Epic Strain in the English Novel* (Fair Lawn, N.J.: Essential Books, 1958), p. 54.

cellaneous Reflections" characterized as "things most *unnatural* and *monstrous*".[8] Shaftesbury's epithets reinforce the identification between the novelty of the genre and the unprecedented nature of its protagonist. Considered more closely, Fielding's own thinking about fiction shows a deterministic bias that almost seems to contradict his liberal views on the importance of character over birth. Whereas his fiction argues that Tom, even if illegitimate, is nevertheless finally worthy to inherit Paradise Hall, in his discursive disquisitions on the nature of fiction Fielding does not hesitate to point out that there are a "Swarm of foolish Novels, and Monstrous Romances" (ix, i) that do not derive from "Nature" (read: literary tradition) but originate from the heated fancy or "distempered Brains" (iv, i) of their authors. He concludes that it is not surprising that "Works so nastily derived should be nasty themselves, or have a Tendency to make others so" (ix, i).

What Fielding's conflation of fictional and human genealogy, however ambivalent, forces to our attention is the high seriousness of his authorial design. *Tom Jones* is meant to be more than a fictional entertainment: it is an attempt to continue and revitalize the tradition of epic. In claiming general truth for his fiction, Fielding also aspired to the *function* of epic: to express not an individual perspective but a transcendent, collective vision, to articulate the voice of his culture, or what Lacan calls its "symbolic order." Fielding's stance suggests that his version of the family romance records and traces a new (but finally respectable) image of man's place in relationship to the All. *Tom Jones* wants to be read as what Northrop Frye calls a "secular scripture."[9]

A large part of Fielding criticism seems to have taken him at his word. Many articles and books "explain" Fielding's moral intentions, his views on Christianity, his ironic didacticism, his relationship to contemporary thought, and so on.[10] My argument shares that outlook, but there is a critical difference between the

[8]Shaftesbury quoted in *Tom Jones,* ed. Battestin and Bowers, vol. i, p. 150n.
[9]*The Secular Scripture: A Study of the Structure of Romance* (Cambridge, Mass.: Harvard Univ. Press, 1976).
[10]Most helpful to my understanding has been the work of Martin Battestin: *The Providence of Wit: Aspects of Form in Augustan Literature and the Arts* (Oxford: Clarendon Press, 1974). The chapter on Fielding refines the insights of his *"Tom Jones:*

traditional interpretations of Fielding's novel in the light of philosophy or religion and the intertextual one that follows. I intend to examine the relationship between Genesis and the novel with a number of questions in mind. What is the point of the intertextual presence of Genesis? How does Fielding change or vary the traditional story? What accounts for the necessity of the deviation? What does Fielding's rewriting of Genesis tell us about the symbolic order and our modern notion of the self?

The first and most important question is Why should Fielding have chosen to model his fiction on Genesis at all? As the first book of the Old Testament, Genesis stands at the beginning of Christian and Hebraic myth and religion. It is a foundational narrative in two ways: it gives an account of the coming into being of the cosmos as well as human beings, and it explains the logos as principle, as the law of creation, the law of becoming. The Christian name for the book, "Genesis" (Hebrew uses *Bereshit,* the first word, meaning "in the beginning"), goes back to an Indo-European root cognate with the English verb *to engender,* suggesting that Christianity has always pictured the creation of the world as a family romance. Genesis is the primal scene of family romance: God the Father begets the world. The passage also tells about the nature of his paternity. It is the Father's verbal creativity, his utterance of the Word, which projects the world. This Word generates a process of differentiation and separation which constitutes identity. It institutes heaven and earth in the act of separating them. There follows differentiation of light from darkness, water from land. Man is identified by his separation from nature, and woman is identified by her difference from man. Even the species of plants and animals are created each "after their kind," and the law of difference which has created the Garden and all that is in it, is represented in the two trees that are marked off from the other vegetation: the Tree of Knowledge and the Tree of Life.

Though Genesis contains two accounts of creation—the first

The Argument of Design," in *The Augustan Milieu: Essays Presented to Louis A. Landa,* ed. Henry K. Miller et al. (Oxford: Clarendon Press, 1970), pp. 289–320, and "Fielding's Definition of Wisdom: Some Functions of Ambiguity and Emblem in *Tom Jones,*" *ELH* 35 (1968), 188–217, rpt. in the Norton Critical Edition of *Tom Jones,* ed. Baker, pp. 817–44.

concerned with the institution of the cosmos and the second with the creation of man and his placement in the Garden of Eden— both stories present the act of creation as the institution of difference and opposition, a process that separates and, in the same movement institutes hierarchy. Thus man is identified by his difference from the animal world and is placed over nature. Adam is set over Eve, Abel is preferred over Cain, and so on, in a pattern that reflects the principle of intellectual ordering and understanding. The law of Genesis might be seen as the Heraclitean logos of differential and hierarchical opposition.[11] Perhaps more pertinently, it is the Aristotelian logical principle of mutual exclusion, which holds that A cannot be both A and not-A (or B) at the same time. The principle of difference and hierarchy in Genesis is the principle of thought itself and the law of the symbolic order. Genesis defines the Father's creativity as the institution and reenactment of this law.

In defining the Father, Genesis also defines his creature, man. The real motivation for the story of Genesis is man's need to define and picture his own metaphysical origin and identity. Thus, Genesis also gives information about the nature of man's consciousness and his awareness of himself as alienated from full presence. Man is identified as different from the Father and from nature. Even before the story of the Fall, man is already separate from the All, from absolute knowledge. Homer Obed Brown depicts the Fall as "a myth grounding distance as estrangement, time as succession, the necessity of error or wandering, and thus of fiction and history."[12] The event of the Fall and its aftermath only crystallizes a state of difference from the All which was present from the beginning. The Fall narrates man's *consciousness* of separation, rather than the fact or event itself.

The story of the Fall is itself a repetitive enactment of the institution of difference and hierarchy with which Genesis begins. The Fall brings about a breach in time, splitting it into a before and

[11]See W. K. C. Guthrie, "Flux and *Logos* in Heraclitus," in *The Pre-Socratics,* ed. A. P. D. Mourelatus (New York: Anchor/Doubleday, 1974), pp. 197–213. This essay is a reprint of the relevant section in Guthrie, *A History of Greek Philosophy,* vol. 1 (Cambridge: Cambridge Univ. Press, 1962).
[12]Homer Obed Brown, p. 223.

after, a *tempus aureus* and a time of leaden despair which is human history. The Book of Genesis thus presents a principle of differentiation, a logos, and enacts it in narrative through and as repetition with a difference. What Genesis seems to argue is that conscious awareness is awareness of difference—without difference no language, no narrative to explain the Fall, no awareness of nakedness, no labor, no sexuality. Consciousness as difference is its own tautological law.

If Genesis, as the story instituting differentiation, is the archetype of narrative, it is also the reason for its necessity. There is something in human consciousness which will not tolerate difference and opposition. The story of paradise lost is usually followed by some version of paradise regained. Narrative both repeats the logos of difference and attempts to overcome it. In his analysis "The First Three Chapters of Genesis," Kenneth Burke diagrams the sequential development of oppositional concepts operative in the story of Genesis, which stand to the left and right of a central axis: to bless–to curse; good–evil; holy–fallen; obedience–disobedience; mortification–fornication; humility–pride; reason–senses; faith–imagination; reward–punishment. These oppositional terms of order cannot rest as they are. The history of religion recounts the mediating terms human beings have used to overcome the unbearable conflict of opposites. Burke sketches a central axis on which he lists a number of mediating terms such as "will as locus of possible choice (*proairesis*) between 'good' and 'evil,'" "patience," and "redemption by vicarious atonement (mercy)." All are important in our reading of *Tom Jones*. Most significant in Christianity, and in our understanding of the novel, is the figure of Christ as symbol of mediation—whom Burke describes as "the idea of a 'perfect' victim to cancel (or 'cover') what was in effect the 'perfect' sin."[13] In Burke's logological analysis the logos of Genesis inevitably generates ambivalence. The radical difference between man and God, child and father, law and transgression, is to be overcome through the imaginative projection of mediating terms that violate the logical principle of the

[13] *The Rhetoric of Religion* (Boston: Beacon Press, 1961), pp. 184–96. Cf. Burke, "Tautological Cycle of Terms for 'Order,'" in *Terms for Order,* ed. Stanley Edgar Hyman (Bloomington: Indiana Univ. Press, 1964).

excluded middle since they combine semantic qualities belonging to the opposing terms. Christ is both God and man. Genesis necessitates narratives that redefine the metaphor of the Fall through metonymic substitution leading to a resolution of the tension of opposites standing at the beginning.

The narrative action of *Tom Jones* constitutes an attempt to readdress the paradox of the Fall and to sketch a solution to the problem of opposition between God and man, order and disorder, which is its premise. While *Tom Jones* claims to be a history—and it does present a very accurate image of England during the Jacobite Rebellion—its contemporary setting does not obscure its underlying mythic intention to depict a universal or general truth about man's being in the world. In sketching the circular quest through which the bastard Tom Jones, as figure for Everyman, regains Paradise Hall, Fielding tries to justify the ways of God to man, as well as to legitimize the natural presence of man as always already secretly related to God.

The Ideology of Change

Like Genesis, Fielding's story begins with a redoubling necessary for representation. The real problem Tom Jones faces is his alienation from a father and his consequent exclusion from title and inheritance. The meaning of Tom's birth outside the patriarchal law, however, can only be given reality, only be remedied through a reenactment of this exclusion. Tom's fall from presence before the story begins is reenacted as a "fall" into the presence of Allworthy, who functions as father to Tom. The sequential introduction of Allworthy, then Bridget, and then infant Tom suggests that Allworthy is the true father. Tom refers to Allworthy as "Father," and Allworthy calls the child "his own Boy" (III, vii). Tom is given Allworthy's Christian name, and Mrs. Wilkins warns that people will think that Allworthy is Tom's real father. Thus Tom's biological but absent father is replaced in the fiction by a substitute father figure, and this redoubling makes a working through of the problem of alienation possible. The fall must be reenacted in history in order to be undone.

From the moment of his appearance in Allworthy's bed, Tom is presented to us as the Dionysian principle of disorder disrupting the equilibrium of Paradise Hall. He is an anomaly, unclassifiable, without nomen; and his unnatural presence questions the very universality of the patriarchal law. It suggests the possibility of presence and life outside the pale of the law. Tom Jones embodies the notion of disruptive otherness. This otherness is ontologically inherent in his *nature;* the fiction, however, portrays Tom's otherness as a quality inherent in his *character.* Tom is welcomed with charity and benevolence, although it soon becomes clear that he is unable to conform to the orderly decorum of Allworthy's household. Tom's violation of the law of property, his poaching, his transgression against the commandment of chastity, the sale of his Bible, his emotional turmoil at Allworthy's illness are understood by the characters in the fiction as signs of a deep "original flaw" of character. Tom is expelled from Allworthy's presence and sent out into the lawless wilderness to the accompaniment of overt echoes from *Paradise Lost: "The World,* as *Milton* phrases it, *lay all before him;* and *Jones,* no more than *Adam,* had any Man to whom he might resort for Comfort or Assistance" (VII, ii). Thus the occasion for the fiction, Tom's alienation from the father, is displaced and historicized as his fall from Allworthy's paternal presence.

The effect of this shift from the problem of Tom's ontological status to that of his character and personal identity is to present not his illegitimacy but his disorderly disobedience—his inability to remain within the requirements of the law—as the real cause of his alienation. Fielding's plot device conflates illegitimacy—birth without sanction of the law—with the sin of Adam and Eve, the first disobedience. The sin of the parent is visited on the child. The original "sin" of illegitimacy is irredeemable and symbolizes an absolute difference between father and child, but flaws in character or behavior, errors of choice, are open to modification and change through education or reform. Fielding's rewriting of "original flaw" as "flaw of character" (and here it is relevant to remember that *karakter* means "imprint" or "inscription") allows for the undoing of its evil aftereffects and opens the way to secular redemption.

The New Testament, *The Divine Comedy, Paradise Regained* are notable examples upon which Fielding might have modeled this secular redemption. He chose, nevertheless, the Hellenic epic that may well be the structural ancestor of the circular quest—Homer's *Odyssey*. The title page of the novel bears the inscription *"Mores hominum multorum vidit,"* Horace's words in the *Ars Poetica* (141–42) echoing the beginning of the *Odyssey*. Elsewhere Fielding claims intellectual kin with both Milton and Homer, calling them "Historians of our Order, and Masters of the Learning of their Times" (IX, i).

Fielding's motive for choosing *The Odyssey* may well have to do with its eighteenth-century interpretation. Pope's translation played a central role in forming and defining contemporary impressions of the figure of Odysseus and the meaning of his quest. In the introduction to his work, Pope points out, following Bossu, that the poet, in contrast to the Schoolmen, who discourse upon virtue and vice in general, addresses himself more closely to the needs of his own country, using the epic to present the moral lesson most appropriate to the contemporary situation. Ulysses' return illustrates the "two Virtues necessary to one in authority, Prudence in order, and Care to see his orders put in execution."[14] *The Odyssey* is regarded as a didactic fable, a mirror for magistrates. This view confirms my suggestion that *Tom Jones* is a quest for the law of the symbolic order. It should also alert us, however, to the inexactitude of the parallel between Tom and Ulysses. Ulysses—father, heir, and monarch—possesses the prudent dissimulation that Tom will learn only a few months before the end of his quest. Tom's lack of experience and his search for a father call up the shadow of Telemachos who set out to find his father. In fact, Fielding's example may well have been Fénelon's *Télémaque*, cited as epic model in the Preface to *Joseph Andrews*. Originally published in 1699, this didactic fable was widely read throughout Western Europe and was brought out in an English translation by Andrew Millar in the year Fielding published *Joseph Andrews*. Fénelon's story about the son—a rather free elaboration of Homer—is a Christian epic rooted in the popular tradition of the Pilgrim's Progress, which details the hero's moral progress toward prudence and virtue.

[14]I found this summary of Pope's meaning in Hunter, *Occasional Form,* p. 186.

The importance of *Tom Jones*'s intertextual connection with Pope's translation of *The Odyssey* and Fénelon's *Télémaque* is the aspect of *Bildung,* education or development, which it lends the novel. Orthodox Protestant Christian doctrine holds that human beings cannot redeem themselves: they are saved through the redeeming sacrifice of Christ. *Tom Jones* suggests, however, that man is capable of redemptive reform of character. He can and must become like the Father. This type of plot, which relies on the development of a character (through *Wanderjahre* or a conversion, for instance) to bring about a return to the *locus amoenus,* deviates from a Christian understanding of the limitations of human nature and capabilities. It presents an image of human beings as dynamic rather than static—not fixed in nature and qualities once and for all but capable of changing and redeeming themselves. In its milder form, it suggests the influence of Arminius; in its extreme, it turns Pelagian and denies the universality of original sin, while undoing the absolute difference between God and man, paradise and the fallen world, myth and history, life and death.

In short, novels that resort to apprenticeship to bring about a return to the place of origin present a secular revision of the story of Genesis which would seem fallacious, almost heretical, from a strictly orthodox, especially Calvinist point of view. They extend the story of the Fall with a narrative account of paradise regained but ignore that this latter fable describes not empirical evidence but a projected event taking place in imaginary, mythic time. Thus the hallmark of the circular quest is a rewriting of Genesis which vitiates the logos of difference instituted at and as the Fall.

We shall return to the notion of a change in character in the next chapter. Here it is important because it allows us to place the rise of the novel in a cultural-historical perspective. Fielding's claim for his new species of writing, his pretension to general truth, was possible because of a general change in contemporary thought which may have occluded awareness of the heretical implications of the fiction. In the early modern period there arose a new form of understanding, a new logic not of classification (of static being) but of definition by means of the process of becoming (history). Foucault suggests that we think of a separate epoch, the classical

age, with its own "episteme."[15] I should like to refer to the change
between, roughly, the fifteenth century and the nineteenth, as a
move from a world view centering on the notion of the Great
Chain of Being to the conceptualization of a Chain of Becoming.[16]
In *The Philosophy of the Enlightenment* Ernst Cassirer provides a
description of the content of that change:

> The scholastic method of definition of a concept by means of *genus
> proximum* (next genus above) and *differentia specifica* (specific dif-
> ference) is more and more commonly recognized as inadequate. The
> object of a definition in this sense is not merely to analyze and
> describe a given conceptual content; it is to be a means for construct-
> ing conceptual content and for establishing it by virtue of this con-
> structive activity. Thus arises the theory of the genetic or causal
> definition, in whose development all the great logicians of the seven-
> teenth century participated. The genuine and really fruitful explana-
> tions of concepts do not proceed by abstraction alone; they are not
> content to divide one element from a given complex of properties or
> characteristics and to define it in isolation. They observe rather the
> inner law according to which the whole either originated or at least
> can be conceived as originating. And they clarify within this law of
> becoming the real nature and behavior of this whole; they not only
> show *what* this whole is, but *why* it is. A genuine genetic definition
> permits us to understand the structure of a complex whole; it does
> not, however, stop with this structure as such, but goes back to its
> foundations.[17]

The definition of human nature and identity through epigenetic
narrative, and as the history of human origin, is facilitated by
increasing belief in the explanatory power of the process of becoming. The epigenetic plot of family romance, which defines the
human being, however ambivalently, as the product of a circular

---

[15] *The Order of Things*, p. 74.

[16] See Frederick M. Keener, *The Chain of Becoming: The Philosophical Tale, the
Novel, and a Neglected Realism of the Enlightenment: Swift, Montesquieu, Voltaire,
Johnson and Austen* (New York: Columbia Univ. Press, 1983).

[17] Trans. F. C. A. Koelln and J. P. Pettegrove (Princeton: Princeton Univ. Press,
1951), pp. 253–54.

journey from origin to end, seemed valid to the eighteenth century because it sketches in the very process of tracing origin a trajectory of difference suggesting real change. The rise of the novel, then, is a central event in the flowering of an ideology of change which has its roots in the optimistic belief of Renaissance humanism in human perfectibility through education. Indeed, the novel is the product and illustration of the eighteenth-century change of attitude by which, according to Cassirer, "the problem of the reconciliation of man and God, with whose solution the great scholastic systems and all medieval mysticism had wrestled, appeared now in a new light. This reconciliation was no longer looked for exclusively in an act of divine grace; it was supposed to take place amid the activity of the human spirit and its process of self-development."[18]

It is the novel, more than any other form of discourse, which depicts and celebrates this activity of the human spirit as self-development[19] and which, at the same time, constitutes a mirror in which human beings can see themselves reflected as self-identical and whole. In the preface to the first chapter of *Amelia,* Fielding defends the novel as the mirror of newly defined human identity:

> Life may as properly be called an Art as any other; and the great incidents in it are no more to be considered as mere Accidents than the several members of a fine Statue or a noble Poem. The Critics in all these are not content with seeing any Thing to be great, without knowing why and how it came to be so. By examining carefully the several Gradations which conduce to bring every Model to Perfection, we learn truly to know that Science in which the Model is formed: As Histories of this Kind, therefore, may properly be called Models of HUMAN LIFE; so by observing minutely the several Incidents which tend to the Catastrophe or Completion of the whole, and the minute Causes whence those Incidents are produced,

[18]Cassirer, p. 138.
[19]Arnold Weinstein, *Fictions of the Self, 1550–1800* (Princeton: Princeton Univ. Press, 1984), shows that each of the fictions he reads plots a self-realization, a history of development which enacts the coming into identity of both the protagonist and the genre.

we shall best be instructed in this most useful of all Arts, which I call the ART of LIFE.[20]

The fiction is intended as both a reflection and an exemplum of what human life means, a mirror that reflects essential features. This fictional imago of man—a mirror-image in which man may recognize the idea of the self and which thus in turn confirms the viability and truth of that idea—in its illusionary reflection confirms and supports the Enlightenment notion of man. What we encounter here is a tautology, a circular process of confirmation and reconfirmation which is no less fallacious, heretical, or imaginary than the logic of the circular quest which informs the narrative that projects this image. As I argued in the previous chapter, the role of the genre of the novel in the constitution of human subjectivity can be understood in the light of Lacan's theory of the mirror stage. Just as our realization of ourselves as separate human individuals is constituted by the first reflection of ourselves as fully outlined shapes in a mirror, so the generic notion of human being as subjective self is mediated by the *Darstellung* of the mirror of epigenetic narrative—at once reflecting and constituting the idea of a distinctly human identity.

The question of the rise of the novel is best understood as part of the general debate about human nature and possibilities which began long before Milton felt the need to justify the ways of God in *Paradise Lost*. It is Pope's contemporary "vindication" in the *Essay on Man* which seems most appropriate here. Writing a few decades before Fielding's fiction, Pope claims for man a separate, medial, paradoxical position in the Chain of Being between stasis and change, matter and spirit. He begins the second epistle with the injunction that man should not concern himself with metaphysics but should study his own nature: "Know then thyself, presume not God to scan, / The proper study of mankind is man." (II, 1–2). These well-known words might be taken as an epigraph for the genre of the novel. Their ambivalence—the line

---

[20]*Amelia*, ed. Martin Battestin and Fredson Bowers, The Wesleyan Edition of the Works of Henry Fielding (Oxford: Clarendon Press, 1983), bk. I, chap. i.

also suggests that the right way of considering man *creates* the idea of man—ties in with the reciprocity and circularity of the mirror image, both in Lacan's theory of the mirror stage and in my suggestion here that the epigenetic plot supplies a mirror to man's illusion of self-identity. Perhaps it is best to leave the final word on this matter, however inconclusive, to Pope himself. He closes his *Essay on Man* with the line: "And all our knowledge is,—Ourselves to know." (IV, 398).

3

The Formal Constitution

of the Self

Men have always had to choose between their subjection to
nature or the subjection of nature to the Self.
                                    —Horkheimer and Adorno,
                                    Dialectic of Enlightenment

My suggestion that the novel functions as a mirror for the
human illusion of self-identity demands a reexamination of *Tom
Jones* to point out those features in the text which allow the reader's
projection of a unified imago of the self. Fielding's fiction, though
greatly praised for its plot, is, in a way, less "well-made" than,
say, *Clarissa,* in that the traces of his workmanship are more visible. Instead of presenting a smooth and unified narrative surface,
the text proves full of ambivalences and inconsistencies. Perhaps
these knots in the narrative web are more evident to twentieth-
century readers than to Fielding's contemporaries. Melvyn New
notes that the ambivalence of eighteenth-century fiction depends
on a "double vision" that tries to combine two antithetical ideas
about man—"man as God's creature, and man as the radical product of his own autonomous will."[1] But such a definitive explana-

[1] "'The Grease of God': The Form of Eighteenth-Century Fiction," *PMLA* 91
(1976), 235–44. Terry Eagleton, *The Rape of Clarissa: Writing, Sexuality and Class
Struggle in Samuel Richardson* (Oxford: Basil Blackwell, 1982), argues the scandal of
Clarissa for a patriarchal society, but Richardson's fictions, it seems to me, do not
subvert the plot of patriarchy. They reconfirm it by depicting woman's transcendence through dematerialization. In *Pamela* this transcendence concerns the bind-
ing of sexuality in marriage; in *Clarissa,* the complete separation of body and soul.
In addition to titillating the reader with descriptions of female sexuality, woman in
the secrecy of her closet, Richardson's novels offer patriarchy the heroic inflation

tion is not enough. I want to dig deeper, to investigate the inconsistencies and "double vision" of Fielding's novel, because they may reveal the hidden motives and the rationale of his modern vision of man. Rather than ignoring the breaks in the web and the folds in the argument, I will focus on precisely such "flaws" in order to uncover the strategy of the constitution of the imago of man.

It is a way of reading encouraged by Freud's exemplary analysis of the Old Testament in *Moses and Monotheism*. Arguing that the text revealed the traces of "opposed treatments," notable in the revisions, mutilations, additions, and reversals of its surface, he suggested the unintentional significance of these distortions:

> Thus almost everywhere there can be found striking omissions, disturbing repetitions, palpable contradictions, signs of things the communication of which was never intended. The distortion is not unlike a murder. The difficulty lies not in the execution of the deed but in the doing away with the traces. One could wish to give the word "distortion" the double meaning to which it has a right, although it is no longer used in this sense. It should mean not only "to change the appearance of" but also "to wrench apart," "to put in another place." That is why in so many textual distortions we may count on finding the suppressed and abnegated material hidden away somewhere, though in an altered shape and torn out of its original connection. Only it is not always easy to recognize it.[2]

Though there are many inconsistencies in Fielding's fiction, I shall focus only on those that play a significant role in the *Darstellung* of a subjective self and in disguising its reliance on the informative presence of the "other."

The first rhetorical shift to notice is a chiastic inversion of cause

---

of the subjective self. Clarissa's pathos is that, as woman, she can undo the violation of her sexual integrity only through the sacrifice of her life. It is perhaps not an accident that *Sir Charles Grandison,* which portrays masculine virtue, fails to interest us. Clarissa's suffering is related to her gender. Richardson's project doubly depends on the "other" as sexually and socially different. Thus, though Fielding's fictions are more openly patriarchal than Richardson's, they may only be less subtle in their configuration of gender and subjectivity.

[2]P. 52.

and effect. When Allworthy discovers Tom in his bed, his as-
tonishment and surprise are great until his "Good-nature" touches
him with "Sentiments of Compassion" for the "little Wretch before him" (I, iii). The reader who opens the novel for the first time
will not be struck by the words *good nature*. It is only after closing
the book that one realizes the extent to which Fielding's argument—which transforms the metaphor of the Fall into the metonymy of return—rests upon his play with the concept of good
nature. Good nature is Tom's most deserving trait of character.
Even when he is in the deepest trouble himself, he demonstrates
his readiness to reach out to others with charity and affection.
Tom's good nature, then, is the quality he shares with Allworthy;
and one of the points of the fiction is to demonstrate that mercy
(exemplified by Allworthy and Tom) is to be ranked higher than
justice (as exemplified by Blifil). Indeed, the opposition between
good nature and strict justice is presented as the vital difference
between Tom and his half brother, in a passage that clearly reveals
the narrator's own preference for mercy over justice:

> Master Blifil fell very short of his Companion in the amiable Quality
> of Mercy; but he as greatly exceeded him in one of a much higher
> Kind, namely in Justice: In which he followed both the Precepts and
> Example of *Thwackum* and *Square;* for though they would both make
> frequent Use of the Word *Mercy,* yet it was plain, that in reality
> *Square* held it to be inconsistent with the Rule of Right; and *Thwack-
> um* was for doing Justice, and leaving Mercy to Heaven. The two
> Gentlemen did indeed somewhat differ in Opinion concerning the
> Objects of this sublime Virtue; by which *Thwackum* would probably
> have destroyed one half of Mankind, and *Square* the other half. (III,
> x)

In this brief passage Fielding delivers his comments on the stricter
forms of Christianity and the rigorous rationality that privileges
law over mercy.[3]

---

[3]Fielding's own position was that of the latitudinarian divines, whose keynote
was tolerance. Glanvill's *Catholick Charity Recommended* comments: "He that is
extreme in his *Principles,* must needs be *narrow* in his *Affections:* whereas he that
stands on the *middle path,* may *extend* the armes of *Charity* to those on *both* sides"

The point is that the preference for charity over justice is not merely a matter of religious doctrine but the motivating principle of the text. In making Tom's good nature the basis of his ultimate accession to Paradise Hall, Fielding himself practices mercy over justice. According to contemporary English law, bastards could not inherit; according to the logos of difference, human beings cannot regain paradise (at least not on their own account). Fielding's suggestion rests upon the heretical attribution to man of a quality that is characteristic of an Allworthy. It is Tom's "natural gentility" of character that allows him to transgress the limits set upon his legal rights as "natural" child—and note how Fielding exploits the plural meanings of the word *natural*.

From a strictly logical point of view, then, the success of Fielding's argument hinges on a chiasmus of cause and effect which is rather similar to the one Cynthia Chase isolated in *Daniel Deronda*.[4] Just as the reader of George Eliot begins to realize that the coherent progress of the story requires the revelation of Deronda's Jewish descent, so the reader of *Tom Jones* cannot help but feel that good-natured Tom must somehow be of good, genteel birth and is perhaps even related to Allworthy. The revelation of Tom's true parentage follows upon the depiction of the "natural gentility" of Tom's character and seems to confirm his moral worth. Thus it would seem that the discovery of kinship with Allworthy is the *effect* of the good nature that had given him the friends who are instrumental in that discovery. But what Fielding presents as effect functions and is felt by the reader as the underlying cause. If Tom had not been a gentleman—and here the reader is well advised to keep Fielding's emphasis on the proper genealogy of his fiction in mind—his character would not have resembled that of an Allworthy. The affinity, the relatedness or kinship, between Allworthy and Tom is the primary justifying given of the fiction, even if the story begins by stressing the difference between Allworthy's apocalyptic order and Tom's Dionysian disorder. The final source of

---

(quoted in Barbara J. Shapiro, "Latitudinarianism and Science in Seventeenth-Century England," in *The Intellectual Revolution of the Seventeenth Century,* ed. Charles Webster [London: Routledge, 1974], p. 303). These words ring with significance in connection with *Tom Jones*.

4"The Decomposition of the Elephants," pp. 215–28.

Tom's character, the principle that allows mediation, is his resemblance to Allworthy. If we read this fiction as a secular scripture addressing man's relationship to the All, we cannot avoid the
realization that Fielding's heretical point of departure, the "unifying idea,"[5] is the secret kinship between God and man which is
manifested in charitable humanity. Here I choose the noun *humanity* on purpose to emphasize the tautology of this reasoning.

I should like to emphasize again, perhaps at the risk of becoming
too emphatic, that the point of my interest in the inconsistencies of
Fielding's text is not a deconstructive demonstration that texts are
always self-contradictory. It is the connection between contemporary thought and the structural peculiarities of the text which has
my main interest. Fielding's rhetorical strategy is significant because it ties in with and elucidates the conceptual configuration of
the Enlightenment view of human perfectibility. The rhetorical
figure of chiasmus or metalepsis supports the *Darstellung* of human
being as subject.

The second peculiarity or irregularity in the texture of *Tom Jones*
which seems significant as an expression of contemporary ideas
about man and his identity is less easily extricated from the web of
the fiction. Instead of one curious knot in the argument, we are
dealing with a method of weaving which relies on the thought
processes found in dreams or slips of the tongue. In other words,
the surface meaning of *Tom Jones* is related to an underlying argument implied in the strategy of building its argument.

Lévi-Strauss's conclusion that myth mediates a logically un-
bridgeable opposition seems significant in connection with *Tom
Jones*. His suggestion that the Oedipus cycle provides a solution to
the dilemma of origin as "born from different" or "born from
same"—earth or sky, nature or culture—seems essentially relevant. The fictional narrative begins, like myth, by establishing a
radical difference in connotation between the two major figures,
Squire Allworthy and the foundling Tom. One represents Apollo-
nian order, the other Dionysian disorder. This semantic opposition
in character and actions present in the early chapters is amplified as

---

[5]I take the term—out of context—from R. S. Crane, "The Plot of *Tom Jones*,"
in *Tom Jones,* ed. Baker, p. 850.

the intrigue develops. Each incident, each new scene, links new features to the connotation established at the beginning. Gradually, Allworthy and Tom acquire, on either side, a cluster of associations that extend the symbolic resonance of their difference; and we may come to read the opposition between them as representing the breach between being and existence, the metaphysical and the physical, or between reason and passion.

But the purpose of the narrative is not to sketch this difference but to resolve it. The action constitutes the slow attempt to undo the initial opposition and to close the fiction with a *coniunctio*. Though Fielding hints at Tom's gradual reform (the semantic redefinition of his "character" to make him more like Allworthy), the reader is not convinced. Critics have worried about the absence of proof of Tom's ability to control his libidinal urges. Does Tom really deserve to become Allworthy's heir? Sophia accepts him, apparently in the belief that the mere assimilation to her world will ensure Tom's reform; but this kind of acceptance suggests that the crucial agent in Tom's transformation is the sacrament of marriage and not Tom's reform of character.

Indeed, there is an ambiguity here that "makes sense" in light of Lévi-Strauss's approach to myth. It is as if the narrative wanted the reader to believe in Tom's worthiness to inhabit Paradise Hall, while it also labors under the necessity to preserve the intrinsic discontinuity between the two orders of reality. The basic premise of the fiction—that Allworthy and what he symbolizes are radically opposed to what Tom represents—would seem to preclude the very notion of complete change or transformation. If Fielding had shown Tom to be fully deserving of Paradise Hall on intrinsic merit, he would have undercut the very premise that justifies the story as "myth" and inspires its necessity in the first place. When Tom is welcomed to Allworthy's bosom, the ambivalent implication is, therefore, that this honor is to be credited to Allworthy's mercy rather than to strict justice. Even Tom himself points this out: "Alas, Sir, I have not been punished more than I have deserved; and it shall be the whole Business of my future Life to deserve the Happiness you now bestow on me" (xviii, x).

Fielding's attempt to resolve the radical discontinuity between Allworthy and Tom through the metonymic substitution of the semantic connotations of Tom's "character" remains necessarily and ambivalently inconclusive. In terms of Christian doctrine, Fielding comes perilously close to a heretical denial of human depravity but preserves the appearance of orthodoxy in allowing the initiative for Tom's assumption to come from Allworthy and Sophia.

Once we have been alerted to the possible presence of primary process thinking, we begin to notice other instances. Another strategy of representation also addresses the mediation between Tom and Allworthy. In his discussion of Hamlet and Oedipus, Ernest Jones points to a mechanism of mythic thought he calls "decomposition," the inverse of the strategy of "condensation," which is characteristic of dreams:

> Whereas in the latter process attributes of several individuals are fused together in the creation of one figure, much as in the production of a composite photograph, in the former process various attributes of a given individual are disunited and several other individuals invented, each endowed with one group of the original attributes. In this way one person of complex character is dissolved and replaced by several, each of whom possesses a different aspect of the character which in a simpler form of the myth was combined in one being; usually the different individuals closely resemble one another in other respects, for instance in age. A great part of Greek mythology must have arisen in this way. A good example of the process in the group now under consideration is seen by the figure of a tyrannical father becoming split into two, a father and a tyrant.[6]

The principle of myth formation described by Jones is familiar in literary studies as "doubling" of character. I cite his description of the phenomenon because Jones points to its underlying psychological and conceptual motivation. Decomposition makes possible the representation (and eventual resolution) of an ambiguity, since it splits the opposing characteristics of a problematic entity into two discrete halves.[7]

---

[6]*Hamlet and Oedipus* (New York: Norton, 1976), p. 131.

[7]Note that Jones does not offer the "standard" psychoanalytic explanation that doubling is evidence of narcissism. See Otto Rank, *The Double: A Psychoanalytic*

While the plot of *Tom Jones* has often been praised for the regularity and balance of its design, apparently no one has recognized that the configuration of the major characters also forms a design. The resolution of the initial opposition hinges on the addition of a supplementary set of characters who double the essential features of Tom and Allworthy as in a looking-glass world. Both Tom and Allworthy are flanked by men who are similar in most respects but the one feature that functions as criterion of differentiation. Thus Allworthy's double is his neighbor Squire Western, his equal in rank, fortune, function (both men are justices of the peace), and marital status (both are widowed and live with an unmarried sister) but his opposite in disposition. This difference in personality, however, paradoxically points to a direct tie. Whereas Allworthy approximates the archetypal figure of the shepherd, Western resembles his opposite, the hunter; in other words, Allworthy embodies the idea of reason, or the soul, whereas Western stands for passion, or the body.

A similar tie exists between Tom and Blifil. They are semi-orphans, half brothers, not very different in age, in need of a secure position in the social hierarchy and therefore dependent on the favor of Allworthy and Western, who have the power and position to fulfill their need. The dispositions of Blifil and Tom (whose name, incidentally, means "twin") are directly opposite and formed by analogy with the qualities attributed to their elders. Tom's characteristic lack of sexual restraint is the socially unacceptable, unsublimated version of Western's passion for hunting, and Blifil's total lack of physical passion ("his Appetites were, by Nature, so moderate, that he was able, by Philosophy or by Study, or by some other Method, easily to subdue them" [IV, iv]) is the unnatural version of Allworthy's prudence and restraint.

Study, trans. Harry Tucker, Jr. (1925; rpt. Chapel Hill: Univ. of North Carolina Press, 1971), p. 86. In this context it is interesting to compare Rank's later statement in "The Double as Immortal Self," in *Beyond Psychology* (New York: Dover, 1958), pp. 62–76, where he suggests that man's desire for immortality and continuity are the impulse behind civilization. The concept of the double, comparable to the primitive understanding of the soul as a kind of shadow, simultaneously provides him with a token of immortality and a pointer toward death.

We might map the semantic relations among these four characters thus[8]:

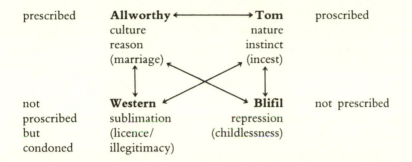

prescribed	Allworthy ⟷ Tom	proscribed
	culture nature	
	reason instinct	
	(marriage) (incest)	
not	Western ⟷ Blifil	not prescribed
proscribed	sublimation repression	
but	(licence/ (childlessness)	
condoned	illegitimacy)	

Drafting the semantic relationships among the four male characters
of the fiction clarifies the central knot of forces which holds the
plot of *Tom Jones* together. The diagram emphasizes the conceptual opposition of Allworthy and Tom, but it also points to the
structural strategy Fielding uses to suggest that this opposition has
been breached. The doubling of the category of the *senex* figure
allows the fiction to suggest subliminally that Tom, through his
marriage to the daughter of Allworthy's double, is joined to Allworthy himself. We have already noted that the sacrament of marriage itself was regarded as a guaranty for Tom's transformation.
This peculiarity of the fiction makes sense not only in terms of
Christian orthodoxy but as an exigency of conceptual structure I
have diagrammed. Sophia figures in the fiction only as a symbolic
stand-in for Allworthy; access to her marks access to Paradise Hall.
And the reader should note that in her personality, her exemplary
behavior, Sophia more closely resembles Allworthy than she does
her own father. She stands for "Amazing Brightness, Purity and
Truth" (VIII, iii). And throughout the story descriptions of Sophia
are notable for their idealization, as Richardson pointed out. In
Tom's lover's discourse she becomes "my goddess" (IV, xiv),
whose "heavenly temper" (V, vi) befits a "Somersetshire Angel"

[8]I presented the argument about *Tom Jones* and the narrative logic of myth in
"The Semiotics of Plot," *Poetics Today* 3, 4 (1982). 89–97.

(x, vii), indeed, "an Angel upon Earth" (xi, iii). Not surprisingly, woman's function in Fielding's grand design is to mediate between father and son, transmitting the torch of patriarchal self-presence from generation to generation.

Mapping the action of the plot in logical terms, we might describe the movement of Tom's return to Paradise Hall more formally and precisely. Thus A (Allworthy) and B (Tom) are intrinsically opposed categories. No mediation between them is possible. The slow metamorphosis of B into A would have denied the very premise of the fiction and undercut its power to refer to ultimate meanings. The novel would have lost its claim to mythic function. According to the basic rule of Aristotelian logic, B cannot be both B and A at the same time. Thus the slow transformation of "Tom" into "Allworthy," though theoretically possible, would have undercut the continuity of identity of B. Tom would have become what Western considers him after he learns Tom's parentage, "another Person" (xviii, xi). The transformation would have vitiated the point Fielding is trying to make: that B—even if presented as radically different from A—will eventually regain a place in Paradise Hall without the radical break of identity necessary in myth, thus, without death and resurrection in this world.[9] The fallacious strategy behind this suggestion depends on the decomposition of categories A and B, into A^1A^2 and B^1B^2; B^1 is then moved into the category of A^1A^2, giving the figure $A^1A^2B^1$ (Allworthy, Sophia, and Tom), on the one hand, and leaving Blifil alone as solitary representative of his undesirable category.

"What happens" in the course of Tom Jones, then, is not just the discovery of the parentage of a foundling. The fiction addresses the problem of illegitimacy by doubling the characters representing the initial opposition and then seems to resolve it by joining half the pair to the representative of the law.

Though the novel presents its message in a more displaced form than myth, Tom Jones suggests the possibility of overcoming the

[9]The narrator of Tom Jones explicitly objects to fictions that suggest that happiness can be earned in this life, considering them false, but his own fiction presents the same message. See Mary Poovey, "Journeys from This World to the Next: The Providential Promise in Clarissa and Tom Jones," ELH 43 (1976), 300–15.

most crucial human problem, that of the Fall and the inevitable dualism and divisiveness clinging to the self-conscious human condition. It is able to do so because of our human capacity for symbolic thinking, using characters or objects as things to think with, working out irreconcilable oppositions by means of rhetorical strategies that can only function or exist when embedded in a narrative process, in language. Thus language—a play of differences, of presence and absence, sign and signifier—which is the ultimate symbol, if not natural sign, of the divisiveness of the human condition, also provides us with the remedy of a narrative logic capable of mediating this split, albeit temporarily, of healing, for the duration of a fiction, the wound left by the severance of nature and culture.

I realize that this discussion of fictional characters in algebraic terms may invite ridicule. It brings out, however, an aspect of Fielding's strategy which would otherwise have remained unnoticed. Tom's assumption into Allworthy's world coincides with, and is morally facilitated by, the use of Blifil as scapegoat for the undesirable qualities that tie Tom to category B. While Tom moves toward Paradise Hall, Blifil, called a "wicked Viper" (XVIII, viii) by Allworthy, is revealed as a scheming devil, the snake in the garden. Thus Blifil's demise marks Tom's conclusive clearing. It substitutes for and coincides with Tom's return. In the final analysis then, the structure of Fielding's plot rests upon a strategy of sacrificial scapegoating, familiar from religion and myth and for some the original moment constituting civilization.[10]

It is this move in Fielding's plot which interests me. Blifil's fall marks and coincides with Tom's ascension. What happens outside Tom's psyche, the discovery of Blifil's hypocrisy, seems to put the seal upon Tom's "good-natured" constancy. On a realistic level, Fielding's strategy of projection makes little sense. While the reader may feel some satisfaction at seeing the culprit punished, Blifil's demise does not signify Tom's transformation. It is only if we understand Tom and Blifil as doubles, as two halves of one coin, that Fielding's strategy makes "sense." Then the final, decisive

---

[10]Freud's *Totem and Taboo* and René Girard's *Violence and the Sacred* are both relevant here.

split between Blifil and Tom substitutes for or signals a process of separation which is taking place inside Tom at the moment of anagnorisis.

In other words, the structure of the fiction can be seen as enacting the split that must take place within Tom to make him worthy of Sophia, or rather Allworthy. The necessity for this repudiation of (a part of) his own nature comes home to him in prison. Locked away on the accusation of murder, told that the woman he took to bed in the inn at Upton is his mother, Tom makes a choice. He will stop projecting the cause of his trouble on abstract forces and locate it in himself: "Fortune will never have done with me, till she hath driven me to Distraction. But why do I blame Fortune? I am myself the Cause of all my Misery. All the dreadful Mischiefs which have befallen me, are the Consequence only of my own Folly and Vice" (xviii, ii). Tom confesses, "I have undone myself" (xviii, v), finds that he has not "been punished more than deserved" (xviii, x), and resolves "not to sin anymore" (xvii, ix). Thus Tom internalizes the prohibitions and dichotomies of the symbolic order. He no longer blames the injustice or cruelty of reality—of fate, in short—for the limitations of human freedom and possibility but allocates responsibility to a part of himself that he will henceforth repudiate, deny, and repress. The split between Blifil and Tom stands for the split within Tom; it is the split that constitutes a "self" acceptable to an Allworthy. The problem of consciousness (its awareness of doubleness), or the problem of human limitations, is resolved through the implicit recognition of a split *in* man. Man himself, to come to terms with the problems of awareness raised by consciousness, constitutes himself as a hybrid being, split into spirit and flesh, body and soul, or reason and instinct.

As I said at the outset of this inquiry into the importance of primary-process thinking in Fielding's text, distortions or gaps in the weaving are important because they point us back to contemporary culture. What the curious mechanism I have outlined suggests is the central place of Fielding's fiction in Enlightenment thought. Its enactment of a split within the self as a structural separation between good and evil will be remembered from the moral guidelines outlined in part 3 of Descartes's *Discourse on Meth-*

od. One of these is "to endeavor always to conquer myself rather than fortune, and to change my desires rather than the order of the world, and in general to habituate myself in the belief that save our thoughts there is nothing completely in our power."[11] Allworthy's emphasis on prudence as "the Duty which we owe to our-*selves*" (XVIII, x; my emphasis) reminds us of the Cartesian maxim of self-mortification. But the similarity to Descartes in turn alerts us to an aspect of Fielding's strategy. The splitting of the self is a rational strategy of domination. Only one's own mind is wholly under control. In splitting himself in two, man constitutes himself as transcendent subject and coherent self in defense against his lack of control over "the order of the world." Thus the logocentric plot of the name-of-the-father illustrates its own assumption in its effect: narrative plot is a device for instituting difference, hierarchy, and distinction (order); and this differentiation is the necessary prelude to a synthetic resolution of opposition in a merging of the self with the symbolic order which suggests transcendence.

What we have come across, then, would seem to have a wider significance. The text of *Tom Jones* provides us with a blueprint of the process of constituting a transcendent self. The strategy by means of which man gains the illusion of subjectivity has, perhaps, been analyzed most critically by Horkheimer and Adorno in *Dialectic of Enlightenment*. Oedipus's answer to the riddle of the Sphinx—"It is man!"—might be taken as the emblem of the central tautological preoccupation of the idea of enlightenment, which is not necessarily limited to the eighteenth-century. Horkheimer and Adorno trace "the notion of enlightenment as progressive thought, back to the beginning of traditional history."[12] It is man's impulse to rational abstraction, constituting a split that suggests subjectivity:

[11]*Philosophical Writings,* trans. N. K. Smith (New York: Modern Library, 1958), p. 113.
[12]P. 44. For an Anglo-American discussion of "the Paradox of Man" in Enlightenment thinking, see Paul Fussell's discussion in *The Rhetorical World of Augustan Humanism: Ethics and Imagery from Swift to Burke* (Oxford: Clarendon Press, 1965). Man is "a flesh-machine of self-destructive depravity fraught with ignorance and vanity, and at the same time inspirited somehow with an *anima* which has it in its power to redeem all defects, except, perhaps, mortality" (p. 44).

The mythic terror feared by the Enlightenment accords with myth. Enlightenment discerns it not merely in unclarified concepts and words, as demonstrated by semantic language-criticism, but in any human assertion that has no place in the ultimate context of self-preservation. Spinoza's *"Conatus sese conservandi primum et unicum virtutis est fundamentum"* contains the true maxim of all Western civilization. . . . The self (which, according to the methodical extirpation of all natural residues because they are mythological, must no longer be either body or blood, or soul, or even the natural I), once sublimated into the transcendental or logical subject, would form the reference point of reason, of the determinative instance of action. Whoever resigns himself to life without any rational reference to self-preservation would, according to the Enlightenment—and Protestantism—regress to prehistory."[13]

Horkheimer and Adorno's discussion of the paradox of Enlightenment may not be notable for facility or transparency, but it helps us understand that, as they put it, the "history of civilization is the history of the introversion of sacrifice" (p. 55). It also alerts us to the sacrificial process constituting both theme and structure of the Bildungsroman, which "translates the painful process of Christian conversion and redemption into a painful process of self-formation, crisis, and self-recognition, which culminates in a stage of self-coherence, self-awareness, and assured power that is its own reward."[14] These words from Abrams's *Natural Supernaturalism* underline, again, the centrality of Fielding's rhetorical strategy. *Tom Jones,* published before the flowering of the Bildungsroman, whose inception is conventionally ascribed to Goethe's *Wilhelm Meister,* nevertheless belongs to the tradition of that subgenre. And what is more, it is at once the limit-text of the genre, which in its awkwardness draws too much attention to the ideological presuppositions of the structure and to the process of constitution of a transcendent self.

[13]Horkheimer and Adorno, p. 29. Spinoza's maxim, in my translation, is: "The effort to preserve the self is the first and only fundamental of virtue."
[14]Abrams, p. 96.

4

The Question of Eve

Et rêve de la filiation masculine,
rêve de Dieu père sortant
de lui-même dans son fils,—
et pas de mère alors.
                    —Stéphane Mallarmé

In the previous pages Tom's quest was presented as a circular quest, and Tom's marriage to Sophia as the confirmation of self-transcendence. While Sophia, like Dante's Beatrice, may represent woman as patriarchal ideal—the feminine as portal of entry to paradise—we should bear in mind that Tom's quest for prudence and constancy is an odyssey marked by encounters with a sequence of Eves, or Liliths, and entailing the rejection of the feminine. The meaning of Tom's self-transcendence has to do with his decision to resist the attraction of female charms. We might understand his peregrination as a sequence of relationships, inverted "marriages," which lead him further and further from the ideal Sophia. His first contact, Molly Seagrim, is the inverse double of the noble Sophia. Cunning, slovenly, and promiscuous, she tempts Tom, as Robert Alter points out, in the counterpart of the Garden, the unregenerate bushes. Though Tom's involvement with Molly indirectly causes his banishment from Paradise Hall, Tom does not learn the lesson that sex outside the law—the sin of his birth—is taboo. On the road to London he meets a Mrs. Waters who is old enough to be his mother; in London—described by Fielding as a den of iniquity—Tom perversely serves the sexual needs of Lady Bellaston. His good nature leading him progressively away from "unadorned nature," he moves "from Molly Seagrim, the plain country flower whose stenches are all of the barnyard variety, to Mrs. Waters, a somewhat more sophisticated roadside blossom . . . to Lady Bell-aston, the subtle hothouse growth that gives off the gamey odor of imminent decay."[1] Alter's phrasing emphasizes the increasing artificiality of Tom's women, which marks his quest as a *via inversa* away from Paradise Hall.

Nevertheless, it is through these adventures with women that Tom reaches the moment of insight which marks his self-transcendence. Tom has to lose himself before he can find himself, and his assumption of identity is predicated "by way" of this purgative quest. Like Homer, whose Odysseus had to surmount the temptations of the virginal Nausicaa, the nymph Calypso, and, most significant, the magic of Circe's reversion to the animal, Fielding would seem to understand the journey to Paradise Hall as a rejection of the dangerous and corrupting allurements of the feminine not bound by patriarchal law. Only when femininity is contained by patriarchy, as Sophia's femininity is, can it be "natural" and wholesome. Outside marriage, the feminine will destroy the drive toward selfhood of the masculine protagonist, will tempt him to inert narcissism or turn him into an animal. The royal road to consciousness of Tom and Odysseus is the process of rejecting the feminine.[2] In order to arrive at Ithaca or Paradise Hall, man must encounter and differentiate himself from the feminine, from nature. The record, or narrative, of that process both constitutes the story of this journey to selfhood and is that selfhood. In short, the archetypal quest for self-transcendence reenacts the rejection of the attraction of the feminine; the progress of the story is the closure of the heterogeneity, the otherness of femininity. The circular quest might more appropriately be called the plot of patriarchy. This reenactment of the exclusion of difference ensures the transmission of masculine authority and patriarchal law which supports the symbolic order. The exclusion of the "other" is both the precondition for and the very law of narrative itself.

[1]Alter, *Fielding and the Nature of the Novel* (Cambridge, Mass.: Harvard Univ. Press, 1968), p. 147.
[2]Norman O. Brown, in *Love's Body* (New York: Vintage, 1966), p. 130, argues that "the self is formed like a nation, by a declaration of independence, a split from the mother or the mother country, and a split in oneself into both mother and child, so as to be self-sufficing."

Why the feminine should be so fearsome to Fielding is not difficult to guess. Tom's anagnorisis in prison coincides with his "discovery" that promiscuity may entail incest: "O good Heavens!
Incest—with a Mother! To what am I reserved?" (xviii, ii). Tom
echoes Oedipus as well as Odysseus, and the prohibition against
incest may be the one universal of civilization. While incest as act
does not, and cannot, take place in the comic structure of the
fiction, the anxiety itself is sufficient to communicate Fielding's
meaning.[3] The acquisition of power, property, and identity requires the subjection of nature and instinct. Calling Tom's alleged
mother Mrs. Waters, Fielding hints what incest threatens, for
water, as Northrop Frye notes, is the traditional symbol of the
"realm of existence below human life, the state of chaos or dissolu-
tion which follows ordinary death, or the reduction to the in-
organic."[4] The mother stands for the archaic or for the lack of
differentiation, for flow and loss of identity and meaning. The
prohibition against incest may well mark the decisive step, the
moment of choice and splitting through which and owing to
which the transition from nature to culture is accomplished. Incest
threatens to abolish the very differences and hierarchies that maintain civilization and identity.[5] In psychoanalytical terms the
Oedipal stage marks the transcendence of the earlier narcissistic
symbiosis with the mother, characterized by orality (undifferentiated incorporation). Incest is literally "*The Spectre*" (xviii, iii) of
Tom Jones; and it is interesting to remember that Fielding's re-
creation of the primal scene of a Garden of Eden without the
presence of old Eve not only depends on eradicating the threat of

[3]Gerard F. Else, *Aristotle's Poetics: The Argument* (Cambridge, Mass.: Harvard
Univ. Press, 1963), p. 420, suggests that "what can be dispensed with is *the act
itself.* The essential thing is the *idea* of a *pathos,* the intention of performing one.
The *pathos* is in fact no more than the lever by which the tragic potentiality is
converted into actuality; and for that purpose—at least so Aristotle gives us to
understand—the intention can serve as well as the act." For an interesting biographical note on the problem of incest in Fielding's writings, see M. C. Battestin,
"Henry Fielding, Sarah Fielding, and 'the Dreadful Sin of Incest,'" *Novel* 13, 1
(1979), 6–19.
[4]*Anatomy of Criticism: Four Essays* (Princeton: Princeton Univ. Press, 1973), p.
146.
[5]See Claude Lévi-Strauss, *The Elementary Structures of Kinship,* trans. J. H. Bell
and J. R. von Sturmer (Boston: Beacon Press, 1969), pp. 3–25.

the feminine but is already prefigured in the single status of both Allworthy and Squire Western. Whether we see the meaning of Tom's quest in psychoanalytical or anthropological terms, we must agree with Horkheimer and Adorno that "men had to do fearful things to themselves before the self, the identical, purposive, and virile nature of man, was formed, and something of that recurs in every childhood."[6]

What Fielding's allusion to incest brings to our attention is the role of Tom's mother, whose dissembling hypocrisy is the origin of all Tom's troubles. In the world of *Tom Jones,* the specter of femininity proves to be not sexuality per se but feminine sexuality, which is assertive, masked, hidden, and duplicitous. A woman can lie about the paternity of her child. It is a Christian cliche that Eve is to be feared as the emblem of both passion and deceit, and if we are to believe the history of philosophy, woman has always represented the otherness or difference that threatens the illusion of self-presence of patriarchy and law.[7] Bridget's secrecy about her relation to Tom withholds his title to the name-of-the-father and places him outside the patriarchal system of transmission of power. Bridget's deceit, like Circe's magic, makes man into "an Animal of a different Species" (VI, i) or a child of literally "nobody" (II, ii). Affection, mothering, the modern connotations of motherhood, are of no concern to Fielding, who aims at fixing the possibility of the anarchic dissemination of meaning and identity caused by the possibility of feminine deceit. The patriarchal law works toward the exclusion of the lie, circumscribing the plurality of the sign and making the issue of the name a matter of legal contract and graphic record. If Fielding's *Tom Jones* is to be contrasted with Richardson's *Clarissa,* then Fielding's and Richardson's very different understanding of the function and nature of writing must inevitably be taken into consideration.[8]

[6]Horkheimer and Adorno, p. 33.
[7]See Lloyd, *The Man of Reason,* especially "Concluding Remarks," pp. 103–11.
[8]See Terry Eagleton, *The Rape of Clarissa.* My suggestion that *Clarissa* is not an antipatriarchal text is substantiated by Nancy K. Miller's argument that the neutralization of female sexuality through death or marriage (as in *Pamela*) helps restore male bonding. See Nancy K. Miller, "The Exquisite Cadavers: Women in Eighteenth-Century Fiction," *Diacritics* 5, 4 (1975), 37–43.

At first glance, what seems most surprising in *Tom Jones* is that Fielding does not blame the mother for her hypocrisy, but in fact, this may not be so surprising after all. The responsibility for and governance of "the principal Fault" of harlotry lie with Allworthy and Western, who fail to "put the Laws in Execution" (v, xii). In a strictly patriarchal scheme of values the possibility of the feminine lie about paternal identity, the specter of otherness, is literally unspeakable, and must be totally repressed from consciousness. The very idea of holding Bridget responsible would lend her autonomy and presence—would acknowledge her as an independent source of origin. Fielding's fiction is radically patriarchal; it visits the sins of the mother on the head of her *son* Blifil. Bridget's hypocrisy and dissimulation are foregrounded in Blifil, whose plot to hide his knowledge of Tom's birth reenacts his mother's dissembling. In mythic narrative the pharmakos represents the menace of undifferentiation. His expulsion to the desert guarantees the stable self-identity of the group. The exclusion of Blifil guarantees the eradication of duplicity and uncertainty about origin from the consciousness of the fiction.

Psychoanalytical theory postulates that the structure of atonement by means of a sacrificial victim is an act of revenge on a substitute. The figure of the scapegoat offers an opportunity to displace and symbolically act out the death wish against the true object of aggression. In Freud's text this is the father, and Freud's suggestion that the father is the archetypical object is taken over by later writers—René Girard, Guy Rosolato, and John Irwin, among others. What we should note in *Tom Jones,* however, is that Fielding reverses Freud's pointer to the father and makes it into the fiction of the mother. The original moment of consciousness, civilization, and language may well be the more archaic one of differentiation from the (m)other—which is covered up, as the guilt of Bridget is repressed in *Tom Jones,* because the text already adopts a strictly patriarchal perspective.

Coleridge, in praising the plot of *Tom Jones* (along with those of *Oedipus Tyrannus* and *The Alchemist*) as one of the three best plots ever planned, calls attention to the novel's charm and "wholesomeness," which may well result from Fielding's success in repressing the presence of otherness from the style, structure, and meaning of his fiction. Coleridge goes on: "To take him up after Richardson is like emerging from a sick-room heated by stoves into an open lawn on a breezy day in May."[9] The reader of *Tom Jones* will remember that it is the sunlight of a breezy May morning which reveals the figure of Allworthy stepping out on his terrace as the glorious incarnation of the idea of benevolent patriarchy.

In retrospect, the story of Tom's circular quest for the name-of-the-father proves to have been concerned from the beginning with the exclusion of the other as feminine or natural. The semantics of meaning of the fiction hinge on a number of oppositions, the one between natural appetite and rational control being perhaps the most important. Natural appetite, or "carnal Appetite" (I, vii), as Allworthy calls it when lecturing Jenny Jones, is the epithet for the "crime" of feminine sexuality:

> How base and mean must that Woman be, how void of that Dignity of Mind, and decent Pride, without which we are not worthy the Name of human Creatures, who can bear to level herself with the lowest Animal, and to sacrifice all that is great and noble in her, all her Heavenly Part, to an Appetite which she hath in common with the vilest Branch of Creation! For no Woman sure, will plead the Passion of Love for an Excuse. This would be to own herself the mere Tool and Bubble of the Man. Love, however barbarously we may corrupt and pervert its Meaning, as it is laudable, is a rational Passion, and can never be violent, but when reciprocal. (I, vii)

Appetite, lust, instinct are base, "Animal" qualities, to which woman, whose appetite produced Tom Jones, seems especially prone. The quest of Tom Jones, of the character as well as the fiction bearing his name, is the transcendence of the physical, the natural and material. Appetite must be transformed into love, copulation into marriage—which ensures the transmission of the name of the father—and the faculty that can work this transformation is the "wonderful Power of Reason" (v, x).

Considered in this "light" the words of Tom's conversion take

---

[9]An excerpt from Coleridge's "Table Talk" of July 1834 is reproduced in *Tom Jones,* Baker, ed., p. 792.

on added meaning. His decision involves a rejection of the feminine as embodied in the goddess Fortune. "'Sure,' cries Jones, 'Fortune will never have done with me, till she hath driven me to Distraction" (xviii, ii). Fortune is the very personification of the quality of unreliability, of deception, attributed to the feminine. It is the "usual Custom" of Fortune to reverse "the Face of Affairs" (xiii, v). Fortune is duplicitous but also materialist and vulgar. Fielding invokes her thus: "And thou, much plumper Dame, whom no airy Forms nor Phantoms of Imagination cloathe: Whom the well-seasoned Beef, and Pudding richly stained with Plumbs delight. Thee, I call; of whom in a *Treckschuyte* in some *Dutch* Canal the fat Ufrow Gelt [Miss Money], impregnated by a jolly Merchant of *Amsterdam,* was delivered: In *Grubstreet*-School didst thou suck in the Elements of thy Erudition" (xiii, i). Tom's moment of decision allows him to turn away from her to another goddess, Prudentia, who personifies the rational power of choice guaranteeing stability, identity, and transcendence of the material. Just as Tom turns away from Molly to Sophia, he transcends his attachment to Fortune by clinging to Prudence.[10] Sophia then, is the emblem of woman as anima, spirit, mind, or *Geist*—her name means "wisdom." In the plot of patriarchy woman, as the means of transmitting masculine power, must first be divested of her physicality, her association with (animal) nature. Her natural function of biological reproduction is spiritualized into a transcendence of nature which is designated as love rather than appetite under the governance of the law.

Fielding's message may be that Tom must renounce his attachment to Fortune, but the fiction itself falls totally under her sway. The word *fortune* has several meanings, and the fiction plays with at least two. Tom is, literally, "a Child sent by Fortune" (xviii, iii)

---

[10]See Battestin, "Fielding's Definition of Wisdom," pp. 827–32. Howard R. Patch, *The Goddess Fortuna in Mediaeval Literature* (Cambridge, Mass.: Harvard Univ. Press, 1927), also opposes Prudentia to Fortuna. The choice between them is analogous to the debate between Passion and Reason in Xenophon's *Cyropaedia*—an educational tract that was a source for Fénelon's *Télémaque*. As Ronald Paulson shows in *Emblem and Expression: Meaning in English Art of the Eighteenth Century* (London: Thames and Hudson, 1975), the choice between Virtue and Voluptas, the choice of Hercules, was a favorite contemporary topos.

to Allworthy's care. He needs fortune in the sense of money to marry Sophia, and he must be fortunate to acquire it. Nor is this acquisitive concern idiosyncratic. Almost everyone in this fiction seems to want to make his fortune: Blifil by ousting Jones, Thwackum and Square through flattery, Honour and Partridge by following Sophia and Tom. Mr. Fitzpatrick runs after his wife's fortune; Squire Western broods about the fortune of his sister; and Mrs. Waters, Tom's alleged mother, is a woman of fortune whose erratic appearance and behavior in the fiction suggests that she embodies the goddess herself. The word *fortune* appears more than 150 times in the fiction. As critics have pointed out, the very structure of the narrative hinges on fortunate and less fortunate coincidences that imperil the verisimilitude of the novel.

From the Olympian point of view of the narrator—whose rational authority as one of the "Registers" of the "Grand Lottery of Time" (ii, i) transcends the limitations of the realm of fortune— these coincidences reflect not the irrationality of fortune but the transcendent design of his own authorial *providentia,* which mirrors that of his creator. Indeed, the narrator himself has already made the choice between fortune and prudence which Tom enacts in the fiction. The point of view of the fiction is strictly transcendent and rational. For the narrator the physical and material aspects of human life, though unavoidable, are of a distinctly lower order. His characters classify themselves by their attitude to nature, and the fictional strategy of presentation suggests that the reader, like Tom, must learn to distinguish between appetite and love, fortune and prudence.

Tom Jones is not only the representation of the process of *Bildung* which leads to self-transcendent subjectivity; it is designed as a model to lead the reader from an unregenerate, "natural" understanding to a higher, transcendent vision. This design is most immediately apparent in the self-conscious commentary of the omniscient narrator. More interesting, though, is its implication in the metaphor of presentation of the fiction. The novel ends and begins with a banquet. The wedding banquet of Tom and Sophia which concludes the fiction suggests the successful sublimation of the libidinal, its assumption into the symbolic order of culture, but the banquet Fielding offers us at the beginning is totally different. The "Bill of Fare to the Feast" which is the prelude to the fiction, promises a spectacle of hearty carnality and presents human nature, the subject of the fiction, under the auspices of such banal foods as Bayonne ham and Bologna sausage. As Maurice Johnson argues, the point of this titillation of the reader's appetite is to engage that reader in a transition from a materialist to a more spiritual understanding.[11] Nature must be sublimated into culture, and the reader who fails to follow Tom's quest will not be able to appreciate the apocalyptic vision, the orderly design of the final banquet or to understand the moral meaning of the fiction. For the unregenerate reader, love continues to "resemble a Dish of Soup, or a Sir-loin of Roast-beef" (VI, i). Fielding's didactic debunking of the reader's supposed materialist expectations demonstrates that this novel, beyond the *Darstellung* of Tom's progress to Sophia, also plots the reader's journey to selfhood.

Tom Jones displays *Bildung* and presents it as a spiritualizing transcendence of the material. Thus the novel reenacts its own initial premise—that Tom's true origin is not his biological origin, his tie to the mother, but, through her, his patriarchal classification, his relationship to Allworthy. Just as material or biological reproduction is overlaid and covered up by the writing of the patriarchal law that empowers the invisible tie to the father, so must the experience of the senses, the appetites of the body, and the randomness of life be made subservient to the transcendent spiritual abstraction.

Although woman is not given originary power in *Tom Jones,* and both Bridget and Sophia serve as instruments of transmission of masculine power (just as the forum or agora facilitates the meeting of man and man), the role of woman proves crucial to the fiction. Horkheimer and Adorno note that Odysseus "loses himself in order to find himself; the estrangement from nature that he brings about is realized in the process of abandonment to nature he contends with in each adventure; and, ironically, when he . . . re-

[11]*Fielding's Art of Fiction* (Philadelphia: Univ. of Pennsylvania Press, 1961), pp. 119–23.

turns home, the inexorable force [of nature] triumphs as the judge and avenger of the legacy of the powers from which he escaped."[12] What is repressed will return, having taken on added mystery and power. If *Tom Jones* illustrates the process of *Bildung* which lends self-identity and patriarchal power, it can only do so by foregrounding the very elements it tries to deny and repress—disorder, chance, sensuality, duplicity, materialism—as the history of the reception of the novel proves. Tom's wanton behavior has long been a point of criticism. Until the twentieth century the novel was considered unsuitable for women in certain circles. We have already noted how Fielding's grand "design" hinges on fortune. Most ironic, however, is that Fielding's plot forces him to commit Bridget's sin of duplicity: he must cover up Tom's origin until the very end. The plot of patriarchy which tries to constitute origin as singular and masculine, which shows how man becomes Allworthy through the exclusion of the "other," uses the very principle it abhors. Without the act of narrative—a representation of the process of transcendence which inevitably entails the presentation of what is to be excluded—the idea of patriarchy could not be. The narrative *is* patriarchy.

Paradoxically, this conclusion adds depth to the idea of a patriarchy that dissolves its claim to singular authority. Even when the story of patriarchy concerns the effort to project and designate the spiritual, the voice, the symbolic order as true and final origin and source of meaning, a close reading will reveal how that constitution hinges on the dismissal, the veiling, or the suppression of the "other"—usually personified in the family romance as female. Thus origin, or arche, is never singular, sole, and whole. There is a shadow of duplicity from the very beginning: there always was and will be a serpent in the garden.

As I have already noted, the formative principle of Fielding's plot is doubling or decomposition. The shade of difference present in and at the moment of origin may be eradicated from the suggested meaning of the fiction but returns to infest the very design as evidence of "the mother." The threat of otherness, which must

12Horkheimer and Adorno, p. 48.

be repressed, returns as the precondition of Fielding's orderly design.

One instance of this self-referential paradox is the split within Allworthy himself. From the beginning Allworthy is presented as "a Pattern" of "true Wisdom" and "Goodness" (VI, iv), the moral center of the novel, its touchstone of true value. Once we are familiar with the outcome of the fiction, the words that introduce Allworthy take on new meaning: "There lately lived (and perhaps lives still) a Gentleman whose name was *Allworthy,* and who might well be called the Favourite of both Nature and Fortune" (I, ii). Allworthy is characterized as possessing the very attributes that are significantly implicated in Tom's fate. Though Tom is endowed with the gift of good nature, he lacks Allworthy's fortune. Moreover, his good nature must be governed by prudence before he can approach the moral status of the exemplary *senex.* Allworthy, however, is presented with the suggestion of eternal immutability, and his single status confirms him as a *deus* figure. Standing alone at the beginning of the fiction, like God, whose singular presence precedes the narrative action of Genesis, he is the alpha and omega of the narrative action.

In the description of Allworthy's dwelling which follows, the emblematic aspect of his character is reinforced. Located on a hill, the estate offers a wide prospect of the surrounding countryside. In addition to the predictable grove, the sloping lawn, there is a lake "which filled the Center of a beautiful Plain, embellished with Groupes of Beeches and Elms, and fed with Sheep," from which issues "a River, that for several Miles was seen to meander through an amazing Variety of Meadows and Woods, till it emptied itself into the Sea, with a large Arm of which, and an Island beyond it, the Prospect was closed" (I, iv). Here Fielding deliberately includes many kinds of English landscape for Allworthy to survey from the top of his hill, as if they were his creation.

Of course, Fielding's description of the situation of Paradise Hall owes much to his acquaintance with the estates of his patrons Lord Lyttleton and Ralph Allen. In addition to its historical significance as a tribute to contemporary English landscape gardening, the description has many symbolic implications. Allworthy's hill is a point of epiphany where the apocalyptic reveals itself to human nature, and the dramatic staging of Allworthy's appearance on the terrace underscores this significance:

> It was now the Middle of *May,* and the Morning was remarkably Serene, when Mr. *Allworthy* walked force on the Terrace, where the Dawn opened every Minute that lovely Prospect we have before described to his Eye. And now having sent forth Streams of Light, which ascended the blue Firmament before him as Harbingers preceding his Pomp, in the full Blaze of his Majesty, up rose the Sun; than which one Object alone in this lower Creation could be more glorious, and that Mr. *Allworthy* himself presented; a human Being replete with Benevolence, meditating in what Manner he might render himself most acceptable to his Creator, by doing most Good to his Creatures.
>
> Reader, take Care, I have unadvisedly led thee to the Top of as high a Hill as Mr. *Allworthy's,* and how to get thee down without breaking thy Neck, I do not well know. (i, iv)

Skirting explicit comparison of Allworthy to God, the text nevertheless makes Allworthy's *imitatio dei* unmistakable. He stands illumined as more glorious than the sun in all its majesty—the symbol of logos and enlightenment, traditionally identified with God's divine wisdom—representing Fielding's conception of the incarnation of a benevolent patriarchy.[13] This patriarchal structure assures the transmission of resemblance between father and son, and just as Tom must grow like Allworthy, Allworthy must resemble his Maker. When he encounters a landlady who dares to claim acquaintance with Allworthy, Tom rebukes her with the argument that human beings are not capable of knowing Allworthy: " 'The Fame of his Goodness indeed,' answered Jones, 'must have extended farther than this; but Heaven only can know him, can know that Benevolence which is copied from itself, and sent upon Earth as its own Pattern. Mankind are as ignorant of such divine Goodness, as they are unworthy of it' " (viii, ii).

[13]Erwin Panofsky, *Meaning in the Visual Arts* (Garden City, N.Y.: Doubleday, 1955), p. 259. On sun symbolism and its religious implications, see H. Rudolf Engler, *Die Sonne als Symbol: Der Schlüssel zu den Mysterien* (Zürich: Melanthius, 1962).

Thus Allworthy, as the emblem of the idea of patriarchy, comes to function in the world of the fiction like God in his creation. It is Tom's relation to Allworthy—not to Sophia—which contains the meaning and argument of the fiction. Allworthy is the referent and touchstone against which Tom must be judged, and his opinion of Tom is the gauge of Tom's fortune. High when Tom is a lad, this opinion falls very low by the time Tom finds himself in a London prison and then rises to unprecedented heights at the close of the story. The pattern of Allworthy's judgment of Tom follows the circular movement of the wheel of fortune and is inseparable from the action of the novel. Thus Allworthy's bosom—like Penelope's bed in *The Odyssey*—is the origin and end of Tom's quest. More significant than his marriage to Sophia, Tom's acceptance by Allworthy as heir and successor marks the closure of the narrative.

The circularity of Tom's rise and fall—implicit in the designation of Allworthy as ultimate origin (thus also end)—presents a logical contradiction. It becomes necessary for Allworthy to banish Tom from his sight in order later to reverse his judgment. The explanation Allworthy himself gives for this reversal is ignorance: "I am . . . ashamed of my past Behaviour to him; but I was as ignorant of his Merit as his Birth" (xviii, ix). But how can someone whose qualities border on the divine be so ignorant? It is a question asked in different forms by almost all critics of this fiction. Even Fielding himself appears to notice the contradiction. In addition to the sudden irony that must deflate the idealism of his introduction of Allworthy, we note his self-justification in presenting the "visible Alteration in *Allworthy's* Mind, and the Abatement of his *Anger* to *Jones*." He continues: "Revolutions of this Kind, it is true, do frequently occur in Histories and dramatic Writers, for no other Reason than because the History or Play draws to a Conclusion, and are justified by Authority of Authors; yet though we insist upon as much Authority as any Author whatever, we shall use this Power very sparingly, and never but when we are driven to it by Necessity, which we do not at present foresee will happen in this Work" (xviii, iii).

Should we, however, blame the reader for feeling that this defense is rather feeble? The author seems to have violated the very rule of "Conservation of Character" he had so warmly defended in an earlier chapter. Fielding claims that Allworthy would have needed the insight of a devil to have surmised the plot of Bridget or Blifil. In fact, however, it seems we cannot escape the conclusion either that Allworthy is less than all-wise and all-knowing (in contradiction of the image Fielding tries to project) or that his character is bafflingly self-contradictory, combining charity with the utmost negligence and gullibility.[14]

At first sight, it perhaps appears that we should revise our conclusion about Allworthy's symbolic significance. Homer Obed Brown argues that Allworthy cannot be taken as an analogue for God the Father either typologically or allegorically.[15] Allworthy is lacking in divine goodness and omniscience. If we regard the story of Genesis not from a devotional but from a structural point of view, however, we may come to an entirely different conclusion. According to Lévi-Strauss, it is a "property of mythical figures the world over . . . that the same god is endowed with contradictory attributes—for instance he may be *good* and *bad* at the same time."[16] The split in Allworthy's character reminds us of a similar problem in the exegesis of Genesis. Indeed, that Allworthy is a "dubious" creation, to use André Gide's word, may be the very proof that he is the god of the fiction.

What returns in *Tom Jones* is the age-old problem of the origin of evil. The dualism of man's experience—the wilderness outside the garden, corruption next to innocence, death in addition to life, mothers as well as fathers—conflicts with the idea of a single origin. Monotheism has always been forced to rationalize God's responsibility for the presence of otherness, for Satan's existence. As Fielding's contemporary Hume put it: "Epicurus's old questions are yet unanswered. Is God willing to prevent evil, but not

[14]A. D. McKillop, *The Early Masters of English Fiction* (Lawrence: Univ. of Kansas Press, 1956), pp. 128–29, calls Allworthy a "rather gullible benevolist." Robert Alter, p. 120, considers Allworthy perhaps "not the only virtuous character who has something to learn in the course of the novel." Most explicit about Allworthy's failure to conform to "normal human nature and conduct" are E. E. Stoll, *Art and Artifice in Shakespeare: A Study in Dramatic Contrast and Illusion* (1933; rpt. New York: Barnes and Noble, 1963); and Andrew Wright, *Henry Fielding: Mask and Feast* (Berkeley: Univ. of California Press, 1965.)

[15]Homer Obed Brown, p. 223.

[16]*The Structural Study of Myth*, p. 227.

able? then he is impotent. Is he able, but not willing? then he is malevolent. Is he both able and willing? whence then is evil?"[17] The dubious duplicity of Allworthy's character is the effect of a structural necessity. In depicting origin as singular, self-identical, and benevolent, Fielding runs into the same problem that has baffled Christian theologians. The metaphysical projection of origin as absolute, although supported by Aristotelian logic, conflicts with human consciousness, which is ipso facto dualistic, for it understands by means of polarities and oppositions. Unity and wholeness are predicated upon the negation of the "other."

Thus our reading of Allworthy's character returns us to the problems inherent in the constitution of the plot of patriarchy. Self-identity and subjectivity are manufactured by the repression of otherness, whether Satanic or feminine; and in the history of Western culture, the two are often allied. But since Satan makes the less likely subject for fictional representation, the history of the novel has usually assigned the burden of otherness to woman. Woman becomes Eve, incriminated in the Fall. And therefore the study of the inscription of the idea of woman in fiction takes on deep importance. In analyzing the semantic charge and structural function of the feminine, we not only bring to light contemporary views about the role and nature of women; we articulate the implicit debate of a culture about its own construction of the subject.

Authority and the "Other"

My analysis of the plot of *Tom Jones* raises a problem: What authorizes a text, a reading, a certain point of view? What legitimizes an interpretation? This question arises not only from an interpretation of Fielding's novel but also from Fielding's reading of his world. Not only is authority the subject of *Tom Jones,* but the thematic concern returns in the self-conscious discourse of the narrator. The quest for Tom's paternity is the diegetic manifestation of a more central concern that also relates to the authority of

[17]*Dialogues concerning Natural Religion,* ed. Norman Kemp Smith (1779; rpt. Oxford: Oxford Univ. Press, 1935), pt. 10, p. 198.

the genre and to the authority of the narrator of this "Invention." In fact, the words "An Author" begin the book.

There is a difference, however, between Tom and his narrator. Whereas Tom is shown in the process of acquiring authority, the narrator claims full authority from the beginning. He presents himself as one of the "registers" of the "grand lottery of Time" (II, i), "admitted behind the Scenes of this great Theatre of Nature" (VII, i), arrogating a degree or kind of authority which vastly surpasses that of the ordinary human being. Fielding dramatizes himself in the fiction, attributing superior insight, superior penetration to himself: "First, then we warn thee not to condemn any of the Incidents in this our History, as impertinent and foreign to our main Design, because thou dost not immediately conceive in what Manner such Incident may conduce to that Design" (X, i). Fielding's role as creator of the fiction is analogous to God's: "For as I am, in reality, the Founder of a new Province of Writing, so I am at Liberty to make what laws I please therein. And these Laws, my Readers, whom I consider as my subjects, are bound to believe in and obey" (II, i). Fielding, the puppetmaster of his metatheater, pictures, designs, and projects his idea of "authority" by analogy with his idea of the ultimate source of patriarchal authority, God himself.

Fielding derives justification for his endeavor from the "good Authority" of the "vast authentic Doomsday-Book of Nature" (IX, i). The word *nature,* of course, does not yet have its romantic connotation. Here it means "the emblematic," what is general, or what culture has determined to be the proper way of understanding. Thus the authority of *Tom Jones* rests upon Fielding's belief that he is, indeed, embodying this general truth, this essential view, this higher vision of the symbolic order. The tautology of this reasoning unexpectedly shows itself to the modern reader in Fielding's choice of metaphor. He speaks of nature as the "authentic Doomsday-Book," thus inadvertently suggesting that the "truth" of his fiction is not original or natural but already written.

From the modern point of view writing is at best a record of speech and does not command credence, but for Fielding writing was synonymous with truth. To this eighteenth-century man of letters the medium itself seemed endowed with presence and authority. If we consider that the institution of patriarchy rests on the cornerstone of legal record—the inscription of the name of the father rather than the oral declaration of the mother, giving true origin—Fielding's belief in the truth of writing begins to make sense.

More telling and perhaps more reliable than the self-conscious commentary of the implied author is his depiction of authority within the tale. The relevant moment in the story occurs toward the end. In the penultimate chapter a penitent Tom tries to convince a reluctant Sophia of his future constancy. Arguing that Tom's constancy can only prove itself in the course of time, she objects, "After what is past, Sir, can you expect I should take you upon your Word?" (xviii, xii). At issue here is the trustworthiness, the reliability, of Tom's promise, his *word,* and since Tom can be taken for Everyman, we might expand the significance of the moment to encompass the question of the relationship of language to truth in general. Tom answers:

> "Don't believe me upon my Word; I have a better Security, a Pledge for my Constancy, which it is impossible to see and doubt." "What is that?" said *Sophia,* a little surprised. "I will show you, my charming Angel," cried *Jones,* seizing her Hand, and carrying her to the Glass. "There, behold it there in that lovely Figure, in that Face, that Shape, those Eyes, that Mind that shines through those Eyes: Can the Man who shall be in Possession of these be inconstant? Impossible! my *Sophia:* They would fix a *Dorimant,* a Lord *Rochester.* You would not doubt it, if you could see yourself with any Eyes but your Own." (xviii, xii)

It is a curious scene, in which the tables seem suddenly turned. The suppliant Tom turns into Sophia's teacher, and the archetypal relationship between the sexes reasserts itself. Tom's moment of assumption is simultaneously a scene of instruction reminiscent of Rembrandt's depiction of Adam and Eve, and Tom's masculine authority to instruct Sophia rests upon her blindness to her own commanding power. Tom shows her the power of her appearance, which can only become visible to her in the mirror, not in Tom's words. The mediation of the mirror is the sine qua non of the resolution of the fiction. It is the visual image, rather than language, which is credited with the power of conveying truth. It seems more "literal" than words. Battestin reads this scene as a literalizing of the Platonic metaphor: Sophia as the goddess Prudence, who is represented in Ripa's *Iconographia* as beholding herself in a mirror. I think the text here also reveals its preconceptions about ultimate authority. Although the implied author may rest his authority on his patriarchal resemblance to the divine Creator, his instrument is not the creative Word per se but its *mimetic capability*. The notion or ideal of mimesis seems itself the source of the authority of the fiction.

We need only turn to the Dedication to see this tentative conclusion confirmed. Here Fielding hammers on mimesis: "To recommend Goodness and Innocence hath been" the "sincere Endeavour in this History. . . . And to say the Truth, it is likeliest to be attained in Books of this Kind; for an Example is a Kind of *Picture,* in which Virtue becomes as it were an *Object of Sight,* and *strikes us* with *an Idea* of that Loveliness, which *Plato* asserts there is in her naked Charms" (p. 7). The authority of narrative and the truth of language, then, reside in their power to provide an "Object of Sight," to give a mimetic representation of the real. The adage *Ut pictura, poesis* also seems to apply to *Tom Jones,* not surprisingly in an epoch designated the Age of Reason, in which reason, as we saw in Fielding's emblematic description of Allworthy, was identified with light, illumination, insight. The mirror of fiction which presents a true "Object of Sight" enacts its own understanding of truth as light, order, and reason. Once more Pope's words seem appropriate: "Unerring Nature, still divinely bright, / One clear, unchanged and universal light" (*An Essay on Criticism,* i, 70–71). Thus the representation of nature represents its own power of seeing, while otherness, the representational function of language or writing, is wholly overlooked. Mimesis, as understood by Fielding, mirrors the assumption of its own feasibility.

The preference for the visual over the verbal is inherent in Fielding's whole understanding of his role: he identified his fiction with theater. All of *Tom Jones* is an attempt to reveal a secret and undo the evil effects of secrecy. Thus the privileging of the more immediate apperception of the visual in the metaphor of presentation of the story ties in with its theme and arises from the same purpose—

to exclude or undo the possibility of duplicity, to fix the plurality of meaning—just as Sophia's image would *fix* a Dorimant. The sin at the heart of the fiction, Bridget's deception, which threatens the self-presence of the name-of-the-father, seems identified with the possibility of the lie, which is, Eco says, the *"proprium* of *semiosis."*[18] Fielding's attempt to fix meaning and patriarchal presence leads to the denial of the sign-function proper to language. He takes the word as index. In fact, Fielding seems to wish to regress to what Foucault calls a "time when words glittered in the universal resemblance of things."[19]

As we saw, the faculty that allows Fielding to see and understand God's "Doomsday-Book of Nature" with immediate apperception, is the principle of reason, which thus ensures the viability of the patriarchal plot. He describes reason thus:

> To give a higher Idea of the Principle I mean, as well as one more familiar to the present Age; it may be considered as sitting on its Throne in the Mind, like the LORD HIGH CHANCELLOR of this Kingdom in his Court; where it presides, governs, directs, judges, acquits and condemns according to Merit and Justice; with a Knowledge which nothing escapes, a Penetration which nothing can deceive, and an Integrity which nothing can corrupt.
>
> This active principle may perhaps be said to constitute the most essential Barrier between us, and our Neighbours the Brutes; for if there be some in the human Shape, who are not under any such Dominion, I chuse rather to consider them Deserters. (IV, vi)

I have spoken of patriarchy as a structure that ensures the resemblance between father and son. Patriarchy wants literal, physical resemblance, of course, but the more important resemblance is ideological. Just as Tom's eventual embrace of prudence makes him like Allworthy, so the faculty of reason marks the likeness between God and man, divine author and writer of fiction. The whole myth of patriarchal self-presence seems summarized in Fielding's personification of reason as absolute knowledge, penetration, and integrity. The resemblance between father and son,

[18]*A Theory of Semiotics,* pp. 58–59.
[19]*The Order of Things,* p. 49.

the mediating quality that eventually makes the son worthy to become a father, is not physical likeness—and cannot be so. The continuity of patriarchy rests upon a symbolic resemblance, and the tie between father and son is always an abstraction, an idea.

In this connection it seems appropriate to remind ourselves of the Christian model for the resemblance between Father and Son, the Trinity, in which the mediating entity is the Holy Ghost, the Spirit itself. Fielding's reason, then, functions like the Paraclete of the Trinity. One might say that the idea behind the fiction is even more patriarchal than the fiction itself. The latter, at least, personifies the successful achievement of relationship between father and son in a trinity that includes a woman, Sophia. (It is interesting to note here that in the Gnostic tradition *Sophia* is the third element in the composition of the Trinity.)[20] The feminine element, however, is fully absent in Fielding's fantasy about the rational resemblance between son and father, or man and God.

I have noted that the idea of achieved relationship between father and son, God and man, rests upon the powers of narrative to project successful mediation. Hence the higher faculty of reason, the abstraction symbolizing mediation, must itself be a projection of the mind validated by its apparently successful embodiment as story. The precondition for Fielding's patriarchy, considered from this perspective, is the orderly design of its fiction.

What all this suggests is that Fielding's claim to authority and that of the new genre, insofar as they were honored by contemporary society, must have rested upon a belief in the viability, let us call it "presence," of the kind of mediation brought about through narrative structure. The structure of narrative itself, understood as mimesis, must have been invested with explanatory power. The vicariousness of mediation *in a medium* must have been overlooked, and the image in the glass of fiction taken for the true figure of man. Thus man's medium, language, and especially, perhaps, its usefulness for the symbolic resolution of contradictions prove the support of his subjectivity. As Lacan also argues, man's image of himself as rational subject is sustained by the mediation of lan-

[20]See Stuart Gilbert, *James Joyce's "Ulysses"* (1930; rpt. New York: Vintage Books, 1955), p. 61, n. 4, who refers to Elena Blavatsky's *Isis Unveiled*.

guage; I would suggest that it is especially plot, or structure, that provides that possibility.

Earlier I discussed Genesis as the archetype of family romance and the primal scene of the institution of the Logos, noting that the Word of Genesis is an analytic word, constituting existence through distinction and differentiation. My conclusions about the function of reason suggest that Fielding's attempt to rewrite Genesis reenacts replacement of the Logos of Genesis with that of John 1:1: "In the beginning was the Word, and the Word was with God, and the Word was God." No longer God's creative utterance, the Word in John is the principle of mediation itself. Ultimately it refers to the figure of Christ—God who appears as man, and man who appears as God: "The Word was made flesh, and dwelt among us." The belief in the historical objectivity and material substantiality of the idea of mediation as figured forth in Christ may well be the implicit rationale and basis for the eighteenth-century belief in the truth, the explanatory power, of narrative fiction.

A Christian, specifically Protestant, subtext to the rise of the novel emphatically announced itself on the continent, as James Engell has shown. Thus Herder grounded his belief in the creative imagination on man's resemblance to Christ. In *Die Schöpfung, ein Morgensang,* he identifies the creative principle as Christ the Logos, and bases man's unity with God on the imagination, the creative force, just as Fielding bases it on Reason:

> And so I am, I am it, yes
> What this God-like form appears!
> I—like God! So moves in me
> Creation's plan.[21]

For an analysis of how narrative structure facilitates the illusion of self-transcendence, the works of Hegel prove most to the purpose, perhaps. In Hegel's philosophy, Christ would seem to function as the symbol of dialectical transcendence. The Incarnation, he

[21]I am quoting from James Engell, *The Creative Imagination: Enlightenment to Romanticism* (Cambridge, Mass.: Harvard Univ. Press, 1981), p. 221.

argues, reveals the differentiated unity of opposites and thus satisfies one of the deepest needs of man's unhappy consciousness. "What satisfies this need," according to the *Philosophy of Religion,* is what "we call the consciousness of reconciliation, the consciousness of the sublation, the nullity of the opposition, the consciousness that this opposition is not the truth, but that rather the truth consists in reaching [*erreichen*] unity through the negation of this opposition, i.e., the peace, the reconciliation which this need demands. Reconciliation is the demand of this need, and lies within it as what is infinitely one, what is self-identical with itself."[22]

It will not surprise the reader of Hegel to find that his *Logic* builds upon the story of the Fall, just as Fielding's *Tom Jones* revises the argument of Genesis. The Adamic legend serves Hegel as a "picture representing the origin and consequences" of the "disunion" of man's consciousness, and philosophy itself is a discursive argument on the method and means of transcending this disunion. That the path toward transcendence, even if articulated philosophically rather than implicitly in the structure of narration, should be very similar to the one sketched by Fielding seems no longer accidental:

Upon a closer inspection of the story of the Fall we find, as was already said, that it exemplifies the universal bearings of knowledge upon the spiritual life. In its instinctive and natural stage, spiritual life wears the garb of innocence and confiding simplicity; but the very essence of spirit implies the absorption of this immediate condition in something higher. The spiritual is distinguished from the natural, and more especially from the animal, life, in the circumstance that it does not continue a mere stream of tendency, but sunders itself to self-realization. But this position of severed life has in its turn to be suppressed, and the spirit has by its own act to win its way to

---

[22]The quotation, from Mark Taylor, *Journeys to Selfhood,* p. 114, is a conflation of several parts from *The Philosophy of Religion.* Another sentence from Hegel which seems especially meaningful in relation to Fielding's idea of reason, is: "Reason is Spirit, when its certainty of being all reality has been raised to the level of truth, and reason is *consciously* aware of itself as its own world, and of the world as itself." *Phenomenology of Mind,* trans. J. B. Baillie (New York: Harper and Row, 1967), p. 457.

concord again. The final concord then is spiritual; that is, the principle of restoration is found in thought, and thought only. The hand that inflicts the wound is also the hand which heals it.[23]

Thus Hegel's dialectic of the constitution of the subject, which hinges on the idea of the spirit or *Geist,* mirrors Tom Jones's journey toward selfhood. Nor is the relevance of this quest for "ghostlier demarcations" limited to the eighteenth and early nineteenth centuries when Fielding and Hegel were alive. Lacan's abstraction of a "symbolic order" seems an elaboration of the strategy of dematerialization and desubstantialization suggested in fictional plot and philosophical argument alike. Just as Fielding excludes the physical from meaning and presence, sublimating instinct as love, Lacan rarefies force into power, the penis into the symbolic phallus. Yet, though Lacan's psychology may be a most appropriate representation of the actual structure of patriarchy and may, for that very reason, have been especially helpful in the analysis of Fielding's fiction, we should be wary to credit it with more than explanatory force. Just as Jones's journey to selfhood can no longer be understood as the model of ultimate reality by the twentieth-century reader, Lacan's model of the self can be recognized as an elaboration of the plot of patriarchy.

This excursion into philosophical discourse should increase our awareness of the mutual determination of fiction and other cultural discourse. Fiction embodies the plot of patriarchy; Hegel articulates it discursively. This plot should also give us pause. If consciousness, seen as *Geist* or spirit, is postulated as the essence of humanity, are we not irredeemably alienated from our material side, expelled from the physical world? Have we not brought about a new repetition of the Fall, an upward fall, an escape from our rootedness in flesh, soil, and matter to an airy insubstantiality? Moreover, does not the emphasis on transcendence also generate a paradoxical glorification of the natural, which now seems mysterious, "other," and forever out of reach? It is a consequence my analyses of *Bleak House* and *Ulysses* would seem to suggest.

[23]*Hegel's Logic,* p. 48.

Horkheimer and Adorno even warn us that the privileging of "Enlightenment" or *Geist* dialectically issues in a fascist idolatry of *Blut und Boden*.[24]

In my reading of the plot of patriarchy I have noted how the viability of the structure depends on its relation to language. For the illusion of full self-presence to be based on language, language cannot be understood as sign, as arbitrary figure of mediation; it must be taken as the graphic record, the fixed inscription of truth and identity. Just as patriarchy founds its authority on repressing the supposed duplicity of the feminine, so it excludes the possible sign-function of language. The question of Eve may well be read as the question of language. The inscription of woman in the family romance correlates with the attitude toward language. The imagined threat of woman's otherness to patriarchal self-presence ties in with a distrust of the dispersive power of language, and as the idea of woman as "other" acquires power (however disquieting the acquisition) in the course of the nineteenth century, so does the acknowledgment of the disseminating forces in language. We might read the history of the inscription of woman in the novel as the history of the genre's relationship with itself. Fielding's claim to authority and his inscription of the feminine seem almost directly opposite to Joyce's (seeming) abdication of authority—his idolatry of Molly, and his bow to the hegemony of language over meaning. Even Dickens is forced to tone down Fielding's self-assured authorial stance (mocked, perhaps, in the figure of Tulkinghorn) to a less forceful, more accommodating one. Apparently, by the middle of the nineteenth century the plot of patriarchy, while perhaps still validated by philosophy and religion, is beginning to lose the self-evident credibility it seems to have had in Fielding's eyes.

[24]Horkheimer and Adorno, "Elements of Anti-Semitism: The Limits of Enlightenment," pp. 168–209.

5

Bleak House and the
Victorian Family Romance

Our solitude has the same roots as religious feelings. It is a form of orphanhood, an obscure awareness that we have been torn from the All, and an ardent search: a flight and a return, an effort to reestablish the bonds that unite us with the universe.

—Octavio Paz, *The Labyrinth of Solitude*

Our classifications will come to be, as far as they can be so made, genealogies; and will then truly give what may be called the plan of creation. . . .

Light will be thrown on the origin of man and his history.
—Charles Darwin, *Origin of Species*

Like my reading of *Tom Jones,* this chapter on *Bleak House* is an attempt to use analytical techniques of reading for a broader purpose, in the light of Cesare Segre's conclusion in *Structures and Time* that a "definition of narrative models must be arrived at from within a study of cultural modeling systems."[1] The narrative model informing *Bleak House,* both Esther Summerson's story and the third-person narrative, is, as in *Tom Jones,* a version of the family romance. The story of the orphan who finds parents or a home is a perennial literary theme, but this process of discovery or recovery is imagined differently from period to period, expressing, perhaps, the deepest, often unconscious, human notions about subjectivity and destiny. Here my argument will be that the pecu-

[1] *Structures and Time: Narration, Poetry, Models,* trans. John Meddemmen (Chicago: Univ. of Chicago Press, 1979), p. 56.

liar revisionary structure of Dickens's family romance can also be detected in the revisionary intent of a contemporary nonliterary text, positivist in inspiration—Darwin's *Origin of Species*—and can be seen as related to the conceptual tensions of the epoch, especially the threat to a patriarchal notion of origin posed by the rise of materialist science.

As my point of departure I have selected a quotation from Paz's *Labyrinth of Solitude* which situates "orphanhood"—the inevitable separation from a full presence—as a metaphor for the human condition as experienced in the modern era. At first sight this term may not seem to apply to *Bleak House,* which presents itself as a story about the corruption of Victorian society, especially the law. The plot traces the fates of those who have had the misfortune to deal with the Court of Chancery, focusing upon the personal history of Esther Summerson, who is ignorant of the identity of her parents. As we shall see, orphanhood, as loss of parents, loss of origin and identity, not only applies to Esther but also summarizes the thematic and structural concerns of *Bleak House.*

Let us begin, then, by defining that aspect of the Darwinian solution which is of importance with regard to *Bleak House.* John Dewey once summarized Darwin's achievement thus: "In laying hands upon the sacred ark of Absolute permanency, in treating the forms that had been regarded as types of fixity and perfection as originating and passing away, the *Origin of Species* introduced a mode of thinking that in the end was bound to transform the logic of knowledge, and hence the treatment of morals, politics, and religion."[2] Darwin's treatise is based on a revisionary strategy that replaces the older, theologic world view of a *scala naturae* founded on the principle of discrete hierarchical levels and a divine creation ex nihilo with a biologic, evolutionary understanding of reality based on the notion of genealogy and natural origin. Thus one might say that Darwin attempted to substitute a metonymical or syntagmatic world view for a metaphorical or paradigmatic one; however, I prefer (while aware of the crudeness of this schematization, to which I shall return later) provisionally to summarize

[2] *The Influence of Darwin on Philosophy* (New York: Holt, 1910), pp. 1–2.

Darwin's strategy as the displacement of God the Father by Mother Nature as the locus of origin.

The modern reader, even one raised in a fundamentalist environment, may find it difficult to realize the unsettling power of Darwin's suggestions about origin. After all, our habit of thinking in biological terms has come to seem natural. But much of what we consider obvious—for example, that a human body is made up of cells, that conception entails the penetration of an ovum by a spermatozoon—was still fairly specialized knowledge in our grandparents' generation. Belief in spontaneous generation of some nonhuman genera was still current, and the baffling phenomenon of biological origin often required the postulation of a transcendental causative agency, a *vis creatrix,* an anima, or entelechy. Our modern understanding of ourselves as sexual beings depends on and testifies to the replacement of a hierarchical world view by an evolutionary or, more precisely, a biological one; and the entrenched nature of our views, which may close our eyes to the pain and profound uncertainty of those who lived through the period of transition, ultimately depends on the creation of biology as a science during the nineteenth century.[3]

In selecting natural history as the matrix of this conceptual change, however, I do not want to suggest that the shift in understanding was limited to the realm of science or originated there. On the contrary, though the general public may not have been aware of all the implications or able to understand the actual processes of scientific investigation, interest in origins and beginnings was in the air.[4] As early as the 1820s there arose a general enthusi-

---

[3]The mid–nineteenth century witnessed the publication of three important theories that helped develop biology as a science: Rudolf Virchow, in *Die Cellularpathologie* (1858), argued that all cells derive from preceding cells; Louis Pasteur disproved the theory of spontaneous generation in bacteria, thus necessitating the conclusion that all organisms come from preceding organisms; Charles Darwin asserted that all species came from earlier species. It was not until 1879, despite the earlier knowledge of the existence of spermatozoa, that Herman Tol, a Swiss physician, actually observed the penetration of an ovum and invalidated the age-old theory that sperm induced a "spiritual" effluence that effected fertilization.

[4]My selection of Darwin's treatise, published seven years *after Bleak House,* as a point of reference is strategic. Though a geological text might have provided an

asm for natural history and especially geology, kindled by popular lectures, introductory booklets, and so forth. The implications of the geological findings about the age of the earth were widely and eagerly discussed because they conflicted with the biblical account of creation. Even poets concerned themselves with this discussion. Byron, for instance, defends his use of Cuvier's account of the creation in the preface to *Cain,* insisting that it did not, in fact, contradict the Mosaic account. But what best captured the popular imagination was the discovery of prehistoric monsters. A model of a dinosaur was reconstructed for the Great Exhibition of 1851, and Dickens's own *Household Words* featured a description of a megalosaurus only a few months before the author started working on *Bleak House.* Indeed, the novel contains an oddly unexpected reference to that animal in its opening paragraph.

This popular interest in science and the primeval should be regarded as more than a mere desire for novelty or sensation. An element of fearful fascination with the disturbing implications of these findings no doubt enhanced their attraction. With the widening realization that human historical origins are not divine, not intrinsically different from those of the rest of the primate world, the problem of human identity becomes increasingly acute. The best-known contemporary articulation of the deeper feelings of the Victorian public is Tennyson's *In Memoriam,* published the year before the first installment of *Bleak House* appeared. Both the beginning and the end of section 56 express the moral threat of the notion of mere biological origin and the poet's agony at having to give up the illusion of superiority over the natural world:

> "So careful of the type?" but no.
> From scarped cliff and quarried stone
> She cries, "A thousand types are gone;
> I care for nothing, all shall go."

example of direct influence, Darwin's contribution to the history of ideas is so representative that I have chosen him as figurehead for the age. Gillian Beer, *Darwin's Plots: Evolutionary Narrative in Darwin, George Eliot and Nineteenth-Century Fiction* (London: Routledge and Kegan Paul, 1983), offers an extensive discussion of the influence of Darwin's ideas. She remarks upon "the sense that everything is connected, though the connections may be obscured," which in turn "gave urgency to the enterprise of uncovering such connections" (p. 47).

"Thou makest thine appeal to me:
  I bring to life, I bring to death:
  The spirit does but mean the breath:
I know no more."

. . . . .

No more? A monster then, a dream,
  A discord. Dragon of the prime,
  That tare each other in their slime,
Were mellow music match'd with him.

O life as futile, then, as frail!
  O for thy voice to soothe and bless!
  What hope of answer, or redress?
Behind the veil, behind the veil.

This desperate lamentation about the looming presence of "Nature, red in tooth and claw / With ravine" provides an intellectual context to the narrative mood of the opening of *Bleak House*. For all the famous realism of the first paragraphs, which situate the reader in a densely concrete, vividly recognizable London suffering the effects of late autumn weather, the novel's initial passage is haunted by the same doubts expressed in *In Memoriam*. Its unique effect depends on a typical Dickensian strategy in which the narrator, while (re)creating a scene, presents it in a manner that points up a vital lack of essence, of rigidly circumscribed identity in the object of description.[5] Everything moves, slides, and slithers while staying in place, not because the narrator would wish us to regard the world under the aspect of process, as modern philosophy might suggest, but because phenomenal reality seems to lack a fixed, definite origin. And without circumscribed origin, there can be no circumscribed identity or shape.

If we look more closely at this description, we see that Dickens's shifting and shimmering outline of London is related to a stylistic

---

[5] Dorothy Van Ghent discusses the fluidity characteristic of Dickens's descriptions of inanimate objects and the reification of his portrayal of people in "The Dickens World: A View from Todger's," in *Dickens: A Collection of Critical Essays*, ed. M. Price (Englewood Cliffs, N.J.: Prentice Hall, 1967), pp. 26–27.

peculiarity. The finite verbs have been elided from the main claus-
es. Action is indicated by present participles, and the passage remains in a continuous present. The evasion of tense suggests the
wish to evoke the absence of time (as linear progression). In a
perpetual present there is no past and future, no beginning or end,
only a perpetual being "in the middest." Implicit is a sense of
uncertainty about what precedes or follows, for the ambivalent
present precludes certainty about origin or destiny. It is the absence of beginning that the narrator seems to stress. Thus, having
accidentally referred to daybreak, he hastens to add a parenthetical
qualification: "if day ever broke" (1).[6]

It is not surprising to note, therefore, that night and day have
become an indistinguishable blur, given up to the supremacy of
fog; that the "death of the sun" has effaced the differences between
climates and seasons; or that, with the collapse of the temporal
distinctions, land, sky, and water have dissolved into an indis-
criminate mixture of mud. Placing this opening passage next to its
prototype, the story of the creation in Genesis, one is surprised to
find that *Bleak House* "creates" its vision of London by the deliberate blurring of precisely those distinctions that in the biblical account had constituted the divine act of original creation—the separation of land and water, darkness and light, and the institution of
the heavenly bodies to mark and measure time. While the setting
remains London, we seem to have moved to a temporal perspective outside biblical or recorded time, a blend of prehistory and
perpetual present which would seem to account for the narrator's
disorientation and the expectation of seeing a megalosaurus on
Holborn Hill.[7]

---

[6]All quotations refer to the Crowell Critical Library Edition, ed. Duane DeVries
(New York: Thomas Y. Crowell, 1971), which is a reprint of the first one-volume
edition of September 1853, cited by chapter number.

[7]It is probably the notion of mud which suggested the megalosaurus to Dickens.
Cf. "Owen's Museum," *All the Year Round*, vol. 8, September 27, 1862, p. 63,
which gives the following description of the prehistoric scene: "For the world was
not then as lovely as it is now, but huge, and monstrous, and uncouth—a mere
seething steaming cauldron of heated mud and turbid water, inhabited by fierce
monsters always warring together." It was, of course, still a general Victorian
belief that monsters generated spontaneously from mud.

The inability to hear what the narrator calls "the rushing of larger worlds" and to "see them circle around the sun" (2), is not peculiar to the beginning of the story. Throughout this account the third-person narrator will betray the deadlock of being bereft of a principle of coherence, a key with which to make firm sense of things. The world he points out to us is not merely fallen or less pristine; it has lost its principle of cohesion. In giving up the belief in a metaphysical patriarchal origin, this world has relinquished the cosmographical conception of the Great Chain of Being in which the hierarchical levels were bound to each other by love. But whereas the informing spirit seems gone, the relics of the older world view, the hierarchical institutions that administer society, live on as the fossilized remains of an earlier age. Thus the "raw afternoon is rawest, and the dense fog is densest, and the muddy streets are muddiest, near . . . that leaden-headed old corporation: Temple Bar," and "hard by Temple Bar, in Lincoln's Inn Hall, at the very heart of the fog, sits the Lord High Chancellor in his High Court of Chancery" (1).

Chancery, then, is the central symbol of the evil aftereffects of this loss of a principle of meaning: instead of justice, this court of law produces endless reams of meaningless writing; rather than provide for the "wards of chancery," the members of this court have made the process of administration self-serving. "Groping and floundering" in a moral fog, like the pedestrians just described, they are "mistily engaged in . . . an endless cause, tripping one another up on slippery precedents, groping knee-deep in technicalities, running their goat-hair and horse-hair warded heads against walls of words" (1). Its most important judge, the Lord High Chancellor, is depicted not as the human representative of the divine prototype, whose prestigious power he still shares in the symbolic order, but as the icon of ineffectiveness. Not a "father," not a provider for the orphans of the world, this lord, lacking the radiance of numinosity, sits at the heart of the moral darkness of the story like the spider in its web, with a "foggy glory round his head," looking into "a lantern that has no light in it" (1). To use a biblical metaphor, chancery symbolizes the death of the "spirit" and the tyranny of the "letter." In this novel crowded with or-

phans, chancery is emblematic of the absence of God the Father
and cause of the bitterness of Mr. Jarndyce's retort to Skimpole
that the "universe makes an indifferent parent" (6).

The narrator's vision also reflects the nobility as a lifeless institution, crumbling now that its inspiring principle has lost the power
to bind. One notes with a sense of irony that the seeds of the
impending downfall of the Dedlock family were planted during
the reign of King Charles I when the English Civil War swept
aside the notion of the divine right of kings, based, of course, on
the sanctity of the hierarchical principle. Though the steps on the
ghost walk predicting the event have rung for several centuries, it
is during Sir Leicester's lifetime that the family skeleton, illicit
relations with "the other party," brings about the end of the lineage. As Sir Leicester is the aristocratic counterpart of the Lord
High Chancellor, his beliefs and preferences personify the de-
suetude of the social structure. Threatened by the political activity
of Mr. Rouncewell, his housekeeper's son, he laments that "the
floodgates of society are burst open, and the waters have—a—
obliterated the landmarks of the framework of the cohesion by
which things are held together" (40). Here again, the narrator uses
the image of flooding water—a traditional symbol of the female,
the "other," the unconscious—to denote the breakdown of the
hierarchical order. He will use it again just before Esther confronts
her dead mother in the wetness of Tom-all-Alone's.

What is important here is that Sir Leicester's fears about the
breakdown of formerly discrete hierarchical levels seem to make
him suspect in the eyes of the narrator, who keeps hammering on
the degeneration of law and aristocracy into things of "precedent
and usage; oversleeping Rip Van Winkles" (2), fossils of an earlier
world view. It is one of the signs of Miss Flite's madness that she
still accords the aristocracy a mystique of presence, firmly maintaining that it is only the best people who are raised to nobility,
whereas the narrator demonstrates over and over again that the
relation between essence and appearance, ideal function and social
actuality, is lost or lacking. As in Dickens's other novels, most
notably *Little Dorrit,* in *Bleak House* the social structure is de-
nounced for having made mediation into a self-contained, inescapable way of life, of which Mr. Jarndyce's perception is perhaps

the clearest in the novel: "Through years and years, and lives and lives, everything goes on, constantly beginning over and over again, and nothing ever ends. And we can't get out of the suit on any terms, for we are made parties to it, and *must be* parties to it, whether we like it or not" (8). Without a relationship to a fixed origin or end, men are forced to live in a permanent halfway house, or as Richard Carstone describes his emotional state, "an unfinished house."

This uncertainty entails problems of identity and role. In their inability to bear the provisional quality of their existence, Dickens's characters reach irritably after an illusionary role or strategy to give their lives identity and outline. Some, like Miss Flite, Gridley, and Richard Carstone, believe against reason in a "Last Judgment" that will retrospectively vindicate their sacrifice of human qualities. Mrs. Pardiggle and Mrs. Jellyby restlessly try to enforce or propagate the ministration of Old Law charity, while neglecting their own children. Harold Skimpole's opportunistic game playing seems especially telling: unwilling to suffer the disillusionment and diminishment of adulthood, he plays the role of the irresponsible, careless child. The supreme irony is that Skimpole, a parent himself, manipulates the orphans of his world into providing for him. Another desperately selfish stance is Mr. Chadband's passionate intensity as a preacher. He perverts "truth" into "Terewth," and all moral distinctions are flattened beneath his oppressively vindictive dogmatism. These assertive stances toward life are subterfuges to escape suffering, refusals of the knowledge that the better characters in the novel patiently bear, a sense of being left without directive, of being an orphan in a bewilderingly complex world. Though modern tastes tend to reject the sentimentality of the novel, it is precisely in his pathos that the figure of little Jo, the orphan, seems to personify the loneliness, the keylessness, the perplexity of most of the inhabitants of *Bleak House:*

And there he sits, munching and gnawing, and looking up at the great Cross on the summit of St. Paul's Cathedral, glittering above a red and violet tinted cloud of smoke. From the boy's face one might suppose that sacred emblem to be, in his eyes, the crowning confusion of the great, confused city; so golden, so high up, so far out of his reach. There he sits, the sun going down, the river running fast, the crowd flowing by him in two streams—everything moving on to some purpose and to one end—until he is stirred up, and told to "move on" too. (19)

Jo's physical and emotional loneliness while looking at the cross, the central symbol of the patriarchal culture that seems to exclude him, stems from lack of education and marks his separateness from the web of cultural traditions and beliefs, the symbolic order. Nevertheless, this inability to interpret the cross, the failure to lend it vital significance, is best read as an ironic displacement of the powerlessness of society at large to find a "key" to unlock a fuller spiritual presence.

French thought has enforced awareness that the tradition of Western culture is founded on a complex of interrelated axiomatic ideas, sometimes labeled, for easy reference, "phallogocentrism"—implying that patriarchal power and the prestige of the written word are the operative principles of our social and conceptual structures. In this view, key, cross, gavel, and sword are symbols of the same ordering principle. And what Dickens shows us in *Bleak House* is not just the aftereffect of the "death of God" but the tottering imbalance of phallogocentrism, the uncertainty about its continuing effectiveness.[8] Thus when logocentrism (to split the term into its component parts) threatens to fail, writing eventuates in meaningless documents, or it turns subversive, as in the letters of Lady Dedlock and her illicit lover, lending a threatening presence to what should have remained hidden or nonexistent, a relationship not sanctioned by logos and law. Similarly, if phallocentrism begins to fail, the traditional relationships within the family break down, especially between parents and children. In addition to Mrs. Jellyby and Harold Skimpole, the patriarchal Mr. Turveydrop, a self-inflated "model of deportment" who lives parasitically on the labor of his daughter-in-law, is an example. Lady

---

[8]The notion of the "death of God" and its importance for nineteenth-century fiction have been dealt with at length by J. Hillis Miller in *Charles Dickens: The World of His Novels* (Cambridge, Mass.: Harvard Univ. Press, 1958) and in *The Form of Victorian Fiction* (Notre Dame, Ind.: Univ. of Notre Dame Press, 1968). I am indebted to his views.

Dedlock, we note with surprise, never rectifies the abandonment of her daughter Esther; whereas little Charley, herself an orphan, must parent and provide for her brother and sister. Relationships between man and wife also become unpredictable: Mrs. Jellyby wields the pen while Mr. Jellyby creeps self-effacingly through the house; Mr. Snagsby lives in terror of his wife, while the Bagnets, a humane couple, play the game of never acknowledging Mrs. Bagnet's superiority to her husband in a pretense of continued conformity, because "discipline must be maintained." Even the most lovable character, Mr. Jarndyce, can no longer assume the power and authority belonging to his place in society. While he emulates divine benevolence, he hides his uncertainty behind the gruffness of a friendly giant. It is only the villain of the story, the lawyer Tulkinghorn, who assumes the full masculine authority connoted by his name (tool-king-horn).

Esther's Quest for Identity

As a novel, *Bleak House* is of course more than a record of the disintegration of our cultural heritage. It would not be a Dickens novel if it failed to offer a solution to the ills and evils it so powerfully evokes, and here we must return to the passage from the conclusion of the *Origin of Species*. Just as Darwin insists that biological research should give up its outdated concern with determining the essential nature of discrete species and study instead the history of their development in order to find "the origin of man" and "the plan of creation," so Dickens proposes to remedy the evil of a disintegrating hierarchical world view by simultaneously tracing connections on several levels which will ultimately sketch the pattern of a new view of origin, a revisionary notion of subjectivity.

In the chapter titled "Tom-all-Alone's," the narrator asks: "What connection can there be, between the place in Lincolnshire, the house in town, the Mercury in powder, and the whereabouts of Jo the outlaw with the broom, who had the distant ray of light upon him when he swept the churchyard-step? What connection can there have been between many people in the innumerable histories of this world, who, from opposite sides of great gulfs, have, nevertheless, been very curiously brought together!" (16). It is in the course of tracing Esther Summerson's illegitimate origin—her "natural genealogy," to use Darwin's phrase—and in neutralizing its unspeakable character that this question is answered.[9] In the process of revealing the secret of Esther's mysterious natural origins Dickens also sketches the failing links in the crumbling social edifice, however tentatively; he transforms what may initially have seemed a random kaleidoscope of Victorian images into a design, even a meaningful design, for Esther's first-person account will outstay the disturbing vision of the third-person narrator and conclude the story with the assurance of personal happiness, secure identity, pattern, and order in a pristine little Bleak House.

As narrative, Esther's quest for identity belongs to the genre of romance. Its suggestive power hinges on the diametrical opposition between good and evil, enemy and hero, which is characteristic of the genre.[10] Whereas society at large is associated with Frye's categories of "winter, darkness, confusion, sterility, moribund life, and old age"—the romance qualities of the enemy—Esther and her substitute family at Bleak House breathe "spring, dawn, order, fertility, vigor, and youth."[11] More specifically, Esther's story resembles that version of the quest for identity to which Freud has given the name "family romance," which, as I pointed out before, revises the actual circumstances of birth and origin, replacing the unacceptable real parents with imaginary others of a higher social standing. Esther's aristocratic mother *is* her biological mother and not the product of a revisionary fantasy; still, Esther's origin is constructed in the course of the story, and

[9]I do not mean to suggest that Dickens's tracing of connections should not also be seen in the light of mid-Victorian literary practice. As Peter K. Garrett points out, "The large loose baggy monsters of the 1840's–1870's meant to transcend the limitations of the individual point of view and envision the life of the whole community" ("Double Plots and Dialogical Form in Victorian Fiction," *Nineteenth–Century Fiction* 32, 1 [1977], 1–18).

[10]See Fredric Jameson, "Magical Narratives: Romance as Genre," *NLH* 7 (1975), 135–63.

[11]*Anatomy of Criticism,* pp. 187–88. See also J. I. Fradin, "Will and Society in *Bleak House,*" *PMLA* 81 (1966), 108.

though the reconstruction is not the revision of the banality of the parents, it is the revision of an even more fundamentally ego-shattering situation, their absence.

When we meet Esther Summerson, she lives in ignorance of the identity of her parents. An apparent orphan, a "child of the universe" (6), as Harold Skimpole euphemistically calls her, her plight is similar to Jo's, even though Esther lives just within the pale of respectability. In her insecurity about origin, she summarizes the emotional condition of almost all inhabitants of the novel, including the third-person narrator. But as the plot unravels, Esther is slowly revealed in her true, mysterious identity: the lonely girl proves to be the daughter of a Captain Hawdon—alias Nemo—who has died in Krook's house, and Lady Dedlock, the most beautiful, most fashionable, most repressively controlled lady in the land. On an unconscious level a father called Nemo ("nobody") may suggest creation ex nihilo or grandiose illusions of virgin birth, but the name, by hiding identity rather than revealing it, also constitutes denial of such illusions. It is the badge of Esther's illegitimacy. She is born outside the law, outside the patriarchal order, and therefore, her godmother tells her, it would have been better had she not been born at all. Without a father, she can never be acknowledged by polite society; she will not inherit a preexisting social identity. Esther's illegitimate existence is so threatening to the social order that her own mother, even after the existence of her daughter has become known to her, cannot acknowledge her. When she is finally forced to do so, her fall brings down with it the towering prestige of the ancient Dedlock lineage.

For this reason this first triangle of the family romance, this first (re)construction of an identity that proves more subversively threatening than its absence, is slowly overlaid and encompassed by a new revisionary triangle, the final one, consisting of Esther, her husband Alan Woodcourt, and the fatherly Mr. Jarndyce, who made it all possible. Esther's story, then, is a double family romance: the narrative practices secondary revision upon its own original (re)construction of origin.

To unravel the secret necessity for this curious strategy, we must return to the situation of the first triangle. Freud argues that when the child is old enough to know the sexual facts of life, his family romance will show evidence of the truth that *pater semper incertus est* whereas the mother is *certissima*. The namelessness of Esther's father and the dangerous presence of her mother would seem to conform to this pattern. Moreover, Freud points out, the romance takes on an erotic orientation, motivated by curiosity about the sexual activities of the mother, often projected as illicit. Had we been engaged in an analysis of *Bleak House* as the reflection of Charles Dickens's personal story, our conclusions would have been predictable.[12] However, Dickens's narrative strategy is his answer to a problem that transcends the discretely individual; the absence of the father and the sexuality of the mother reflect the threat of the new ideas about the origin of human beings and the creation of the earth, of a suddenly powerful and prolific Mother Nature dethroning the ancient figure of God the Father. In the light of Lacan's reinterpretation of Freud, a widely cultural and psychoanalytic interpretation of *Bleak House* as family romance would seem to be possible. In other words, if the narrative progresses as a secondary revision of Esther's identity, it is because her illegitimacy stands for the uneasy suggestion of a purely biological, nonphallic, nontranscendental notion of human origin. And this notion must, finally, be repressed from the consciousness of this Victorian novel.

Though the author cannot and will not openly discuss the symbolic implications of Lady Dedlock's motherhood, its unconscious presence provides the impetus for his long and revisionary narrative. As we shall see, it is Esther's quest for her mother, as well as her need to come to terms with her own female sexual nature, which necessitates the many twists and turns of this fiction. This pattern is seen most easily in a comparison of the two triangles of Esther's family romance. The difference in the second is the absence of the mother and Esther's newly acquired status of married woman—even mother. Would it not have been easier to construct a plot in which Lady Dedlock died before the story began? Such a plot would have obviated the necessity of removing her from the

---

[12]On Dickens's Oedipal problems and their reflection in his work, see L. J. Dessner, "*Great Expectations*: 'The Ghost of a Man's Own Father,'" *PMLA* 91 (1978), 436–49.

scene in order to suggest a happy ending with greater force. But it would also have deprived the novel of its wide social panorama. Indeed, it is Lady Dedlock's sin and its contagious aftereffects, connecting Chesney Wold, Tom-all-Alone's, chancery, and Bleak House, which together produce the panorama of Victorian society for which we especially value the novel. Therefore, the problem of female generativity, though not alluded to in the text, is its central inarticulated nexus and motivating impulse, forcing it through endless visions and revisions to "answer" its underlying question.

Since the overwhelming question remains implicit in the structure of the narrative and is never openly articulated, the importance of Lady Dedlock's sexuality for Esther's accession to her own motherhood is far from self-evident. To discover it we are forced to scrutinize Dickens's revisionary family romance with an eye to its structural and symbolic ambiguities. It is at the moments of puzzling ambiguity, when the unconscious irradiates the text with its peculiar numinous aura, that the public and the personal, the familiar and the subversive, have been welded together by the poetic imagination. In a text dealing with identity and origin, what better starting point can we select than the ambivalence of Esther's "self"?

Like many other fictions, *Bleak House* represents a character's quest for subjectivity in the image of the search for a permanent house or home.[13] In this, as in her orphanhood, Esther is representative of what moves and motivates the other inhabitants of *Bleak House,* who live in a "Ruined House" (one of the projected titles for the novel), an "unfinished house," or at best, in the disenchantment of a "Bleak" house. Through the analogy of sympathetic magic, Esther's search, leading her from the foster homes of her earlier days to the boarding school of the Miss Donnys and on to the quasi permanence of her stay at Bleak House, is redemptive of all the others.

The crucial point, however, is that, though she is at first greatly

---

[13]Gaston Bachelard, *The Poetics of Space,* trans. M. Jolas (Boston: Beacon Press, 1969), p. xxxii, states that with "the house image we are in possession of a veritable principle of psychological integration. . . . [It] would seem to have become the topography of our intimate being."

honored and tempted by Mr. Jarndyce's offer to make her the mistress of Bleak House, Esther cannot and must not accept his benevolence. She must move on to her own detached home. It is only after she has been described as happily at ease amidst husband and children, living in a small-scale model of Mr. Jarndyce's Bleak House, that the novel finds its end. It is Esther's assumption of the detached house then, rather than her renewed beauty or the discovery of her parents, which marks the fulfillment of her quest. Yet the little house is not so detached after all; there is a curious ambivalence in its symbolic connotations which condenses two different—in fact, opposed—aspects of Esther's hard-won identity. Most obviously, as a place separate from the corruption of society and from the fatherly Jarndyce, it seems to indicate Esther's social, moral, and emotional autonomy. On the other hand, in its odd metaphorical relation to Mr. Jarndyce's house, of which it is the exact replica, down to the most insignificant detail, almost as if houses spawned little ones, Esther's final house would seem to mark her as reproductive, generative, sexual. The little house is also the nest, and we see Esther referring proudly to her own two little girls.[14]

Looking back over Esther's development as a character, one notices that the ambivalence of the final symbol of subjectivity has been present in Dickens's portrayal of her all along and reflects an underlying ambivalence in the novel's notion of human identity. From Esther's earliest moments of conscious reflection, her awareness is structured by the tension between her true but unmentionable natural identity and the necessity to secure a place and role in the patriarchal social system from which she is excluded. As she gathers from her godmother's unrelenting insistence that it would have been better not to have been born at all, the anniversary of her birth is a symbol of evil and sinful disgrace to those

[14]In *Dickens on the Romantic Side of Familiar Things: "Bleak House" and the Novel Tradition* (New York: Columbia Univ. Press, 1977), p. 61, while discussing the notion of "the uncanny" (*das Unheimliche*), Robert Newsom refers to Freud's view that the home is ultimately the mother's womb. Although his book is also a study of the "romantic side of familiar things" in Dickens's novel, Newsom does not view them under the aspect of the family romance. He sees "familiar" and "romantic" as opposites and accounts for the novel's texture in terms of the tension between them.

sharing the secret of her origin. Esther's way of coping with the social and emotional isolation of her position is to deny that deepest, most natural part of herself, which in her childish understanding merely seems to keep the "wound" of the day of her birth open. This "natural" self, on which her own generativity and full womanhood depend, she projects upon her doll, the only one to whom she opens her heart. But this child ought never have been born at all: departing for school, Esther buries her doll in the garden. Simultaneously, she sets out to win social approval with the vow "to repair the fault I had been born with (of which I confessedly felt guilty and yet innocent) . . . and [to] strive as I grew up to be industrious, contented and kind-hearted, and to do some good to some one, and win some love to myself if I could" (3). From the very beginning, then, Esther's self is split into two halves, one "buried" and unmentionable, one obsessively concerned with conformity to patriarchal views of feminine identity. Whereas Fielding's hero Tom Jones reached maturity after the constitutive rejection of his own feminine side, Esther's struggle for selfhood would seem to take place at two levels simultaneously: one quest for sexual identification with the (m)other, the other for substitutive fatherhood and a place in society.[15]

[15]The critical view of Esther as a flawed character has lately superseded the earlier indictment of her character as insignificant, hypocritical, or falsely sweet. Alex Zwerdling argues in "Esther Summerson Rehabilitated," *PMLA* 88 (1973), 432, that "Dickens' interest in Esther is fundamentally clinical: to observe and describe a certain kind of psychic debility. The psychological subject matter of Dickens' later novels demanded a new narrative technique, in which the character could present himself directly. . . . Esther Summerson is Dickens' most ambitious attempt to allow a character who does not fully understand herself to tell her own story." Though I do not disagree with Zwerdling, I am not here concerned with psychological realism. I focus instead on Esther as a function in a narrative strategy, an "actant" in a story, to use A. J. Greimas's term. From this analytical point of view the dualism of Esther's character is related to Taylor Stoehr's conclusions in *Dickens: The Dreamer's Stance* (Ithaca: Cornell Univ. Press, 1965), which point to the many instances of doubling in this novel. Apart from the two voices and their contrary visions of the world, doubling has led to the creation of many pairs of characters which are "projections onto separate characters of the conflicting impulses of the dreamer. Through them Dickens conveys the ambivalence and complexity of his dream meaning without expressly stating it" (p. 167). Stoehr believes the function of the double plot is to keep social and sexual problems from intermingling. In my view both plots are concerned with the same ontological problem of identity.

Initially, the attempts to earn a place in society and the protection of a father figure occupy the foreground of the narrative. At the Miss Donnys', and then at Bleak House, Esther persistently attempts to blot out the shame of her birth by trying to become an "original" herself. As everyone agrees, she is a model of deportment—a "pattern young lady," as detective Bucket praises her—obsessively creating order out of disorder and postponing the disintegration of society at large (domestically reflected in the state of Mrs. Jellyby's closets) by her unrelenting diligence and the protection of her household keys, which she jingles to the refrain of "Esther, duty, my dear." Indeed, Esther's attempt to lock out the "original sin" leads her further and further away from selfhood to the perfection of an imaginary, obsessive role, and to speaking to herself in the third person; when her substitute father and guardian finally offers to marry her, it momentarily seems as if Esther will become, like her biblical namesake, a queen of starry purity.[16]

For all Esther's exertions to earn an unfallen status, at moments of emotional crisis the repressed image of the doll revives in her memory, bringing with it softer sensations. When the young lawyer Guppy proposes marriage in the chapter entitled "Signs and Tokens," her own refusal leaves her perturbed: "I surprised myself by beginning to laugh about it, and then surprised myself still more by beginning to cry about it. . . . I was in a flutter for a while; and felt as if an old chord had been more coarsely touched than it had ever been since the days of the dear old doll, long buried in the garden" (9). A similar reaction marks Esther's first meeting with her mother, whom she has never known and who is still a mere stranger to her: "And, very strangely, there was something quickened within me, associated with the lonely days at my godmother's; yes, away even to the days when I had stood on tiptoe to dress myself at my little glass, after dressing my doll" (18).

[16]The biblical Esther, a Jewish orphan and the ward of Mordecai, was chosen by the Babylonian king Ahasuerus to replace his wife Vashti, who had refused to appear dressed in nothing but the royal crown at a banquet held for the princes of the realm. Queen Esther was noted for a feminine diplomacy and manipulative respect for authority which allowed her to save her people from the extinction planned by Haman.

Thus, beneath the narrative strand that moves toward Esther's social rootedness, there is the concern with the buried but stirring insistence of the original "wound" or "sin" of the relationship to the (m)other. Whether the Victorian era was as repressive about sexual matters as it has been reputed to be is a matter of dispute, but it is certain that Esther's confrontation with the feminine, nonpatriarchal sexuality of her mother is present in the fiction only at the level of implication, and it occurs in hardly perceptible stages. The first begins on the crucially important evening of Esther's contact with Jo, who will transmit the mysterious and highly contagious disease that originates from a rat scurrying from Captain Nemo's pauper grave in Tom-all-Alone's. At that moment, though Esther has not yet learned the identity of her mother—or even of her existence—she has the "undefinable impression" of "being something different from what I then was" (3). As Mark Spilka and Taylor Stoehr have suggested, this disease, never given a name in the novel, is symbolically related to the unbridled sexuality of Esther's parents; and "smallpox" is indeed close enough to "pox" to assume a sexual connotation.[17]

In addition, smallpox, a disease that leaves marks on the face, suggests the castration "wound" of nonphallic origin. The imagery in which Esther describes the experience of her illness is suggestive of a successful archetypal quest for identity: she recalls the sensation of crossing a dark lake and of laboring, like a worm, up colossal staircases. This confrontation with the uncanny taboo—the return of the repressed—does not, however, lead to the blinding insight achieved by a figure like Oedipus (though it strikes her with temporary blindness). Here is the anagnorisis when Esther looks at the pockmarks on her face:

> My hair had not been cut off. . . . It was long and thick. I let it down, and shook it out, and went up to the glass upon the dressing-table. There was a little muslin curtain drawn across it. I drew it back; and stood for a moment looking through such a veil of my own hair, that I could see nothing else. Then I put my hair aside, and looked at the reflection in the mirror. . . . I was very much changed—O very, very

[17]Spilka, *Dickens and Kafka: A Mutual Interpretation* (Bloomington: Indiana Univ. Press, 1963), p. 214; Stoehr, *Dickens*, pp. 143–44.

much. At first my face was so strange to me, that I think I should have put my hands before it and started back. . . . Very soon it became more familiar, and then I knew the extent of the alteration in it better than I had done at first. It was not like what I had expected; but I had expected nothing definite, and I dare say anything definite would have surprised me. (36)

In this revelation, in which Esther's social self finds her true self fearsomely un-*familiar* we recognize the same gesture of moving aside the hair to look at the face which marks the revelatory moment of Esther's later identification of and with her mother. Indeed, the frightening face surrounded by copious hair is an image of the Medusa's head, the visual representation, as Freud suggested, of castrated female sexuality that turns the beholder into stone.[18] At one level, then, as a suggestive foreshadowing of the later event, this passage seems to imply Esther's confrontation with the otherness within herself. It might be taken to suggest Esther's acceptance of the biological truth of her origin (without so much as touching the hem of Victorian respectability.) However, in the evasiveness of the final phrases, refusing to accept loss or otherness in denying the existence of a previous expectation, her repression of the reality of her biological self is renewed.

Consequently, her illness, rather than integrating these selves, increases the need to maintain separation from the split-off image of the doll, evident in Esther's relationship to Ada Clare, who—like Charley, Esther's little maid—is a reincarnation of the long-buried doll. Charley's wide-eyed tininess suggests the childhood confidante, but Ada has the doll's "beautiful complexion" and "rosy lips" and is, moreover, an idealized alter ego. Unlike Esther, whose nicknames (Mother Hubbard, Dame Durden, Mrs. Shipton) connote sexlessness, Ada represents feminine sexuality through her betrothal to Richard; in contrast to Esther, burdened with a sense of her own unworthiness, Ada seems bright, beautiful, good, and unblemished. No wonder that Esther seems to love Ada almost more than herself. When Ada marries Richard, Esther hopes to live with them, keeping "the keys of their house" and "happy for ever

---

[18]"Medusa's Head," *Standard Edition,* vol. XVIII, pp. 273–74.

and a day" (14). When her longing thus to reconstitute the triangle of family romance is not fulfilled, Esther is wild with grief. At night she steals to Ada's house and listens to the sounds within! During her illness, it is Ada's pure beauty that must at all costs be protected from the disease. Ada's perfection, the token that she has had no contact with the blight of natural female origin clinging to Esther, is "the light" in Esther's blindness. During her illness Esther seems to feel that if she fails to preserve this idealized version of herself uncontaminated and intact, she cannot continue to live: if Ada is allowed to look upon her marked face for only one moment, Esther will die.

Esther's continued fear of revealing her face to Ada marks her unchanged refusal to accept herself as her mother's daughter. She cannot admit that her self-identity is based on a relationship, however negative or repressive, with the "other." From this point of view, it is highly significant that the chapter whose central event is the relatively restrained recognition of the kinship between Esther and her mother should end in a reunion of much greater emotional intensity between Esther and Ada. Here we see Ada play the role of mother, accepting Esther's face, "bathing it with tears and kisses, rocking [her] to and fro like a child, calling [her] by every tender name that she could think of" (36). Only after Esther has truly accepted the familiarity of her mother's "sin" will she change positions with Ada: Esther will have a romance and start her own family while the widowed Ada moves back to Bleak House to take care of her guardian.

This moment of acceptance comes after another confrontation with the "sin" from which all corruption in *Bleak House* has sprung, after another archetypal descent, which, unlike Esther's illness, is a confrontation with real death. It is the death of Lady Dedlock, who has completed her own circuitous return to the reality of the past and lies dead at the grave of the man "who should have been her husband," in the spot from which all corruption in the world of this novel takes its origin. This final image of Tom-all-Alone's is the "primal scene" of narrative motivation. From here has arisen the subversive threat to hierarchical distinctions, the threat of a breakdown of the walls of subjectivity which ensure the operative power of such concepts as race, class, sex, and age—the threat of which the narrator asserts, "His Grace shall not be able to say Nay to the infamous alliance" (46). Esther's journey toward this heart of London's darkness, undertaken to "save" her mother from the final deed, leads her between darkness and dawn into a mental state between waking and dreaming through a "labyrinth of streets" in which the reality she had always known seems so changed that "great water-gates seemed to be opening and closing in my head, or in the air; and . . . the unreal things were more substantial than the real" (59). She has just confessed that it seemed as if the "stained house-fronts put on human shapes and looked at" her. In the light of the house symbolism of the novel, this image seems a hallucinatory realization that the stain of Tom-all-Alone's is also her own but cannot yet be admitted into consciousness. Thus, when she arrives at the entrance to this enclosed place—the curiously Victorian version of the *hortus conclusus* (the image of the Holy Virgin)—she still cannot relate its otherness to herself: "The gate was closed. Beyond it, was a burial-ground—a dreadful spot in which the night was very slowly stirring; but where I could dimly see . . . houses . . . on whose walls a thick humidity broke out like a disease. On the steps at the gate, drenched in the fearful wet of such a place, which oozed and splashed down everywhere, I saw, with a cry of pity and horror, a woman lying—Jenny, the mother of the dead child" (59).

But this last phrase is not final; it is to be revised into the "dead mother of the living child." The truth about her own face will come home after a gesture we remember from Esther's illness: "I lifted the heavy head, put the long dank hair aside, and turned the face. And it was my mother, cold and dead" (59). At last, then, the unfortunate girl has owned her mother, has looked the evil of her birth in the face and accepted it as her own; from this moment, the taboo on her sexuality is lifted. Avoiding the mistakes of her mother, Esther does not marry the elderly Jarndyce, who calls her "my child," but confesses her hitherto unacknowledged attraction to Alan Woodcourt.

Thus Esther's quest for identity and subjectivity, depicted in a fiction that represents the society and the ideology of Western culture one hundred years after the publication of *Tom Jones,* embodies those differences. Whereas Tom's quest led to the transcendent repression of the mother, Esther must learn to acknowledge her presence and to understand the sterile effects of total repression. It is as if Dickens's fiction foreshadows the psychoanalytic process. It should be noted, however, that the process of recognition never finds its way into the discourse; it must remain implicit.

The Presence of the "Other"

Within the framework of the internal logic of this fiction, Esther must confront the otherness of her origin to gain full acceptance of her own identity and thus bring the narrative to a satisfactory closure. But the scene is equally necessary on the discursive level of the text—in terms of the organization and structure of the fiction as a whole. Lady Dedlock, like Blifil in *Tom Jones,* functions as scapegoat. She must die in order to cleanse and purify—to exorcise—the implications of Esther's recognition. *Bleak House* is as much the inspired page, the literary signifier that proclaims the redemption of the loss of presence resulting from original sin by means of the steady exercise of Victorian virtue; it provides the "key" of duty and order, the fig leaf to shield Victorian eyes from what they know is there. This curious strategy of simultaneous concealment and revelation is inevitable, since fictional discourse, exemplum and sustenance of the cultural order, cannot move outside the bounds of logocentrism without imperiling the grounds of its own existence; the repression or exclusion of the heterogeneous lends connectedness and meaning to the fiction. A full recognition and acceptance of Lady Dedlock's otherness would have destroyed the hierarchical order in which the binary pair father-(m)other is positioned in the *scala naturae.* Letting Lady Dedlock live, reconciling her with her husband and daughter, would have opened the floodgates and erased the principle of cohesion upon which the revisionary narrative strain depends—something we see happen in Joyce's *Finnegans Wake* or Pynchon's *Gravity's Rainbow.*

Though Dickens has obvious problems controlling the vision he evokes, he eventually stems the threat of engulfment not only by killing Lady Dedlock but also by revising the notion of the father in a strategic diversion reminiscent of the replacement of the castrating primal (Mosaic) father of the Old Testament by the figure of Jesus in the New Testament—of the Old Law by the New—allaying the threat of retribution by a reduction in authoritative power (even of his own authority in the fiction) and an emphasis on charity or agape.

The "old fathers"—Lord Dedlock and the Lord High Chancellor are, as I noted earlier, the most prestigious examples—have proven "Krooks," negative forces, hoarding life and energy for self-serving purposes; though Lord Dedlock's love for his wife redeems him to a certain extent, he is shown to us first and primarily as the typical embodiment of a reactionary force that aims at maintaining the status quo of the old dispensation. The first "new father," Mr. Jarndyce, on the other hand, is notable for the generosity with which he provides for the orphans of chancery, fulfilling the duties of the Lord High Chancellor out of love. A spokesman for Dickens's views, he consciously keeps himself aloof from legal and political entanglements and tries to preserve a prelapsarian enclave of sweetness and light in his home. To Esther he soon becomes a "father" whose goodness seems of divine origin, and he remains a source of inspiration till the end of the story, when she writes that at the moment the "sun's rays descended . . . upon his bare head. I felt as if the brightness on him must be the brightness of the Angels" (64).

What is important with regard to Dickens's revisionary strategy, however, is that the father figure Jarndyce is reluctant to assume authority. He appears to need the love of his wards so much that he condescends to eradicate the social and emotional differences that separate them by proposing to marry Esther. This he does—appropriately in the context of both his position as a *deus* figure and the importance of "writing" in this novel—in a letter. As a literary figure, Mr. Jarndyce seems to derive from the familiar eighteenth-century type of the benevolent gentleman. He resembles Allworthy, as the critics have repeatedly pointed out. But if we compare him with Rousseau's M. de Wolmar in *La nouvelle Héloise,* with which the plot of *Bleak House* has striking structural and thematic similarities, we cannot help noting how much more "romantic" Dickens's figure is. Jarndyce eventually renounces possession of his promised bride Esther and arranges for her marriage to the man she secretly loves. This version of the *senex* or, by extension, *deus* figure seems to result from the need to accommodate the wishes and allay the fears of the subjectivity of the writer, who does not or cannot identify with the overtly patriarchal figures of power and veers toward imaginative empathy with the underdog. The fact that Esther's marriage and her little house are, in the final analysis, made to seem dependent on the providence of this "new" father—rather than on the hard-won insights of her own experience—amounts to a neutralization of Esther's heterogeneity by this revised (and obviously effective) version of the myth of paternal origin.

The highly romantic replacement of the Lord High Chancellor's faded numinosity by the "brightness of the Angels" radiating from Jarndyce tells us something about the place of this fiction in literary history, but more significant as an indication of its specifically Victorian aspects (and here we finally verge back to our starting point in Darwin's *Origin of Species*) is the substitution of detective Bucket for Tulkinghorn as the agency that penetrates the secret of Lady Dedlock's otherness and resolves the mystery of origin.

Of all the characters Dickens has created in *Bleak House,* Tulkinghorn is the most mysteriously evil and the most convincing. Perhaps it is because he is in effect the "king," the most powerful and the most traditionally masculine personality on Dickens's stage, that his presence haunts the reader as it does Lady Dedlock, or it may be because of his curious relationship to the feebleness of the Lord High Chancellor: what indicated the latter's failure, his inability to inspire and shine, becomes, with an inversion, the very source of power for Tulkinghorn. In his black clothes—which, peculiarly enough, never shine but seem "mute, close, irresponsive to any glancing light" (2)—he is like a black hole in space, a burned-out star, drawing everything around him within the radius of his hoarding power. In his insufficiently lit room everything is locked away in a perverse exaggeration of Esther's proud housekeeping, but here even the key is hoarded and kept out of sight in a peculiar inversion of the castration motif. Tulkinghorn has no emotional ties to other people, no passions to break the rigidity of his black armor; his only desire is the acquisition of knowledge and secrets and "holding possession of such powers as they give him, with no sharer or opponent in it" (36). In a world where the key, the symbol of patriarchal power, is lost or unintelligible, Tulkinghorn has sent out to embody this key himself, to be "all in all." While the feminine figure of allegory hangs over his head like the sword of Damocles, he "cuts her dead" and ignores what her name implies—the inevitable presence of otherness, the curse of writing—spying and prying all the while to contain the threatening secret of Lady Dedlock, to "cut her dead" through the force of his presence.

As Joseph Fradin suggests, Tulkinghorn, like Krook, is "allegorically" self-destroyed by the repression of his own deeper emotions—unrestraint and passion, embodied in Lady Dedlock's maid Hortense.[19] His place in Sir Leicester's confidence and in the pursuit of Lady Dedlock is taken by another servant of the law, detective Bucket, who is in a sense the hero of the novel. In contrast to Tulkinghorn, he dispels the darkness and fog of origin, leading Esther to the moment of revelation in the pauper graveyard. Similarly, Bucket's power, seemingly preternatural—he is omnipresent, he has attendants everywhere, he penetrates secrets, and he moves about with infallible aim—is not the hoarding power of the older man but the power of youth, mobility, sympathy, and wit. If Tulkinghorn as representative of an outworn ideal of masculinity is almost a *dio boia,* Bucket is the incarnation of the optimistic vitality of a newer version, based on the nineteenth-century belief in the power of scientific investigation. Like Mephistopheles' shining and increasing key in *Faust* (according to C. G. Jung, a symbol of the phallus, like Tom Thumb and other "dactyls"),[20] Bucket's extended forefinger leads Esther down to the crucial place, the realm of the mother. It is Bucket's forcefulness that unlocks Esther's sexuality. And in making Esther's revelation dependent upon the agency of the detective, Dickens seems to be offering an additional replacement for the faded numinosity and effectiveness of the primal father(s) of this fiction, in the form of a newer hero and a more socially constructive use of power.

[19]"Will and Society," pp. 103–4.
[20]*Symbols of Transformation: An Analysis of the Prelude to a Case of Schizophrenia,* trans. R. F. C. Hull (New York: Harper, 1962), pp. 124–28.

Dickens's strategy for containing the disruptive heterogeneity of the female, or of nature, through the replacement of the old father(s) by new fathers, is itself the revisionary movement we recognize from the family romance, lending an extra, literal edge to his well-known avowal in the Preface of having "purposely dwelt upon the romantic side of *familiar things*" (my emphasis). Indeed, it would be foolish to blame Dickens for a lack of intellectual consistency, for revealing and repressing at the same time. Not only is *Bleak House* a fiction, aiming at a different kind of truth from that sought in a work of philosophy, but the mind, as it expresses itself in language, cannot step outside the very play of polarities that make significance and communication possible. It would have been inconceivable to let *Bleak House* take the course of *Ulysses* or *Finnegans Wake*, where Molly Bloom and Anna Livia Plurabelle flood the discursiveness of form, structure, and language with their otherness. Without Jarndyce's benevolence and Bucket's intervention, Esther's children could not have been born.

Moreover, Dickens's revisionary strategy, if we compare it with Darwin's, proves suggestive of a conceptual pattern not limited to fiction but characteristic of the age. Darwin, though he creates a work of science, must, like the writer of narrative, cut and tie the strands of his argument to arrive at a convincing, meaningful conclusion. Rereading the last chapter of the *Origin of Species* one notes that the threat to human self-respect implied in an evolutionary notion of origin—that man is not created separately in God's image, or, even worse, that there is no definite moment of transcendental origin—is lessened by the author's implied suggestion that a revised interpretation of the biblical account might picture the creator as a prime mover impressing his laws upon matter, not as the anthropomorphic father shaping his children in clay.

The Obscurity of Origin and the History of the Novel

The polarities of father–mother, creator–matter are intrinsic to human thought, whether fictional or scientific; it is not their mere presence or opposition but their internal relationship, how they inform a narrative strategy or a scientific argument, which is significant for the epistemological concerns of an age. Thus, this analysis of the symbolic structure of *Bleak House* need not lead us into a self-spun tropological net. On the contrary, if the analogy with the conceptual structure of the *Origin of Species* has a function, it is to help us gain a clearer vision of the development of the novel in relation to the ontological concerns of the age in which it comes into existence and which it embodies in turn. In other words, *Bleak House* as a fiction is not merely the personal nightmare of its author or a literary pacifier superficially reflecting, but removed from, the strife of historical existence. As a work of serious and compassionate art it expresses in its peculiar fictional form a mid-nineteenth-century conceptualization of an ineradicable human problem, and consequently, its narrative strategy assumes significance as the self-reflection of human subjectivity as it was experienced and understood in the Victorian age.

Further, as I shall try to show, *Bleak House* clarifies the transition from an earlier plot structure predominant in popular fiction (and in Dickens's own earlier novels), the simple family romance, to that typically Victorian form, the detective story. Both share features of hidden origin and miraculous, sudden recovery.

Though *Bleak House* has many features of the older family romance, the moment that resolves the original blight, the discovery of the dead mother at the entrance to Tom-all-Alone's, is reached only after a deliberate, organized search, directed by a trained professional. Unlike the popular family romance, which assumes that identity is there merely waiting to be discovered, *Bleak House* is notable for its fairly early revelation of origin (in itself a reconstitution) and its lengthy process of bringing Lady Dedlock, the criminal, to what is in terms of Victorian narrative logic her justly deserved end. But this logic is Victorian not only because it emphasizes the process of excommunication rather than simple discovery: the nature of what is communicated is of equal importance. Thus, in the light of psychoanalytic theories of the detective story, it is curiously appropriate that the moment at Tom-all-Alone's, while not a revelation of the crime of murder, should be both the revelation of a moment of pathetic death and a displaced version of the primal scene. In her analysis of Poe's "The Murders in the Rue Morgue," Marie Bonaparte writes: "The unconscious source of our interest in narratives of this type lies, as Freud first led us to recognize, in the fact that the researches conducted by the detective reproduce, by displacement onto subjects of a quite different nature, our infantile investigations into matters of sex."[21] In other words, the detective story, displacing the primal scene onto a scene of violence, offers readers an opportunity to allay their fear and curiosity without having to acknowledge it.

But what is "primal scene" but another term for the moment of biological origin? And if it is true that biological origin as a problem is characteristic of the Victorian age, can we not, in turn, explain the origin and popularity of the detective story as the fictional reflection of the deeper, unconscious concerns of the age? Unconscious concern with origin can account, however, for only one aspect of the mystery story, its fascination with violence. As a fiction privileging organized investigation, rational detection rather than accidental discovery, the detective novel is also the fictional form of an era that has committed itself to a belief in the liberating efficacy of scientific research. As Geoffrey Hartman writes, "It explains the irrational . . . by the latest rational system."[22] The "whodunit" is the poor, or less prestigious, stepsister of a scientific treatise like the *Origin of Species,* and Darwin's insistence that we "possess no pedigrees or armorial bearings" (i.e., traceable and emblematically fixed origins), that "we have to *discover* and *trace* the many diverging lines of descent in our natural genealogies" (my emphasis), conforms to what the detective novel, in its characteristically displaced form, does.

Probably because it is an experimental search for an adequate

---

[21] "The Murders in the Rue Morgue," *Psychoanalytic Quarterly* 4 (1935), 292. The connection between detective story and "primal scene" was first brought to my attention by Geoffrey H. Hartman's "Literature High and Low: The Case of the Mystery Story," in his *The Fate of Reading and Other Essays* (Chicago: Univ. of Chicago Press, 1975). Hartman speaks of "one definitively visualized scene to which everything else might be referred," a "scene of suffering" or a "*to pathos*" (p. 207). His argument also refers to the work of Charles Rycroft, "The Analysis of a Detective Story," in his *Imagination and Reality: Psychoanalytical Essays, 1951–61* (London: Hogarth, 1968); and Geraldine Pederson-Krag, "Detective Stories and the Primal Scene," *Psychoanalytic Quarterly* 18 (1949), 207–14. I have relied on all these works.

[22] "Literature High and Low," p. 209.

form, *Bleak House* is both more primitive and less displaced than the more sophisticated work of Dickens's friend Wilkie Collins and his acquaintance Poe, though the indebtedness to "The Purloined Letter" (1845) seems especially great.[23] Thus, what Hartman calls the "scene of suffering" is displaced by a scene of recognition both more clearly sexual and more ambivalent than the central event in the crime mystery. I say more ambivalent because in the detective novel, according to Geraldine Pederson-Krag, the "parent for whom the reader (the child) has negative Oedipal feelings" is represented as the pitiful victim, whereas Lady Dedlock, the dead mother, is both victim and criminal at once.[24] *Bleak House* shows us in the moment at Tom-all-Alone's a whodunit off guard, and this lesser depth of its "buried life" seems to provide unique insight into the generic moment of transformation from family romance to detective novel.

With this realization we have arrived at a better position from which to judge the validity of my initial assumption—that Dickens's concern with orphanhood in *Bleak House* and other writings and the revisionary tactics with which he excommunicates the threat of otherness from the surface level of his novel should not be seen as merely reflecting a personal psychological need or the artis-

---

[23]We know from the very beginning who the criminal is: a woman whose prominent social position places her in the public eye. Moreover, the "crime" relates to a piece of writing, a personal letter, suggesting illicit personal relations. Along with the gusty autumn weather of the setting, the analogy extends to the similarity in character of Tulkinghorn and Mr. D——, who hoard the secret, and their replacement in the plots by the detectives Bucket and Dupin. An interesting psychological interpretation of Poe's story, which places it centrally in the discussion about Western phallogocentrism, while by analogy confirming my reading of *Bleak House,* is Jacques Lacan, "The Seminar on 'The Purloined Letter,'" trans. Jeffrey Mehlman, in *French Freud, Yale French Studies* 48 (1972), 38–72. Lacan's interpretation has been criticized by Jacques Derrida in "Le facteur de la vérité," *Poétique* 21 (1975), 96–147. For an exposition of Lacan's analysis, see Shoshana Felman, "On Reading Poetry: Reflections on the Limits and Possibilities of Psychoanalytic Approaches," in *The Literary Freud: Mechanisms of Defense and the Poetic Will,* ed. J. H. Smith, Psychiatry and the Humanities 4 (New Haven: Yale Univ. Press, 1980). Dickens had met Poe in Philadelphia during his American tour of 1842 and had promised to find an English publisher for *Tales of the Grotesque and Arabesque.* Though publication of "The Purloined Letter" postdates their meeting, it seems unlikely that Dickens, who had kept in touch with Poe, would not have read it.

[24]"Detective Stories," p. 209.

tic credo that "in all familiar things, even in those which are re-
pellent on the surface, there is Romance enough, if we will find it
out."[25] Dickens, as the strategist of his narrative, is an analogue of
the energetic detective Bucket, searching and finding out with his
pen (guided by his pointed forefinger) the (dis)closure of Esther's
illegitimate origin.[26] Just as Bucket's mysterious powers dissolve
the anxiety of his world, Dickens's narrative magic wipes the cob-
webs of doubt from the Victorian sky, giving his audience on an
unconscious level what it needs to pull through, the reassuring
message of the *familiar* myth and its reassertion of the presence of
the father.

[25]From "A Preliminary Word," in the first number of *Household Words,* March
30, 1850.

[26]Dickens had originally pictured his authorial persona for *Household Words* as a
"certain SHADOW, which may go into any place, by sunlight, moonlight, star-
light . . . and be supposed to be cognizant of everything." This image reminds
one rather suggestively of Bucket's omnipresent omniscience. See Edgar Johnson,
Charles Dickens: His Tragedy and Triumph (New York: Viking Press, 1977), p. 356.

6

The Difference of *Ulysses* and the Tautology of Mimesis

Dead, but still with us, still with us, but dead.
—Donald Barthelme, *The Dead Father*

Ulysses is an extremely complex and deliberately elusive text, whose ambivalence has inevitable consequences for the reader. Unless we reduce the text to the clear-cut categories of our own understanding, we are forced to follow a path of interpretation which may seem wayward and circuitous, a reader's odyssey. Instead of the fairly traditional interpretive approach appropriate in reading *Bleak House* and *Tom Jones,* the analysis of *Ulysses* requires the simultaneous release of a goal-directed argument and recourse to a theoretical approach: the examination of Joyce's ambivalent poetics and their effect upon the constitutive conventions of the genre. For the sake of clarity, I have used separate headings to mark the stages of my circular quest upon the sea of difference of *Ulysses*. The argumentation itself is continuous, however, and necessary for the more straightforward interpretation of Joyce in the chapter that follows.

Ulysses is a story of homecoming, like *Tom Jones* and *Bleak House*. Taking its title directly from the Homeric prototype, it announces itself as a rewriting of the venerated epic model, an adaptation *sub specie temporis nostri*. To recreate the ancient myth in a manner appropriate to our time is an epic ambition indeed, and one which ensures an author a place in the long list of poets, including Sophocles, Euripides, Dante, Shakespeare, Calderón, Kazantzakis, and many others, who have turned to the story of Homer's epic for the architecture of their own work.

The decision to rewrite *The Odyssey* is not merely an attempt to partake of the prestige of other artists who have accomplished the transposition. It is also an attempt to claim for the genre of the novel the prestigious status of the epic, to make the resultant work of fiction into a central text that articulates, mirrors, and confirms the notions of origin and identity informing a cultural community. In choosing Homer as prototype, Joyce explicitly fulfils an epic intention already implicitly present in Fielding's *Tom Jones*.

Anyone familiar with *Ulysses* will know that this novel is indeed epic in scope, but it is also what William Carlos Williams has called "a reply to Greek and Latin with the bare hands." One crucial difference separating Joyce's version of the wanderings of Ulysses from all others is this: in making the epic possible for the modern world, Joyce refused to follow the tradition of clear-cut resolution, of recovery of origin, identity, or title. Leopold Bloom's return to the bed of his wife Molly is not a climactic *coniunctio;* the meeting of Bloom and Stephen is unconvincing as an emblem of permanent bonding. The imperfection and absence of bliss that characterize Joyce's evocation of the events of June 16, 1904, also mark the ending. With the characters in the fiction, the reader is denied the *catharsis* of a totalizing perspective. There is no closure, no resolution of contradictions. One misses even what Stephen Dedalus calls a "swelling act." *Ulysses* frustrates the reader's expectations. Its ambiguous open-endedness undercuts the habit of thinking in terms of the final reward at the end of the quest, the apotheosis of meaning as reward for protagonist as well as reader. Always more self-conscious than his critics, Joyce himself called his novel an "epical forged cheque on the public" (*FW* 181, 16),[1] and the ingenuity with which critics have tried to resolve its open-endedness testifies to our disappointment.

This refusal to satisfy the reader's desire for a sense of "paradise regained," however suburban its dimension, is the most striking mark of Joyce's difference from Dickens. At times almost losing control over his proliferating fiction, Dickens nevertheless visibly struggles to steer its panorama of futility and anarchy toward the

---

[1] See Tillyard, *The Epic Strain in the English Novel,* pp. 187–95, for a discussion of *Ulysses* and the tradition of epic.

modest happiness of the ending. Like Fielding before him, he creates order out of disorder; he clears the fog. His instrument is not Fielding's *vox auctoris,* nor is it Esther's key; it is the writing stylus. The realist novelist does not unlock or record an already ordered world. Instead, the creative activity of the writer redeems a world in which the symbolic order is crumbling.[2]

As we saw, the highly revisionary structure of *Bleak House* implied the threat of chaos because the traditional instruments of patriarchal order—most notably the social hierarchy as embodied in Lord Dedlock and the law as exemplified by Tulkinghorn—were no longer powerful enough to repress the awareness of the presence of the idea of the "other," personified as the (m)other of material origin. Dickens's homecoming to a smaller replica of the original Bleak House lacks the power and glory of Fielding's return to Paradise Hall. And the move from phallus to pen as symbolic instrument of order, which Dickens's fiction implies, appears to be a strategic salvaging compromise, enforced by the rise of the curtain of repression on the other partner in the primal scene. One of the questions that must be addressed in a discussion of Joyce is whether his refusal—or is it inability?—to provide closure in *Ulysses* is the result of an even greater awareness of the presence of the "other."

It is a question that must wait till a later chapter, however. First we must arm ourselves for a struggle with Joyce's protean difference and must sketch, at least in generalized fashion, the literary historical context of the transition from *Bleak House* to *Ulysses.* From a traditional literary historical perspective, one might simply conclude that the family romance as an intrinsically meaningful structure seems to have lost most of its force by the middle of the nineteenth century and that Joyce's deviation from the model is a logical consequence of the tendency of the age. After all, contemporary authors were generally searching for new structures of meaningful representation. In Dickens's invention of detective

[2]The assumption that so-called classic realism, whatever that may be, presents a mirror reflection of the world is, of course, naïve. Dickens's conception of writing places him firmly in the romantic tradition of the creative imagination.

Bucket to resolve the presence of Lady Dedlock, for example, the new form of the detective novel shifts the excitement of discovery and understanding from the fabula to the story.[3] And this shift of emphasis from events to the representation of events in language—to telling—proliferates toward the end of the century in the novels of Conrad, Ford, and Henry James. Taking a wide cultural-historical view, one might understand the emphasis on memory, on the process of reworking experience rather than aiming at the accurate representation or definition of objective events, as a literary analogue for the process of psychoanalysis which Freud developed more or less at the same time in Vienna.

It might have been an elegant and seemingly satisfactory perspective to relate Joyce's refusal to close the family romance of his fabula to the ongoing process of interpretation privileged by the late nineteenth century. Or noting that in *Ulysses* the doubling of characters no longer provides the cathartic resolution it had in *Tom Jones,* one might simply have concluded that by the end of the nineteenth century doubling had become an autonomous explanatory force for rationalizing and naturalizing events and incidents—as if reality, or rather the human psyche itself, were suddenly understood as potentially double. Even if we limit ourselves to literature in English, the number of plots that do not resolve their doubling but exploit it is convincingly large. Oscar Wilde moralized *The Picture of Dorian Gray;* Stevenson suggested the psychic cohabitation of a Dr. Jekyll and a Mr. Hyde, Henry James turned the screw of the alter ego in many of his stories. That the reading public accepted this convention suggests that the modern assump-

---

[3]See Mieke Bal, *Narratologie: Essais sur la signification narrative dans quatre romans modernes* (Paris: Klinksieck, 1977), for a refinement of the theory of Gérard Genette. "The Narrating and the Focalizing: A Theory of the Agents in Narrative," *Style* 17 (1983), 234–70, is the English translation of Bal's chap. 1. A short introduction to narratology in English is Mieke Bal, *Narratology: Introduction to the Theory of Narrative,* trans. Christine van Boheemen (Toronto: Univ. of Toronto Press, 1985). Throughout this analysis I shall use *fabula* for "a series of logically and chronologically related events that are caused or experienced by actors." *Story* is a "fabula that is presented in a certain manner" (Bal, *Narratology* p. 3). The story of the detective novel does not end with the revelation of a murder. That is its point of beginning; it ends with the revelation of the murderer.

tion of division in the human psyche, though still thrilling, was no longer an overwhelming threat. No longer was doubling an instrument of mediation, and we might have rationalized Joyce's ambivalent refusal to let Bloom oust Boylan or Stephen oust Buck as expressing contemporary awareness of the complexity of human motivation.

Doing so, we would have had very prestigious support in the theory of Edward Said, who suggests that the typical plot pattern of what he terms "filiation"—"father and son, the image, the process of genesis, a story," in short, the epigenetic structure of mimetic realism which I have called family romance—is replaced by another configuration, another logic, which is characterized by discontinuity, paragenesis, construction, and "the brother."[4] Even more recently, Robert Caserio, citing Said, says that modern novels "welcome what we can call the end of filiation by emphatically saying farewell to the family plot."[5] There is evidence enough, then, to assume that the structure of the family romance has simply lost some of its informative presence by the beginning of World War I. And our first reaction to Joyce's ambivalent use of the structure might simply have been to see it as part of the general move toward open-endedness at the turn of the century.

As I hope these pages will demonstrate, doing so would have been a great pity, for I believe close examination of the open-endedness of *Ulysses* may reveal something quite different: underlying assumptions, problems of conceptualization and personification relating to representation itself. The Joycean text (and perhaps the whole move toward open-endedness) rests upon the strategy of using the successful inscription of the "other" (in Joyce, woman) as legitimation for the new signifying practice. In fact, if family romance as epigenetic structure is discarded, it is replaced by a different conceptualization of origin and identity which in the final analysis proves equally mythic. At least, that is what these chapters will argue, but we will have a long and winding journey to go before I can demonstrate the validity of that conclusion.

[4]*Beginnings: Intention and Method*, pp. 65–66.
[5]*Plot, Story, and the Novel: From Dickens and Poe to the Modern Period* (Princeton: Princeton Univ. Press, 1979), pp. 235–36.

The Deliberate Ambiguity of *Ulysses*

The opening scene of *Bleak House* presented the threatening spectacle of a blurring of all distinctions, the universal destruction of the cultural order, indeed, the undoing of the logic of separation instituted at the beginning of the world. The fog threatened the logos of Genesis which marks not only the beginning of history but the very essence of language and thought. What frightened Dickens enough to drive him to undo that horror in the writing of a long, long tale proves attractive to Joyce. Joyce deliberately creates obscurity. Dickens's idea of "fog everywhere" becomes snow in Joyce, "general all over Ireland," reducing the distinct polarity between black and white into a universal grey that resolves the last story in *Dubliners*.[6] That the meaning of the ending of *Dubliners* is not very clear, may, in fact, be a case in point. As early as these stories, Joyce was drawn to the deliberate creation of ambiguity, to a way of writing which wipes out the wall of difference separating oppositions and breaks the frames of identity which support the logos of noncontradiction. Dickens's nightmare is Joyce's pleasant dream. And after *Dubliners,* his strategy will be more and more deliberate ambiguity, more use of language to undo differences rather than to affirm or create them. It is a heretical way of writing which culminates in the free "chaosmos" of *Finnegans Wake.*

Since Joyce's struggle with the logos is most clearly evident in the later fiction, it may be wise to begin with a brief excursion to *Finnegans Wake.* There the first thing readers notice is the tinkering with the single identity of a word as framed by the convention of its spelling. In combining two signifiers, *twilight* and *toilette,* Joyce allows the resultant single word, *twalette,* to resonate with a combination of traditionally distinct significations. This blurring of categories inheres in a revision of the material part of the sign. It is this self-inscription of the "other" into the graphic symbol, the graven image of meaning, which produces a double or even plural signification. The word evokes more than one concept *at once,* implying that the object of reference of a text is never singular, never clearly circumscribed, always includes the presence of other-

6(London: Jonathan Cape, 1927), p. 255.

ness. The advantage of this strategy of writing with "double dye" is precisely its ambiguity. It both affirms and denies identity. It keeps the conventional meanings while revising them; it violates the principle of single identity, while not wholly destroying it; it erodes the very logic/logos of signification without a total deterioration into chaos; it questions the self-evidence of the logos of Genesis, while remaining within its domain. Of course, *Finnegans Wake* shakes more cornerstones of Western metaphysics. Here, however, it is sufficient to remind ourselves that the language of this capstone to Joyce's oeuvre seems deliberately designed to reflect a decentering ambivalence toward the central logical axiom of Western thought.

The example of *Finnegans Wake* should alert us to the possible complexity of *Ulysses*. Few bodies of work are more coherent than Joyce's; the same revisionary desire underlies all his fiction, even if his works become more and more radical in expressing it. *Ulysses* too, then, hinges on a tinkering with the logos. Though this tinkering may not be so immediately apparent as the graphic fraction of *Finnegans Wake,* it is very unsettling, as the critics of the novel have increasingly begun to recognize.

The peculiarity of *Ulysses* is not the erosion of the self-identity of the signifier. Though *Ulysses* too, especially in "Sirens," plays with the spelling and combination of words, its ambiguity is different. It resides not within each individual concept but in the blurring of the conventional cultural connotations of signs, styles, and secondary modeling systems, by means of a practice of writing which deliberately subverts the binary oppositions upon which meaning rests. Origin and end, consciousness and unconsciousness, father and son, cause and effect, male and female, body and soul, sacred and profane—to list only those categories that come immediately to mind—are cut adrift on the sea of meaning and suspended in a linguistic medium that itself undoes the distinction between fabula and story.[7]

Wyndham Lewis, a very perceptive critic of his contemporaries, called *Ulysses* a "jellyfish structure." It seems an appropriate meta-

---

[7]For a more conventional reading of Joyce and the logos, see Dwight Eddins, "*Ulysses:* The Search for the Logos," *ELH* 47 (1980), 804–19.

phor for a text in which all identities are unsettled, all outlines blurred, and which invalidates, however subtly, the principle of discrete subjective identity which underlies the possibility of signature and meaning. The word *jellyfish,* however, carried a pejorative connotation for Lewis, who wanted to demonstrate the lack of backbone and structure in Joyce's writing. He considered Joyce's refusal to choose and mark limits objectionable, an indication of decadence. I view the fluidity of *Ulysses,* however, as a deliberate practice of decentering and depolarization which should be seen in the larger context of the strategies of signification of the Modern episteme.

The blurring of opposites *of* the text is represented *in* the text in the "parallactic" thought processes of the modern Odysseus, Leopold Bloom, who typically thinks in oxymorons: "Dirty cleans" (IV, 481), and "Poisons the only cures" (V, 483). This last expression ironically brings to mind Derrida's discussion of "La pharmacie de Platon" in *La dissémination.*[8] The resemblance is no doubt accidental; the paradox of pharmacy is one of the platitudes of the tribe which went into the composition of Leopold Bloom as *homme moyen sensuel.* It may, nevertheless, alert us to the possibility that the ambivalence of Bloom's spiritual father, his typical thinking in terms of *both/and,* which is the subject of this chapter, has affinities with Derrida's ambivalent questioning of the logocentrism of Western metaphysics. In his writings Derrida demonstrates familiarity with *Ulysses* and *Finnegans Wake.* His address at the Ninth International James Joyce Symposium at Frankfurt, June 1984, titled "*Ulysse* Gramophone," points to *Ulysses* and *Finnegans Wake* as precursors to *La carte postale* (which explicitly refers to Joyce). Most telling, however, is the *imitatio* of Joyce's strategy of writing in *Finnegans Wake* in Derrida's coinage of *différance* and his verbal play in *Glas.*[9] But even apart from these natural signs of Joyce's influence on Derrida, it seems valid to conclude that what Joyce attempts through his style of writing is similar to what

---

[8](Paris: Seuil, 1972), pp. 69–81.

[9]In "Two Words for Joyce," *Post-structuralist Joyce: Essays from the French,* ed. Derek Attridge and Daniel Ferrer (Cambridge: Cambridge Univ. Press, 1984), pp. 145–60 (published after this chapter was completed), Derrida admits his indebtedness to Joyce and refers to "La pharmacie de Platon."

Derrida tries to attain in his readings of philosophy—an unsettling of the conventional categories of thought, of the hierarchizing strategy by which we order reality and structure representation, always a decentering that tries to unsettle the logos and not to undo it.

In my reading of Dickens I pointed to Darwin's revision of the structure of origin as a contemporary analogue because I wanted to amplify my suggestion that the structural peculiarity of Dickens's fiction was not individual to him but an expression of the semiotics of Victorian culture, the ideology of the epoch. To give resonance to the view that Joyce's struggle with the logic of noncontradiction gains in scope and general cultural significance if it is seen as the expression of a Modern questioning of origin as self-identical, I might have referred to the Heidegger of *Identity and Difference,* whose essay "The Onto-theological Constitution of Metaphysics" raises the question of the complicity between Western languages and metaphysics.[10] Another obvious choice would have been Freud, whose invention of the praxis of psychoanalysis (not the theory, as explained by Otto Fenichel) implies, as Peter Brooks argues, the erosion of the concept of an original event or fabula that is to be uncovered through the discursive activity of memory.[11]

Nevertheless, I have chosen Derrida, even if he is not Joyce's contemporary, for a number of reasons. First, it is possible to understand and define Freud and, to a lesser extent perhaps, Heidegger in two very different, almost mutually exclusive ways that we might label "structuralist" and "poststructuralist." This is, incidentally, also a problem that applies to Joyce himself. My view of *Ulysses* through *Finnegans Wake* and through Derrida produces a different understanding than would a reading of Joyce with a symbolist or naturalist bias. Joyce through the eyes of Eliot is far different from the Joyce of Kristeva and Philippe Sollers. And since I believe that Joyce, more emphatically than Freud or Heidegger, expressed the query about origins of Modernity so that

[10]*Identity and Difference,* trans. Joan Stambaugh (1957; rpt. New York: Harper and Row, 1969), pp. 42–75.

[11]"Fictions of the Wolf Man: Freud and Narrative Understanding," *Diacritics* 9, 1 (1979), 72–84.

many of us "are still learning to be" his "contemporaries," as
Richard Ellmann expresses it so well in the biography, I do not see
the gap in time as an objection.[12] It is not incredible that Joyce, as
early as 1922, expressed what philosophy is only now making discursively available. Thus Derrida's revisionary strategy seems the
most appropriate analogue here. Moreover, Derrida's concepts
and terms, such as "under erasure" and "supplement," provide me
with the only set of critical terms I know which is adequate to
denote Joyce's ambivalent strategy of writing.[13]

Intertextuality as a Model for Ambivalence

The relationship between the title and the text offers a good
starting point for a discussion of the ambivalence of *Ulysses*. The
title of the novel raises the expectation of a re-creation of the
ancient myth of the wanderings of Ulysses, but the unsuspecting
reader will find on opening Joyce's Homer that Ulysses seems to
have disappeared. At first sight, the text offers little to confirm the
suggestion of the title—that *Ulysses* is part of the long tradition of
retellings of the epic theme.[14] Exercising ingenuity and aided by
the Gilbert and Linati schemata, however, the reader will soon
learn to see the eighteen episodes of the novel as parallels, however
tenuous, to stages of the circular quest of the wily Ulysses.[15]

Yet the truth remains that apart from the title and Buck Mulligan's schoolboy pedantry of "*Epi oinopa ponton*" (i, 78) and
"*Thalatta! Thalatta!*" (i, 80)—a reference to Xenophon's *Ana-
basis!*—there is little to suggest the shadow of Homer. I am not
arguing that Joyce's version of the family romance has no structural or other relationship to the epic. I merely want to note that

[12]*James Joyce,* new and rev. ed. (New York: Oxford Univ. Press, 1982), p. 3.
[13]For an explanation of the meaning of the terms, see Gayatri Spivak, Translator's Preface to Jacques Derrida, *Of Grammatology* (Baltimore: Johns Hopkins
Univ. Press, 1976), pp. ix–lxxxix; or Jonathan Culler, *On Deconstruction: Theory
and Criticism after Structuralism* (Ithaca: Cornell Univ. Press, 1982).
[14]See W. B. Stanford, *The Ulysses Theme,* 2d ed. (New York: Barnes and
Noble, 1964).
[15]With the exception, of course, of "Wandering Rocks," which derives from the
myth of the Argonauts.

the connection between title and text is suggestive and intriguing rather than explanatory. The presence of the title makes the reader wonder what the author's point may have been. How does Bloom relate to his avatar Ulysses? It is difficult to believe that this character, whom Mark Shechner terms "oral passive," could be the reincarnation of the wily wanderer.[16] All heroism in the Homeric sense is gone. On the other hand, there are similarities. Bloom is versatile and inquisitive like the Achaean, and a reader willing to suspend disbelief might discern some analogy between his wanderings through Dublin and the stages of Odysseus's return to the arms of Penelope. But the parallel remains ambivalent and unclear. Bloom is *both* different from *and* similar to the classical hero.

Not surprisingly, the critical discussion of the relationship of *Ulysses* to *The Odyssey* has a long and respectable history.[17] Though Larbaud and Pound preceded Eliot, Eliot's essay in the *Dial* in 1923 forms a notable starting point for later critics, and it is useful to repeat Eliot's words here, even if only as an example of the reductive simplification critics have had to bring to bear upon Joyce to make univocal sense of him. Eliot wrote:

> In using the myth, in manipulating a continuous parallel between contemporaneity and antiquity, Mr Joyce is pursuing a method which others must pursue after him. They will not be imitators, any more than the scientist who uses the discoveries of an Einstein in pursuing his own, independent, further investigations. It is simply a way of controlling, of ordering, of giving a shape and significance to the immense panorama of futility and anarchy which is contempo-

---

[16]See Shechner, *Joyce in Nighttown: A Psychoanalytic Inquiry into Ulysses* (Berkeley: Univ. of California Press, 1974). I do not quote Shechner out of disagreement. On the contrary, I have found his book very illuminating. It is a pity, however, that psychoanalytic terminology almost inevitably seems to imply a value judgment.

[17]It is summarized in Wolfgang Iser, *The Implied Reader: Patterns of Communication in Prose Fiction from Bunyan to Beckett* (Baltimore: Johns Hopkins Univ. Press, 1974). Iser shows that there are two basic critical positions, dependency and analogy. His own argument, that the text reveals "irreducible differences" (p. 200), is very similar to the point I am making here. There is a distinction, however. Iser considers the "irreducible differences" produced by the text to be mimetic of "life," whereas I place Joyce's difference as a strategy of signification which corroborates Modern notions of origin.

rary history. It is a method already adumbrated by Mr Yeats, and of the need of which I believe Mr Yeats to have been the first contemporary to be conscious. . . . Instead of narrative method, we may now use the mythical method.[18]

Eliot praises Joyce for the innovation of using myth as a device of structure, a principle of order which *gives significance*. Yet he blithely disregards the fact that the relationship of epic to novel is rather tenuous and not simply imitative. In fact, it is different at a very crucial point. The homecoming of Leopold Bloom, the wandering hero, which should have provided closure and resolution and thus the meaning of the novel's progress, is at once a return to and, in a certain sense, a continued exile from his Penelope. The reader's expectation is ironically perverted because Leopold and Molly do not resume their marital relations. Seen against the light of Homer's example, the homecoming of *Ulysses* is ambivalent and frustrating. What strikes the reader most is the lack of closure. Still, Eliot praised Joyce for using the myth. But his praise, then, cannot have regarded the way Joyce used it but the mere fact of use. What Eliot reads into Joyce—as his praise of Yeats (and later Frazer) in the same passage would seem to corroborate—is his own idealization of myth, the hypostasis of structure as intrinsically meaningful. How can the mere presence of the structure of myth, though used to subvert its cathartic function, redeem the futility and anarchy of contemporary history? Such a redemption, indeed, is only conceivable if structure is itself Platonized as the origin of meaning.

If Eliot overvalues structure to the extent of disregarding the subversive strategy of its use, Pound almost dismisses the importance of the epic prototype. In the *Mercure de France* of June 1922, he speaks of this "more or less exact correspondence" as "a matter of cooking."[19] Elsewhere he wrote, "These correspondences are part of Joyce's mediaevalism and are chiefly his own affair, a scaf-

[18] "*Ulysses,* Order and Myth," *Dial* 75 (1923), 480–83, rpt. in *James Joyce: The Critical Heritage,* vol. I: *1907–1927,* ed. Robert H. Deming (London: Routledge and Kegan Paul, 1970), pp. 270–71.

[19] "Pound on *Ulysses* and Flaubert," extract from "James Joyce et Pécuchet," trans. F. Bornhauser, *Shenandoah* 3 (1952), 9–20, rpt. in Deming, pp. 263–65.

fold, a means of construction. . . . The result is a triumph in form . . . with continuous inweaving and arabesque."[20] Even though I disagree with Pound about the importance of the prototype, I have quoted his words here because they suggest a way of conceptualizing Joyce's ambivalence which is neither dismissive nor distorting.

Pound directs our attention away from the relationship between the two texts to the process of writing. The meaning of Homer's presence is not its function as point of reference for either difference or identity, he suggests. The epic was of personal importance to Joyce in the process of composing the novel. And yes, of course, Joyce's infinite pains in inventing suitable analogues for Homeric attributes and incidents have found ample documentation in his letters to Frank Budgen. First he would try to determine the meaning of something in *The Odyssey,* for instance the magic substance moly. Then he would exert all his ingenuity to find a modern parallel that should be as unobtrusive as possible. Thus for Joyce himself the transposition of the epic was a double process: of mastery and appropriation and then of covering the traces of that process, of decreation. The point is that what Joyce did consciously and deliberately is what all texts do unconsciously. All writing predicates itself upon previous structures, meanings, or texts. There is no novel ex nihilo. The bite of Pound's suggestion, then, is not that he refers us to the biography of the author but that Joyce's writing strategy proves emblematic of the intertextuality of all writing.

And in giving the title *Ulysses* to his fiction, in not fully covering the tracks of the struggle with the epic precursor but blatantly advertising it, Joyce makes his text into a deliberate emblem of the Modern understanding of the process of writing, which holds that writing never begins with an imitation of reality but always with another text—however unconscious the author may be of his reliance upon the prototype. The "beginning" of *Ulysses,* its title, advertises that the text has its "origin" in language and literary

[20]"Ulysses," originally the "Paris Letter" to *The Dial,* June 1922, in *Literary Essays of Ezra Pound,* ed. T. S. Eliot (1954; rpt. London: Faber, 1974), p. 406.

history; it is Joyce's conscious projection of his own understanding of the nature of the literary text.

But if the title points to the intertextual, that is, ambivalent mode of the novel, that reference itself is ambivalent. The title is not *The Odyssey,* not even *Odysseus,* but *Ulysses,* a name that is not listed in the "Index Nominum" of the Greek dictionary. It is an English version of the Latin "Ulixes." Thus, this title, which points to the epic, also marks the text's revisionary difference from the classic narrative. The title as sign functions as an epitaph, marking the last remains of *The Odyssey.* In giving his novel the title *Ulysses,* Joyce incorporated Homer into his fiction as the para-doxical presence of a defunct absence.

If we conceptualize the relationship between epic and novel in this way, Joyce requires of us a way of understanding which is not an irritable reaching after either/or but a more inclusive, complex vision that accommodates the "other" within the subject. In other words, we learn a strategy of reading which is no longer subject to the strictly bracketing demarcation of identities of the logos. *Ulys-ses* is both an *imitatio* and a parody of the epic, both a re-creation, an affirmative *Bejahung,* and an ironic undoing, *Verneinung.* How-ever obliquely, it weaves and unweaves at the same time. If the title is now *Ulysses* and no longer *The Odyssey,* the texture is woven by a Penelope forever precluding possession.

The struggle to find an escape from the Scylla and Charybdis of an oppositional winding "all upon two spools . . . black, white; right, wrong," as Gerard Manley Hopkins put it in "Spelt from Sibyl's Leaves," is dramatized in Stephen Dedalus's grappling with different ways of conceptualizing the relationship between origin and copy, father and son, author and text, under the permanent threat of the final breakdown of meaning. From his letters and critical writings, too, we know of James Joyce's lifelong interest in philosophers and poets whose ideas broke through the binarism of Aristotelian logic. Giordano Bruno, Blake, and in a different way Ibsen, each kicked the axiom of the excluded middle, while Vico unsettled the polarity of beginning and end in a model of *ricorso.* It may very well be that Joyce's crossing out of the presence of *The Odyssey,* putting it "sous rature," as Derrida might say, reflects his personal difficulty in overcoming the paralyzing rigidity of Irish Catholic schizophrenia and binarism portrayed in *Dubliners* and *A Portrait of the Artist as a Young Man*. However this may be, the fact is that the deconstructive relationship of the novel to the epic as marked by the title is not limited to the title. On the contrary, as we shall see, this ambivalent practice pervades every aspect of the text. Whatever *Ulysses* presents, creates, or constructs is immediately deprived of full self-presence and put "under erasure."

The Novel under Erasure

At first the general unsettledness in *Ulysses* may not be so apparent. Our usual process of reading is one of labeling and identifying. We place characters, actions, and attributes into the mutually exclusive pigeonholes of semantic connotation provided by our culture and education. Especially when we are experienced readers, we become very adept at finding meanings and oppositions that to less experienced readers may seem almost arbitrary. Opening *Ulysses* to the first page, then, one is ready to order the information of the text in the usual way. Stephen Dedalus is the "good guy," and Buck Mulligan the antagonist. But on longer acquaintance with the text this opposition proves not so simple, and each attempt at pigeonholing places the reader in the role of Cinderella's stepsister, who had to cut off toes to fit the slipper. Indeed, *Ulysses* teaches us to read without a "rage for order."

The fiction begins with the evocation of a crisp and beautiful morning, seen from the top of a tower. In the tradition of Western literature, the tower, the navel or "omphalos" in Mulligan's word, is, as Frye writes, a "point of epiphany."[21] It shares this privilege with mountains and other high places that function as *axes mundi,* places of revelation where the irreconcilable opposites of the transcendent and immanent are brought into communion. One might extend the symbolic import of the tower to a comparison with the

---

[21] *Anatomy of Criticism,* p. 203. See also Mircea Eliade, *The Sacred and the Profane: The Nature of Religion,* trans. Willard R. Trask (New York: Harcourt, Brace and World, 1959). Stuart Gilbert discusses the tower as "omphalos" in *James Joyce's "Ulysses,"* pp. 51–56.

moment of transubstantiation in the Mass. Both imply the "meeting" of physical and metaphysical, the transformation of matter
into spirit. As Buck Mulligan's intoning of the *Introibo* indicates,
Joyce played with this connotation. I deliberately chose the verb *to
play*, however, because the possibility of reading the Martello
Tower as a point of epiphany is at once deflated by Buck's dis-
respectful treatment of the sacred, which perverts (not inverts) the
opposition between sacred and profane. The first scene of *Ulysses*
will not allow itself to be "read" according to conventional schemata. We can no longer label the tower a place of epiphany, but
neither is it simply the place where the sacred is profaned.[22] The
presence of the idea of the sacred lingers, even if under abuse.
Indeed, as Ellmann points out, the crispness of the morning and
the lucid beauty of the scene preserve the feeling of a new dawn, an
unfallen beginning.[23]

The reader might try to neutralize the disturbing presence of
Buck Mulligan with the argument that he is just a character in a
scene and that his mockery serves to define his status as antihero to
Stephen Dedalus. Even so, the fact must be faced that Stephen,
too, profanes, though his motivation may be less reprehensible.
The parodic version of the Apostles' Creed in "Scylla and Charybdis" floats in his stream of consciousness. "Oxen of the Sun"
presents Stephen as the ringleader of a group of irreverent medical
students, boisterously misbehaving in a hospital where a woman is
giving birth to a child. It is a moment charged with symbolic
significance, emphasized by the narrator's allusion to the watch of
the shepherds at Bethlehem, and the beginning of the Gospel of
Saint John, which recounts the "birth" of the logos, the Word. We
read: "so and not otherwise was the transformation, violent and
instantaneous, upon the utterance of the word. Burke's! outflings
my lord Stephen, giving the cry" (XIV, 1391). I shall return to the
problem of the usurpation of material production by signification
in the next chapter. Here I only want to note how the narrator
presents Stephen. It is to him that the privilege of uttering the
word is given. That word, however, the name of a pub, intrudes

[22]See also Iser, pp. 204–5.
[23]*Ulysses on the Liffey* (New York: Oxford Univ. Press, 1972), p. 8.

as a bathetic violation of the sacred mystery of birth. In other words, the reader impatient to define ("to set limits to") the characters, will not find in the text itself sufficient confirmation to simply stick the label "profane" on Buck, "pious" on Stephen.[24]

Even more disconcerting is the realization that the text as a whole deals again and again with ideas of the sacred in terms very similar to those of Buck's perversion of ritual. What the reader encounters on opening *Ulysses* is not a simple inversion of "fair is foul" like the blight of *Bleak House*. Buck's profanity is a condition different only in degree. Mulligan cannot be used as scapegoat. If Buck and Stephen are the Tom and Blifil of *Ulysses,* this instance of doubling no longer mediates. The opening scene of *Ulysses* leads the reader into an endless maze because it cannot be read clearly by selecting one connotation from a pair of opposites. The situation on top of Martello Tower on the morning of June 16, 1904, precludes and perverts the possibility of choosing between hero and antihero, sacred and profane; it deliberately unsettles the discrete distinction between standard semantic connotations and associative meanings.

What applies to the opening scene of the novel applies to what follows too. It is possible to unravel scene after scene in this way, but our discussion of Joyce is part of a more general discussion of the logocentricity of the novel as genre. Rather than continue this analysis of the microlevel of the text, therefore, I want to show that the ambivalence that unsettles the stability of meaning of the individual scene also affects the constitutive conventions of the genre. The absence of living origin marked by the title of the novel is a blueprint for the workings of the text as a whole. Knit into the stitches of the design, the looseness that is the hallmark of Joyce's authorship decenters the assumption of the presence of the father upon which the novel as genre rests.

[24]A surviving fragment of text in fair copy from an early draft of *A Portrait of the Artist as a Young Man* shows that as late as 1912 or 1913, Joyce was still working on a tower scene for that novel. His earlier intention had been to write one for *Stephen Hero*. In the context of a discussion on endings and beginnings, it is ironic to note that the planned conclusion of the earlier novels eventually crystallized as the opening scene of *Ulysses*. See A. Walton Litz, *The Art of James Joyce: Method and Design in "Ulysses" and "Finnegans Wake"* (London: Oxford Univ. Press, 1961), pp. 132–41.

This decentering is most immediately obvious with regard to the notion of the literary character. To depict human character, unique individuality, the complexity and irreducible presence of the psyche, has been one of the central preoccupations of the novel. Especially in the late nineteenth century, character was the central focus of fiction, and of literary criticism. The fiction and essays of Henry James are still an admirable testimony to this focus, and it is not surprising that much of the theory of the novel in England and the United States should have been influenced by James's ideas. Character should be "round," not "flat," capable of surprising the reader, as another novelist put it, and the sequence of incidents and events must find its justification and explanation in the psychology of the character.[25]

Taking a long historical view, this emphasis on the importance of character in fiction is the reverse of the priority of action over character which Aristotle had posited in his *Poetics*. The most recent approach to character in fiction seems to return to the Aristotelian preference for structure. Taking the structure of language as its example, it understands fictional character as the product of the signifying practices of a text and classifies it by analogy with the different parts of a sentence as senders, receivers, etc.[26] If the "Jamesian" psychologizing school grounds mimetic practice in the assumption of an absolute presence outside the text, some of the (post)structuralist theorists would argue that it is the illusionary practice of fiction making, writing, which creates and supports the illusion of presence. It is not my purpose here to argue for or against either point of view. I need to provide this context, however, to show that what Joyce in his unweaving of epic plot makes clear about character is that neither a psychologizing nor a strictly structuralist point of view can be held without repressing awareness of the other possibility.[27] They are in fact opposites, like the polarity of

[25]W. J. Harvey, *Character and the Novel* (Ithaca: Cornell Univ. Press, 1965), is a very readable example.

[26]On character, see especially Philippe Hamon, "Pour un statut sémiologique du personnage," in *Poétique du récit* (Paris: Seuil, 1977), 117–63; A. J. Greimas, "Les actants, les acteurs, et les figures," in *Sémiotique narrative et textuelle,* ed. C. Chabrol (Paris: Larousse, 1973).

[27]James H. Maddox, Jr., *Joyce's "Ulysses" and the Assault upon Character* (New Brunswick, N.J.: Rutgers Univ. Press, 1978), is a recent example of the traditional

father and mother, and one cannot exist independently from the other—even if that other is kept unconscious. The ambivalence of Joyce's text alerts us to the idea that structure and self are mutually created and exist by virtue of their polarity.

Let me explain this idea by a closer look at Joyce's irreverent play with the convention of character in the text. Indeed, in his decentering of the logic of noncontradiction Joyce unsettles the axiom of self-identity which informs the fictional convention of character. I do not mean that Joyce plays with the possibility of multiple personality when he gives Bloom the alter ego of Henry Flower. This device is a source of pathetic comedy that does not really confuse the reader, who understands that the words "Bloom mur: best references. But Henry wrote: it will excite me" (XI, 888) present Bloom pretending to write a business letter while he is in fact addressing his secret correspondent Martha Clifford. Joyce's iconoclasm consists in something else. In the course of *Ulysses,* he repeatedly violates the convention that the experience and mental activity of a fictional character are particular to that character and are circumscribed, framed, by that character's individual consciousness. There is an unspoken rule that the words uttered belong to the character who speaks them, are tied to the person of a particular character and will not simply crop up in the stream of consciousness of another character in the fiction unless clearly marked as borrowed or remembered. Sometimes Joyce's playfulness is so subtle that the reader hardly notices or easily finds a way to rationalize the discrepancy. When we come across: "God, we must simply dress the character" (III, 174) in "Proteus," we may take it as Stephen's natural elaboration upon the idea of clothing introduced by his memory of "my Latin quarter hat." However, the reader who has noticed that beginning a sentence with the word *God* is characteristic of Buck Mulligan—the signature of his linguistic identity—will begin to wonder. Turning back to "Telemachus," this reader will find that virtually the same

---

Anglo-American approach to character, making in its own admirable way the point that Joyce opens up to his characters. It is a point also made by MacCabe, *Joyce and the Revolution of the Word.* MacCabe's views are similar to my own, though his method and theory are different. My indebtedness to his readings of "Sirens" and "Cyclops" will, I hope, be clear.

words figured there: "God, we'll simply have to dress the character. I want puce gloves and green boots. Contradiction. Do I
contradict myself? Very well then, I contradict myself. Mercurial
Malachi. A limp black missile flew out of his talking hands. —And
there's your Latin quarter hat, he said." (I, 515–20). The phrase
that at first seemed part of Stephen's musings while walking on
Sandymount Strand now proves related to Buck Mulligan's
presence.

The curious thing, however, is that neither in "Telemachus"
nor in the later chapter is the phrase preceded by the dash that
introduces direct speech in *Ulysses*. The phrase can only be an
utterance of Mulligan's which Stephen mentally recalls, then,
without directly attributing it to a source, perhaps an association
with the Latin quarter hat? In leaving out the visual mark that
distinguishes direct speech from stream of consciousness, Joyce
loosens language from its determinate origin, a specifically individual human source. If we did not know that a sentence beginning "God . . ." belonged to Mulligan, there would have been no
problem. We would have taken this as Stephen's thought. But
what or who guarantees the reader that Stephen, too, may not
begin a sentence in the way Mulligan does? After all, speech habits
are contagious. Joyce makes us conscious that the idea of character
in fiction rests upon a convention. If a character is "characterized"
by a personal idiom or by idiosyncrasies of speech, this diction or
these idiosyncrasies are, within the scope of the fiction, to be
limited to that character alone. Thus the distribution of qualities
and the preservation of differences, the ordering of the fiction,
generate the impression of individuality.

The instance cited here is one of the many cases in the text where
Joyce seems deliberately ambiguous. Is he teasing us? If so, in
precisely what way? We shall never be able to tell for sure in this
instance whether Joyce reneged on the convention or not, but
there are other places in the text which leave no doubt that the
convention is being deliberately flouted. Molly's text in "Circe,"
for example, presents the expression "Nebrakada! Feminum!"
(XV, 319) which had earlier featured in Stephen's stream of consciousness in "Wandering Rocks" as "*Nebrakada feminum*" (X,
861). While Bloom ponders the ending of his letter to Martha in

"Sirens," he suddenly falls into the words spoken by Stephen in his discussion of Shakespeare in "Scylla and Charybdis": "Too poetical that about the sad. Music did that. Music hath charms. Shakespeare said. Quotations every day in the year. To be or not to be. Wisdom while you wait. In Gerard's rosery of Fetter lane he walks, greyedauburn. One life is all. One body. Do. But do. Done anyhow. Postal order, stamp" (XI, 904–10). But language always returns in a way slightly different from the "original" version. "Scylla and Charybdis" had: "Do and do. Thing done. In a rosery of Fetter Lane of Gerard, herbalist, he walks, greyedauburn" (IX, 651–52). The repetition is always marked by a slight difference, as if to question even the very notion of *Wiederholung*. Joyce's ambivalence is indeed inexhaustible.

The shorthand symbol, the "sound sense sympol" (*FW* 612.29), of character in fiction is the name. The name seals the discrete self-identity of the literary personage, as it does the self-identity of the individual person in real life. But there are differences, and by exploiting the conventionality of the name in fiction, Joyce alerts us to the logic of noncontradiction upon which our sense of individuality as human beings rests. In everyday existence we relate a name to a living presence of flesh and blood, but we also use names of persons whose objective existence has been suggested to us by language but whom we have never seen. How do we know President Reagan exists? Only because the media tell us. The name suggests, evokes, and confirms the presence of the subject of news, events, incidents, stories we know from hearsay. In writing a novel an author may introduce a name, suggesting the fictional existence of a certain person, but if this person is to become a "character," the name must correlate with more information about the subject—thoughts, adventures, attitudes and so on. Certain adventures and specific utterances are correlated with and centered upon the name of the subject. The singular identity of the name supports the singular identity of the literary subject. If Joyce questions the convention that speech patterns identify characters, it should not surprise us that he also opens the frame of the name which brackets individuality.

Again, the strategy of deconstruction is carried furthest in *Finnegans Wake*. There, Margot Norris writes, "characters are fluid and interchangeable, melting easily into their landscapes to become river and land, tree and stone, Howth Castle and Environs, or HCE. We find in the *Wake* not characters as such but ciphers, in formal relationship to each other."[28] Moreover, these ciphers—or *karakters,* to use the Greek word for the imprint that gives identity to the coin—are distributed over the text in many different configurations. Thus fluidity has come to replace self-identity, and the "name" is no longer separate from the speech, stories, and so on that flesh out the character of the name but is interwoven with them. The name is knitted into the words of the text, which are both its product and its source. In thus fusing name with the story belonging to that name, Joyce makes it impossible to ask the question of priority, of origin. Which is first, character or action? He makes them into functions of each other. What this practice makes us realize, is that naming itself is part of the logos of noncontradiction of our culture. The writing at birth of the name into the social register or family Bible marks the person as an individual subject of the history of his life.

In contrast to *Finnegans Wake, Ulysses* gives its characters conventional names, but it does defamiliarize and unsettle the convention of the name. In rewriting Bloom's name as "O'Bloom, the son of Rory" (xii, 216), in referring to Buck Mulligan as "Puck Mulligan" (ix, 1125), or in translating "Henry Flower" (Bloom's alias) into "Henry Fleury," Joyce punctures the self-identity of the name as the anchor of signification. Translating the name, he shows us that names, too, are part of the semiotic system of signification. The question "What's in a name?" (xvi, 364), to which we give little thought in everyday existence, is problematized in *Ulysses.* For Stephen, names are impostures. They deceptively suggest unique individuality, but "Cicero, Podmore, Napoleon, Mr Goodbody. Jesus, Mr Doyle. Shakespeares were as common as Murphies" (xvi, 363–64), he points out. And Stephen's question within "Eumaeus" is the question of "Eumaeus."[29] What is the relationship between person and name? Is it their correlation that constitutes individuality?

Whether names were also "impostures" for the author of *Ulysses*

---

[28] *The Decentered Universe of "Finnegans Wake": A Structuralist Analysis* (Baltimore: Johns Hopkins Univ. Press, 1976), p. 4.

[29] For an analysis of the styles of *Ulysses,* see Karen Lawrence, *The Odyssey of Style in Ulysses* (Princeton: Princeton Univ. Press, 1981).

is impossible to say. We know that Joyce "read" names as signs. He saw a secret affinity between himself and Freud because the German word for *joy* is *Freude,* for example. Still, the way names are handled in *Ulysses* is so blatant a violation of the convention of self-identity that one gets the impression of deliberate parody. "Sirens," which tries to bend the style of the chapter to its musical subject, plays a number of variations on the theme of the name "Bloom," beginning with: "Blew. Blue bloom is on the" (xi, 5), and continuing with "Blowho" (84), "Bloowhose" (149), "greaseabloom" (180), to end with "Seabloom, greaseabloom" (1284). At the moment when the music reaches its greatest intensity, Bloom's identification with the voice of the singer, Simon Dedalus, suggests the name "Siopold" (xi, 752). This fusion of two names occurs elsewhere in the text as "Stoom" and "Blephen" (xvii, 549, 551) and asks the question of discrete individual identity. Is character or individuality a potential fluidity anchored by the name? If the practice of creating character in fiction is supported by the logic of noncontradiction, how does the logos determine or influence our understanding of ourselves as selves in everyday life?

These examples are taken from a text that is riddled with mocking lists of names. In religious practice the recitation of a litany renders homage to the mystery of divinity. The names for Christ in the New Testament indicate the ineffable mystery of his incarnation. Joyce turns this motivation upon its head. His lists of names deflate the suggestion of presence inherent in the name and point out that names, especially in their written form, are signs. A list of saints shows that sanctity inheres in the capital letter *S:* "S. Anonymous and S. Eponymous and S. Pseudonymous and S. Homonymous and S. Paronymous and S. Synonymous" (xii, 1696–98), and the euphonic names themselves also parody the conventions of naming. A comparable list of members of the clergy shows us how the graphic symbol of the letter marks and institutes hierarchical and social difference. Thus "the very rev. William Delaney, S.J., L.L.D." is marked as different from "the rt rev. Gerald Molloy, D.D." (xii, 927–28). Then there are lists of foreign names, where the signifier, because it evokes incongruous English words, erodes all reverence for the name: "the Grandjoker Vladinmire Pokethankertscheff, the Archjoker Leopold Rudolph von Schwanzenbad-Hodenthaler . . . Count Athanatos Karamelopulos" (XII, 559–62). But even if Joyce's game with names, especially in "Cyclops," turns into a debunking parody, the almost obsessive energy and force of it all testify to the continuing power of the idea of the name. After all, the name as idea is at the heart of Western culture. The name of God, "I am that I am" of Exodus 3:14, expresses the assumption of self-identity of the logos. *Finnegans Wake* rephrases this as "I yam as I yam" (*FW* 604.23), thus fracturing self-containment by introducing the overtone of the Latin word *iam,* "already," suggesting difference at the heart of identity. But however much Joyce may struggle against the logos, whatever games he plays with names, the question raised by his writing cannot change the ineluctably informative presence of the logos, except by tittle or iota. "The first and the last rittlerattle of the anniverse" can never be more than the paradoxical question "when is a nam nought a nam" (*FW* 607.11–14). It is a question that ambivalently affirms in denying.

One of the most disturbing effects of Joyce's deliberate violation of the logos of noncontradiction relates not to the idea of character within the text but to the identity of the character projected by the text, the author. The idea of the author as source of the language that constitutes the novel would seem a sacrosanct convention of literature—but not to Joyce. Implicit in his refusal to respect the convention that character is identified by speech is the erosion of the figure of the author as Fielding pictured him, the subject of his own province of writing.

This erosion is best illustrated by employing the insights of the structural analysis of narrative, which proceeds by asking three questions: Who speaks? Who sees? Who acts? These functions of articulation, perception, and performative action can be distributed in different combinations according to the narrative mode. The question "Who sees?" relates to "focalization" or point of view. But how do we know "who sees"? An answer to this question requires an analysis of style and idiom to determine whose consciousness filters perception. Our example may be the sentence from *A Portrait of the Artist* that caught the eye of Wyndham Lewis and Hugh Kenner: "Every morning, therefore, Uncle Charles repaired to his outhouse but not before he had greased and brushed scrupulously his back hair and brushed and put on his tall hat."[30] Kenner argues that the verb *to repair* is not a slip of Joyce's pen, a fall into vulgar cliche, as Lewis thought it. On the contrary, Joyce deliberately bends his style to the personal idiom of the character, in this case Uncle Charles. While the narrator speaks about Uncle Charles, the mediation of the activity described is colored with Uncle Charles's idiom. Kenner calls this the Uncle Charles principle.

This instance from *A Portrait of the Artist* suggests that the question of point of view is somehow tied in with the notion of the semiotics of a consistent and coherent "personal" idiom. We note again that the correlation between voice and character is an arbitrary convention relying upon distributive selection and ordering and naturalized by the collective cultural discourse. Who sees, for instance, in this passage from "Cyclops"? "And there came a voice out of heaven, calling: *Elijah! Elijah!* And he answered with a main cry: *Abba! Adonai!* And they beheld Him even Him, ben Bloom Elijah, amid clouds of angels ascend to the glory of the brightness at an angle of fortyfive degrees over Donohoe's in Little Green street like a shot of a shovel" (XII, 1914–18). The passage is narrated by an anonymous narrator whose sudden turn to biblical idiom suggests that he bends his style to his subject Leopold Bloom whose wounded consciousness overreacts to the humiliation just suffered by picturing himself in apotheosis. But this assumption, which raises more questions than it answers (why choose a biblical idiom for Bloom?), is rudely deflated by the last words "like a shot of a shovel." Stylistically and semantically, they jar with the preceding words of the sentence, evoking rather the presence of the vulgar pubster who supposedly narrates "Cyclops." But can focalization change so abruptly within the compass of one sentence? Or should we understand this instance as another of Joyce's reminders that stylistic identity, that is, voice, does not necessarily tally with personal identity?

Did Joyce want to present an image of language as no longer tied to human consciousness, language as autonomous? It is true that

[30] I quote from Kenner, *Joyce's Voices* (London: Faber and Faber, 1978), pp. 16–17.

styles and discourses seemingly lead their own independent lives in
Ulysses, turning up when and where and as they list. It is a peculiarity that presents a problem of interpretation at the macrolevel
of the text. What is the central point of view of the novel itself?
How can we circumscribe, identify, personify the implied author
as source of his text? The classic humanist personification of the
author as a single being with a single, unified point of view, is
questioned by the practice of *Ulysses.* Who narrates the novel? Or
should we ask, "Who narrate the novel?" or perhaps, "What narrates *Ulysses?*" The polylogued nature of the text has driven one
critic to conclude that *Ulysses* "deconstructs any possible author";
another postulates a single author who plays different roles, one of
which is "the arranger"; and a third sees the progression of stylistic
experiments as an odyssey in itself.[31] Again, it is not my intention
to solve the problems that beset Joyce critics; eventually we shall
have to adapt our tools of analysis to the complexity of Joyce. My
argument, however, does not bear upon an interpretation of the
text but upon the preconceptions of its praxis. I merely want to
remind my readers that Joyce, in transgressing the limits that
frame the identity of styles and voices, has placed the conventional
anthropomorphic model of understanding authority "under
erasure."

The Structure of the Text and the Structure of the Self

Ultimately our activity as scholars is directed toward a better
understanding of ourselves as human beings and of the culture we
create. My analysis of the ambivalence of *Ulysses* derives its validity and justification from the reflection of the unsettling of the
weaving of the text in the unsettling of human identity within the
story. If *Ulysses* is emblematic of Modern writing, as I think, this

[31]The quotation "deconstructs any possible author" is from MacCabe, p. 90; the
arranger theory from David Hayman, *"Ulysses": The Mechanics of Meaning* (Englewood Cliffs, N.J.: Prentice-Hall, 1970); Karen Lawrence takes the journey
metaphor as framework for her analysis. Brook Thomas, *James Joyce's "Ulysses":
A Book of Many Happy Returns* (Baton Rouge: Louisiana State Univ. Press, 1982),
offers an extensive discussion of the configuration of authority of *Ulysses.*

analysis of the novel will also pertain to an understanding of modern humanity and its awareness of itself. As Joyce is different from Dickens, the existential mode of the inhabitants of the city he describes is proportionately different from that of Dickens's Victorian characters. *Ulysses* presents the pre-Oedipal, fragmented, or narcissistic personality psychoanalysts find so prevalent today.

This very broad claim needs some substantiation, however brief. That the ending of *Ulysses* frustrates the reader's desire for climax, I have said many times. But the ideas of *coniunctio,* of communion, of the return to paradise, in short, the paraphernalia of closure do not just disappear from the consciousness of the text. They are incorporated into the consciousness of the characters as the presence of their absence. Just as the title proclaims the death of *The Odyssey,* the blissful happiness of resolution informs the text as permanent and unattainable desire. Both Bloom and Stephen, clad in mourning throughout the day, dream of perfect bliss (oriental fruit and gardens), desire full self-possession, and muse on places of epiphany and apotheosis. But their author makes it clear that this persistence of desire is not the anticipation of later fulfillment but a chronic condition of life in Dublin on June 16, 1904. The citrons of Agendath Netaim may hold Edenic associations of immortality "like that, heavy, sweet, wild perfume. Always the same, year after year" (IV, 208–9). They may even guarantee their owner the permanent inscription of the name, "entered for life as owner in the book of the union," which resides at "Bleibtreustrasse 34" (German for "Stay True Street"); but it is a paradise that has lost its ideal status. In Dublin "Nobody owns" (VI, 365). Nobody reaches the Promised Land; nor is there a return to Paradise Hall.

In fact, there is no such thing as epiphany in *Ulysses*. Though the text is sprinkled with a profusion of high places—Martello Tower, the Peak of Gibraltar, Nelson's Pillar and Howth Hill—as well as a profusion of symbols of communion—chalices, grails, cups of cocoa—these symbols seem to have lost efficacy. Any peak experience is, at best, a memory. The memory of making love to Molly on Howth Hill, for example, haunts Bloom throughout the day, but this memory is the mother of desire, and his stream of consciousness is suffused with the acutely painful awareness of the absence of present bliss, so that the advertisement for "Plumtree's potted meat" becomes resonant as the image of the grail Bloom lacks. Molly's adultery, too, seems almost more a symbol of the imperfection inherent in reality than an act of personal betrayal. If Bloom, unlike Stephen, is not preoccupied with the Fall in a theological sense—with the implied possibility of redemption—he is fascinated by the physical mechanics of falling: "Thirtytwo feet per second per second. Law of falling bodies: per second. They all fall to the ground. The earth. It's the force of gravity of the earth is the weight" (v, 44–46). At the end of the story Bloom will fall asleep, satisfied with the melons of Molly's posterior as the substitute for the Edenic fruit. Open-endedness, then, the absence of climax, the permanency of acutely unsatisfied desire, is not only characteristic of the plot of *Ulysses;* it marks the personality of its characters.

While Joyce's depiction of the permanent insistence of desire in the makeup of his heroes is highly affecting, it also provides the basis for a more general insight. What Joyce shows as the reality of Bloom and Stephen suggests the recent emphasis on open-endedness and desire in French literary criticism and psychoanalysis. Translating our conclusions about the lack of resolution in *Ulysses* into Lacanian idiom, we might say that Bloom accepts his own castration. Walking by a horse, Bloom notices: "Gelded too: a stump of black guttapercha wagging limp between their haunches. Might be happy all the same that way" (v, 217–19). If Joyce illustrates what French psychoanalysis theorizes, Joyce's depiction of modern man is not an expression of merely personal views but the reflection of a more widely held revision of the idea of what human nature and human identity are. Joyce's revolution, not of but against the Word, may be a very powerful expression of a tendency generally present in Western culture.

We might even rephrase what Joyce shows us in the words employed by Jean Laplanche in his revision of Freud and say that "Bloom opens himself up to death"[32] or, in the terms of this argument, to the "other." In the course of his wanderings through

[32]*Life and Death in Psychoanalysis,* trans. Jeffrey Mehlman (Baltimore: Johns Hopkins Univ. Press, 1976).

Dublin, Bloom's consciousness shows an acute awareness of the presence of death. The idea of death is not something to be repressed, cosmeticized, or exploited for sentimental thrills as in a cheap Victorian novel. For Stephen and Bloom the presence of death is part of life, and thoughout the day both have acute experiences of nothingness. Stephen is threatened by the fear of being engulfed by the tie to his mother. Bloom has horrifying visions of the void. Immediately after his blissful vision of the oriental fruit in the Holy Land, he has a countervision of the Dead Sea. It is a vision of death so intense that it threatens to annihilate Bloom's consciousness. But in the syntax of *Ulysses* this moment functions not as a descent into an underworld, as part of a purgative quest, but—like the lack of fulfillment of desire—as a permanent aspect of life. In Dublin the advertisement for Plumtree's potted meat is printed beneath the obituary notices.

Thus our interpretive reading of character in *Ulysses* returns us to the theoretical problem of Joyce's denial of logocentric order. What we notice as peculiarities of Joyce's representation are secondary effects of the primary refusal to order his text (and the reality it represents) in terms of oppositions. Life and death are mutually exclusive concepts, but Joyce breaks the circle framing the identity of life to incorporate the awareness of death. The Dead Sea is *in* the Holy Land. In short, it seems to me that the "clue" to *Ulysses* as representation and as structure resides in Joyce's iconoclastic denial of the logos of polarity. The ideal is no longer absolutely ideal but part of the real; macrocosm and microcosm fuse; life and death are no longer wholly different. Hence, there is no mediation, no quest, no change or development of character, no resolution, and no climax. The action of *Ulysses* remains firmly moored in medias res or to recall the complaint about open-endedness from *Bleak House,* "in the middest." In Dublin it is always already "the morning after."[33]

The attentive reader will argue that the ending of *Ulysses* entails more than the reconciliation of Molly and Bloom, that the novel, in fact, features more than one quest. Is there not also Stephen Dedalus's search for a father? Of course, *Ulysses* interlaces two quests; one for the m(other) and one for the paternal principle, the

[33]See Ellmann, *Ulysses on the Liffey,* p. 8.

logos. But the point is that if Bloom's return to Molly ambivalently undercuts the possibility of a clear, univocal interpretation, the
meeting of Stephen and Bloom comes trailing even darker clouds
of ambiguity. The history of Joyce criticism abounds with inge-
nious constructions of their relationship, none of which is ultimately convincing.[34] My own view is that *Ulysses* mocks the reader's expectation of resolution. At the conclusion of "Eumaeus,"
Bloom and Stephen are walking "towards the railway bridge, *to be
married by Father Maher*" (XVI, 1887–88). The words from the bal-
lad irrupt into the consciousness of the text as if to reflect the
unconscious truth about quest structures. Nor does it seem merely
accidental that the parodic *moment suprême* of the paternity theme
features the image of a mirror. When Bloom and Stephen look into
this mirror together, what appears is the face of a paralyzed Shakespeare. Lynch's attendant cry "The mirror up to nature" (XV,
3820) creates a link between this incident in "Circe"—the "unconscious" of the novel—and the theory of mimesis. It is as if the text
would suggest that contraries never fuse, except in the paralyzed
or paralyzing medium of the Aristotelian imitation of an action.

The Question of Family Romance

Sometimes "The longest way round is the shortest way home"
(XIII, 1110–11), and it is only after a long discussion of novelistic
conventions and their relation to the notion of (self-)identity that

[34]The possible interpretations have been surveyed by Richard Kain in "The
Significance of Stephen's Meeting Bloom: A Survey of Interpretations," in *Fifty
Years: "Ulysses,"* ed. Thomas F. Staley (Bloomington: Indiana Univ. Press, 1974),
pp. 147–61. Kain summarizes and extensively discusses all theories, then lists
summarily (p. 159): "1. Isolation: the meeting is fortuitous and unimportant, a
demonstration of modern keylessness or of the existential position of man. 2.
Creativity: Stephen becomes a discoverer of mankind, through communion with
Bloom. 3. Ambiguity: Joyce seems to indicate a subtle relationship of himself,
Stephen, and Bloom. 4. Trinitarian: Joyce seems to indicate a subtle relationship of
Molly, Stephen, and Bloom. 5. Classical Temper: the book reveals the wholeness
and complexity of life. 6. Existential: Bloom and Stephen reach a point of crisis,
the outcome of which is problematic. 7. Biographical Fact: *Ulysses* dramatizes a
crucial personal experience of the author. 8. Psychological Projection: Stephen and
Bloom are fictional surrogates for Joyce's own conscious and subconscious
drives."

we return to the basic discussion of plot. It is as if the absence of closure in *Ulysses* itself forced us to take this circuitous route. Only after witnessing the universal disarray in the texture of the fiction are we in a position to realize how fundamental the logos of oppositional difference has been to the generic identity of the novel. When contraries begin to overlap, and A can be both A and B at the same time, we have entered a world in which nothing is clearly distinct or itself. Cause and effect, inside and outside, physical and metaphysical, transcendent and immanent, male and female, ideal and real, and especially origin and end lose their absolute, essential status. The tension between them will not be strong enough to necessitate mediation, and therefore, the circular quest, the family romance of Western culture, loses its mystique of presence. Why generate more stories about a return to origin if the idea of origin is no longer compelling?

This is, indeed, the question of *Ulysses*. But it is not all *Ulysses* brings to our attention. As a fiction, Joyce's re-creation of the epic remains within the general category of the circular quest. The reader's suspicions about the generic orthodoxy of the fiction are only confirmed in the last three chapters. In raising the expectation of closure and circularity and simultaneously frustrating the demand he himself has created, Joyce turns the convention inside out. He shows us the loose threads of workmanship, the knots, the blurrings of the pattern, which fiction conventionally keeps at the back of the embroidery. The design can still be recognized, but what emerges is the question of the meaning of this anomalous order. *Ulysses* is the one novel I know which manages to create this double image of simultaneously weaving and unweaving a fiction, showing us plot in deconstruction. Of course, there are many works of fiction which dramatize fiction making. The example cited most often may well be John Barth's *Lost in the Funhouse*. The difference is that Joyce's novel is not metafictive, not explicitly about fiction making but about a city, about people and their emotions. *Ulysses,* nevertheless, raises the question of the relationship between the structures of our fictions and the structure of human identity because it weaves and unweaves its image at the same time, while metafiction tends to foreground its self-consciousness.

Joyce is uniquely ambivalent, as well as uniquely successful. His quarrel with the logos did not tumble his fiction into chaos. Instead, he discovered a way of writing which incorporated chaos into the *kosmos* (the Greek word for order) of his design as "chaosmos." But the text is, of course, highly heretical. In the realization that it cannot refuse or escape the logos, it tries to rewrite the logos and to open it to what it must necessarily exclude.[35] It turns the very vehicle of the logos, language, against its own principle of exclusive order. Instead of tailoring the representation according to the conventional syntax of the circular quest—distributing roles and identities, and excluding the "other" from articulation in language—Joyce adopts an allusive strategy of incorporative writing not to return the repressed but to flaunt difference.

As I argued, *Ulysses* is the epitaph not only of *The Odyssey* but of the informative presence of the epigenetic structure itself. It mockingly preinscribes all the ideas, concepts, notions, subjects, stories, myths, sciences, quests, religious doctrines that epigenetic structure offers as meaningful. If traditional plot structure mirrors the ordering principle of Western metaphysics, Joyce jumbles the whole of Western discourse as if to parody what the structure of the circular quest had always entailed. His method should not be seen as a symptomatic return of the repressed but as his deliberate orchestration and articulation of what the syntax of identity is about. In his séminaire on Joyce, Lacan coined the word *sinthome* for Joyce's strategy of enunciation. (Thus Lacan, too, had recourse to the Joycean strategy of writing with "double dye," as if to demonstrate once again that no existing critical term covers Joyce's ambivalent practice.) Joyce himself spoke of *Ulysses* as a "kind of encyclopedia" in a letter to Carlo Linati of September 1920.[36] The medieval word *summa* might also be useful here, since it denotes the inventory of all existing knowledge. Whatever word we choose, the point is that "this chaffering allincluding most farraginous chronicle" (xiv, 1412) includes and incorporates allusions

---

[35]As is argued by MacCabe, who personifies the "other" as the desire of the mother. The next chapter will discuss my reasons for disagreeing with this anthropomorphic and essentializing representation.

[36]Richard Ellmann, ed., *Selected Letters of James Joyce* (New York: Viking, 1975), p. 271.

to all other stories and discourses, all versions of family romance—Sinbad, Robinson Crusoe, the Ancient Mariner, the Wandering Jew, the Flying Dutchman, and Captain Nemo, not to forget Cinderella and Little Lord Fauntleroy.[37] Perhaps it is again Wyndham Lewis who provides us with the appropriate words, even if we do not share his meaning. In *Time and Western Man,* he spoke of *Ulysses* as a "catafalque" of Western culture, an "immense nature-morte."[38] If we translate *nature-morte* into the English "still life," the point becomes more pressing. *Ulysses* is a circular quest deprived of its informative presence, its life. And it is the presence of this defunct structure in literary history which in turn forces us to examine the question of the psychological and ideological function of the structure while it was still alive.

In his seminal discussion, *The Sense of an Ending,* Frank Kermode pointed out that the pattern of our fictions mirrors our myths. Linear progression toward an apocalyptic ending evokes the Christian concordance of beginning, middle, and end. I could not agree more if Kermode means that both myth and narrative show the same pattern of composition. He seems to imply, however, that narrative imitates myth, that myth is prior and narrative secondary. This suggestion is itself the result of the process of ordering information by means of the epigenetic plot—assigning a beginning and a consequence, a model and a copy. The awareness Joyce forces upon us, however, is that plot, putting things in order and in line, is not just an aspect of myth, hence story, but the central ordering principle of our culture. It is the logos upon which our whole civilization rests. Stories do not have plot because they imitate myth. Stories have plot because plot, as logos, informs our minds, our perception, our selves, and our society. In creating stories then—that is, in consciously exercising the faculty for ordering—we project the very essence of culture, of humanity, and also of religion.

[37]Allusions in the interior monologue of Stephen Dedalus may suggest that Joyce was familiar with Freud's essay on family romance, probably through Rank. See Jean Kimball, "Family Romance and Hero Myth: A Psychoanalytic Context for the Paternity Theme in *Ulysses,*" *James Joyce Quarterly* 20 (1983), 161–74.

[38]*Time and Western Man* (London: Chatto and Windus, 1927), pp. 91–130, offers "An Analysis of the Mind of James Joyce."

For literary theorists this realization is a double bind. Can we still speak of mimesis? What mirrors what? If the essential order of story mirrors the syntax of the self or if the social structure is predicated upon the ordering processes of the logos, it is impossible to argue that fiction imitates life. Fiction is not only a mirror of life, it is also a mirror of the mediating mind and the medium that creates the picture of life. Like many other theoretical problems, this one has found a place in the stream of consciousness of Stephen Dedalus, who argues in "Scylla and Charybdis": "Maeterlinck says: *If Socrates leave his house today he will find the sage seated on his doorstep. If Judas go forth tonight it is to Judas his steps will tend.* Every life is many days, day after day. We walk through ourselves, meeting robbers, ghosts, giants, old men, young men, wives, widows, brothers-in-love, but always meeting ourselves. The playwright who wrote the folio of this world and wrote it badly. . . . is doubtless all in all in all of us" (IX, 1042–51).

Instead of mimesis as a one-directional operation, Joyce's deconstruction of plot suggests that we should understand the relationship between fiction and world as a double process, a simultaneous and mutual confirming constitution of presence. The shape and presence of "life" are mirrored in narrative. At the same time, the order of the objective world confirms the order of story. Like Stephen's *amor matris,* subjective and objective genitive, the idea of mimesis is tautological. Self and world, language and reality mirror and sustain each other in a single act of mutual polarity. Indeed, in Joyce mimesis has become a semiotic process that has no knowable origin.

That it took a Joyce to enforce this understanding upon our awareness is not surprising. To live in the illusion that fiction mirrors life or even the converse, to postulate that language creates reality (the *Darstellung* or *creatio* view), is easier on our understanding because it allows the safety of a fixed point of origin and truth. The semiotic model I am proposing here, however, makes truth a matter of correspondence and congruence between the logos and structure of our fictions and those of history.

And once we are capable of envisioning a semiotic model of representation without irritably reaching after firm fact, we may also begin to understand the tautology of the plot structure that has formed the subject of discussion in these chapters. If this type of plot typically proceeds by postulating an opposition and then resolving it, it mirrors not only the pattern of a Fortunate Fall but the splitting into inside and outside, origin and copy, of mimesis itself. Indeed, it is the repetitive enactment in language, the organization of the fiction, which allows us to forget or repress the tautology of representation which is so deflating to our self-esteem as the "apex" of God's creation. What Joyce has done by opening the circle of that structure is to include the outside in the texture of his fiction. The process of unconscious doubling by means of which the logos predicates itself is enunciated *in* the doubleness of Joyce's representation. The "double dye" (*FW* 185.32), of his "dividual chaos" (*FW* 186.4–5) is the "logical" consequence of lifting the repression upon the process of splitting by means of which the logos maintains its self-evidence.

Perhaps we are now in a position to account for the Joycean strategy of ambivalence. The central importance of the issues raised by Joyce's quarrel with the logos, both for the theory of literature and for culture, precludes the rationalization of the difference of *Ulysses* in terms of the psychology or biography of the author. Even if Joyce's exile from traditional ways of representation was made necessary by his confrontation with the deadlock of Irishness, the implications of his attempt to fly by that net are of general cultural significance.

Indeed, what Joyce suggests about the metaphysics of identity and structure has since the fifties found articulation in the discourses of philosophy, psychology, and sociology usually labeled poststructuralist. I have taken Derrida as analogue in my analysis of *Ulysses* because his insights and terminology helped me articulate certain peculiarities of Joyce's text. In doing so, I may unintentionally have made Derrida the figurehead of an international development in Western thought which in the United States is often criticized as "narcissistic."[39] It will not come as a surprise that I do not share the view that Joyce, Derrida, or all of Modern thought

---

[39]Gerald Graff, *Literature against Itself: Literary Ideas in Modern Society* (Chicago: Univ. of Chicago Press, 1979); Christopher Lasch, *The Culture of Narcissism: American Life in an Age of Diminishing Expectations* (New York: Norton, 1978).

stands for a regressive or reductive simplification. Instead of taking the circularity and ambivalence of Modern discourse as a moral or psychological deficit, I should like to see it as the outcome of a real and perhaps even baffling concern with what Emmanuel Lévinas has called the "violence" of metaphysics[40]—or in the terms in which I have conducted my argument, a greater tolerance for the presence of the "other."

It is not by accident that *Ulysses* places the "other," as Jew, center stage and that the story shows again and again how the social order structures Bloom's exclusion and victimization. *Ulysses* can be read as an illustration of the mechanics of prejudice which proves a caricature of the divisive ordering of the logos. "Cyclops" particularly is an anatomy of prejudice. At a pub whose customers have the mistaken notion that he has just won money at the races, Bloom's failure to stand a round is identified as Jewish behavior by the nameless narrator. "Mean bloody scut. Stand us a drink itself. Devil a sweet fear! There's a jew for you! All for number one. Cute as a shithouse rat" (XII, 1760–62). Apparently, the nameless one has a blueprint for ordering his world in which Jewishness is identified with avarice (Jew = miser) and the Jew is stereotyped as the "other"—that which is different from the self. In this world of mutually exclusive categories, unacceptable qualities are projected upon the "other." That Joyce should have chosen the figure of the one-eyed Cyclops, blinded by Odysseus's exploitation of the doubleness of the word *outis* ("no one"), as symbol for his chapter on rhetoric and prejudice, seems wholly appropriate. It is an indication, perhaps, of Joyce's own intention in exploiting the sign-function of language to counter the violence of "single vision," of turning language against its own powers of conjuring presence.

What "Cyclops" emphasizes once again is the extent to which the logic of noncontradiction is interwoven with the self-identity of the ego. Structure supports the illusion of self-sufficiency and projects the awareness of doubleness outside upon the "other."

---

[40] *Totality and Infinity,* trans. Alphonso Lingis (Pittsburgh: Duquesne Univ. Press, 1969). It should be understood, however, that Lévinas does not refer to the violence *of* metaphysics but to the complicity between philosophy and violence.

Thus the self can hide its own inner division from itself. In *Anti-Oedipus,* a plea for the liberation of desire from the restriction of structure, Deleuze and Guattari argue that the triangular model of father, mother, child—the triangle of the circular quest—is society's straightjacket for the self. Though I question the possibility of the liberation of flow and desire which Deleuze and Guattari postulate, their theory of the Oedipal structure as a hardy perennial articulates an insight already implicit in Joyce. Guattari thinks that "the work of the analyst, the revolutionary, and the artist meet to the extent that they must constantly tear down systems which reify desire, which submit the subject to the familial and social hierarchy. (I am a man, I am a woman, I am a son, I am a brother, etc.) No sooner does someone say, 'I am this or that' than desire is strangled."[41]

We might wish to understand Joyce's ambivalent reluctance to close *Ulysses,* then, as a reluctance to complete the predication of single definition. Alone on Sandymount Strand after his vicarious experience with Gerty MacDowell, Bloom finds a stick and begins to write in the sand. He begins by tracing a capital *I.* But as he is writing, the illusion of the desire for permanence which writing implies forces itself into awareness. He continues "AM A" and then desists without completing the predicate with a *nomen.* One might take this abortive sentence as an allusion to God's self-definition: "I am Alpha and Omega, the beginning and the ending, saith the Lord" (Revelation 1:8), but to do so would only add another symbolic dimension to the fact that Bloom's impulse to define himself in writing fades before the completion of the act, as if he no longer believed in the self-identity suggested by the fixity of closure. But if Bloom does not complete his writing, he does begin. In that respect his open-ended sentence reminds one of the inconclusiveness of *Ulysses* itself. Instead of a complete predication that confirms origin and identity, the ambivalence of *Ulysses* points to the meaning of predication and structure. *Ulysses* is the story of story.

Joyce ends, then, where Dickens begins, with obscurity. The

---

[41]*Anti-Oedipus.* I am quoting from Arno Munster, "Psychoanalysis and Schizoanalysis: An Interview with Félix Guattari," *Sémiotext(e)* 2, 3 (1977), 77–86.

Dickensian use of the pen as the instrument for uncovering and tracing order is almost inverted by Joyce. The pen is used to try and scratch out the clear demarcations, the brackets and boundaries that create an illusion of absolute presence but also exclude the "other." For Joyce the pen is not a symbol or instrument of the logocentric cultural order, nor is it the masculine phallus or one of its erect substitutes. In *Finnegans Wake,* a text riddled with references to letters, ALP's mamafesta may be taken as an image of the text itself. ALP, indicated in Joyce's notes by the Greek uppercase delta, is associated with flow and feminity. It is a curiously unorthodox symbolization of authority which will be examined more closely in the next chapter.

7

The Syntax of Return:

"Still an Idea behind It"

> The only possible step that remains is to stand on the very
> ground from which logic arose and to overturn it.
> —Heidegger, *An Introduction to Metaphysics*

The ambivalence of *Ulysses* precludes the possibility of reading it as the mirror of a stable, unified reality outside itself. There is no single origin outside the text to anchor and fix its meaning, since the idea of origin was erased as the verbal cosmos came into existence. Though the reader, beginning with the allusion of the title, receives many suggestions about how to decode the text, none of them leads to a unified view. The mirror of Joyce's fiction displays a host of random scratches that mockingly refuse to center on any imago projected by the reader's viewpoint. The semantic ambivalence of the text, its deconstruction of the traditional logos, subverts the validity of all interpretations and all metalanguages or discourses in which a unified interpretation might be rendered. Whoever dares "to explain" *Ulysses,* will eventually discover that the strategy of exclusion, of choice, always necessary to arrive at intellectual validity and logical coherence has already been subverted by the incorporative stance of the text itself. *Ulysses* precludes mastery by interpretation, and whoever engages the text with the traditional aim of making coherent sense of it will eventually come face to face with Joyce's mocking signature. Of course, this is a feature long recognized by such sensitive readers of Joyce as Fritz Senn, who instituted a practice of reading which does not aim at mastery or totalization but patiently follows the antithetical weavings of Joyce's webs, delighting in paradox.[1]

Less versatile critics, however might be reduced to a state of paralysis similar to that of the inhabitants of Joyce's Dublin. Certainly, the inclusiveness of the text raises a question about my argument. How is it possible to persist in discussing *Ulysses* as family romance—even in the context of what seems a history of family romance—once one is forced by its peculiar organization to recognize that *Ulysses* is a deconstruction of the family romance, a decreation that seems to suggest that epigenetic models are based on preconceptions of patriarchal presence.

Let me repeat that my overall aim is not to sketch the process of a linear development, of direct and causal continuity. If the gist of this chapter is to demonstrate that a designation of single origin ultimately also informs *Ulysses*—however much the text may try to elude the determination of traditional epigenetic structures—it is because I want to show that fictional representation always implies an argument about the nature of reality, even when the text tries to undercut traditional notions of origin. Instead of arguing the continuous historical development of the story of origin, I wish to emphasize its ubiquitous necessity for meaning. Even if the text erodes the notion of single origin in its attack upon the logic of noncontradiction, what we are presented with will eventually prove a revised view of origin, another, newer conceptualization, never a *Darstellung* without order. In the previous chapter I suggested that Joyce's strategy of questioning the logos showed affinity with the insights of Derrida, presenting the possibility of applying the results of an analysis that follows the Derridean argument. If Joyce suggests a revision of the conceptualization of origin, that same conceptualization may very well inform and underlie the deconstructive stance of Derrida. It is a question to which we shall return later.

First let us proceed with the analysis of *Ulysses*. The effect of Joyce's deconstructive text is to force his reader to a deconstructive

---

[1]See Senn, *Joyce's Dislocutions: Essays on Reading as Translation,* ed. John Paul Riquelme (Baltimore: Johns Hopkins Univ. Press, 1984).

method of reading. If we do not want to fall victim to intellectual paralysis, we must turn the weapon of the text against itself. Instead of the traditional questions "What does it mean?" or "How does it work?" the Joycean text and, as I implied, the Derridean one, too, suggest another query: "What is the rationale of the otherness of the text?" What makes it possible, desirable, or necessary to create texts that pervert the logos by a self-inscription of the "other"? Or in more specifically literary terms, what allows a text both to belong to a genre and to destroy the idea of genre from within, to tell a story and to alert the reader to the artifice of "character," the violence of "plot," the idealism of the structure of family romance? What I shall analyze, then, is no longer the shape of family romance *in* Joyce's writing but the family romance *of* his writing, how the syntax of his text constitutes a return to the idea of the (m)other. But in order to do that, I must trace my way back to the ending of the novel.

In referring to the ending of *Ulysses* in the previous chapter, I tacitly avoided choosing between the meeting of Stephen and Bloom and Bloom's homecoming as the conclusion of the story. If anything, I have privileged the father-son plot. The reader may object that there is an additional chapter that presents itself as the ending of the fiction, but my hesitancy was not without justification or precedent. Karen Lawrence concludes *The Odyssey of Style* with "Ithaca." A. Walton Litz calls "Ithaca" "the end of *Ulysses* as novel and fable" and attributes symbolic significance to the dot, the period that concludes the chapter: "'La réponse à la dernière demande est un point,' Joyce instructed the printer on his typescript, and that point contains a double meaning. As a full-stop it marks the conclusion of Bloom's day, the terminus of the novel's literal action, but as a spatial object it represents Bloom's total retreat into the womb of time, from which he shall emerge the next day with all the fresh potentialities of Everyman. Like the Viconian *ricorso,* the final moment of 'Ithaca' is both an end and a beginning."[2] Indeed, in a letter to Harriet Shaw Weaver, Joyce himself suggested, not without justification, that "Ithaca" was "in

[2]"Ithaca," in *James Joyce's "Ulysses,"* ed. Hart and Hayman, p. 404.

reality the end as *Penelope* has no beginning, middle or end."[3] "Penelope," as memory, reflection, and dream, may seem to stand outside the sequence of events of the history. But is the depiction of action (events in time) the real meat of a novel? If "Penelope" stands outside the action, Molly's memories significantly add to the reader's insight into the events of the day. Molly's last word ends the representation of Dublin, even if it does so in an act of seeming recapitulation. In fact, one might make a convincing case that the fabula of *Ulysses* itself is twined, that Stephen's quest for a father is placed next to Bloom's quest for a (m)other, and that each of the two strands has its own conclusion—hence the doubleness of the ending.

Instead of thus naturalizing Joyce's ambivalence, which extends itself even to the notion of the ending, I want to investigate the structural function of "Penelope" in the syntax of the novel as text. Why the repetition? What justifies or necessitates the extension of the story with a chapter staging the "other"—a chapter of words rather than action, of fantasy rather than fact, of libido rather than ratio?

My suggestion is that "Penelope" should be seen as the *mise en abîme* of the otherness, the difference, of *Ulysses* itself. As a *ricorso* it is self-contained, separated from the action. It presents itself as an afterthought, an "ek-static" supplement to the main body of *Ulysses*. Still, even if "Penelope" stands outside and apart, the flow of its language, transgressing the boundaries set by syntax and decorum, continues the stylistic practice of the text as a whole. In fact, it presents it in a concentrated and heightened form. We might say that "Penelope," by repeating, clarifying, and intensifying the style of writing in the body of the text, affirms and signs the alterity of *Ulysses*.

As I have already suggested, the most striking stylistic quality of Molly's monologue is its absence of traditional punctuation. The flow of the eight sentences (8 as symbol of the Virgin Mary, as well as the lemniscate denoting infinity) is often read, as Joyce said

---

[3]Letter of October 7, 1921, from *Letters of James Joyce,* ed. Stuart Gilbert (London: Faber and Faber, 1957), p. 172.

he intended it to be read, as the representation of the "other," as feminine language—alogical, flowing, inconsequential, and in every way the opposite of the masculine logos of predicative meaning. However, if we forgo a mimetic view of the figure of Molly and try instead to define her syntactic function in the texture of words—the text called *Ulysses*—Molly's language proves more than the speech of a woman or even the idea of woman. Undermining the possibility of discrimination, distinction, and denial, "Penelope" suspends the either/or of logic into a both/and (or neither/nor) as well as an or/rather. But the preclusion of distinct meaning and identity, though embodied differently in "Penelope," is the characteristic quality of *Ulysses* as a whole. Thus the final chapter is not only different from the body of the text in that it stands outside as a *ricorso*, it is simultaneously the continuation, almost the summary apotheosis, of the text's earlier self-inscription of the other. "Penelope" presents the concentrated essence of the style of the text, and its achievement retrospectively affirms and confirms the otherness of the work as a whole in structure, style, and theme. "Penelope" presents itself as both the capstone and the cornerstone of *Ulysses*, its arche and its telos.

It might, therefore, be interesting to have a closer look at Molly's style. The style of otherness of the language attributed to her may teach us about the otherness or the idea of the "other" of the text as a whole and about the dependence of the latter on the former. And since we are engaged in an analysis of Molly's style as a figure for the style of *Ulysses*, it may be most appropriate to concentrate on those "Mollyisms" that are to be found not in "Penelope" but in the main body of the text.

It is Molly's husband Leopold who lovingly remembers the typical quality of his wife's style in "Lestrygonians": "Met him pike hoses she called it till I told her about the transmigration. O rocks!" (VIII, 112–14). Apparently, Molly asked Bloom to explain the meaning of the word *metempsychosis*. Wanting to know, to possess a word—the logos—is a common preoccupation of the major characters in the novel, but unlike Stephen, who desires an apocalyptic word, Molly is not interested in a revelation of meaning to redeem the obscurity of quotidian life. Nor does she desire learning, power, or transcendence. What she wants are "plain words," and I am inclined, in view of Joyce's predilection for puns, to read "plain" as also designating the geographical opposite of the high place of epiphany. Molly, then, does not desire epiphany; on the contrary, she seeks liberation from the obfuscation of meaning brought about by a logocentric culture. Thus the word *metempsychosis,* one of the leitmotivs of the novel and a term that haunts Bloom, the reincarnated Ulysses, throughout the day, is rendered in four plain English words—plain, because the ordinariness of these words deflates the connotations of intellectual and social rank clinging to the Greek term. Molly turns Greek into the speech of an uneducated Irish housewife, just as Joyce turns the Greek epic into an Anglo-Irish novel. Moreover, these words are plain because they redirect the reference to a transcendent signified, an intangible mystery of the soul, to common, familiar English words already in use in Anglo-Saxon days, referring to the piece of clothing covering the least spiritual part of the body. It is as if Molly's "voicing" of the written word of the text—making it at once different and the same—echoes it in such a deflatingly revealing way that we seem to overhear the uncanny voice of original otherness, an otherness outside *doxa,* subverting the fixity of conventional meaning in an obliquely sly, knowing way. We might regard "met him pike hoses" as a rendering of the unconscious of "metempsychosis," and take Molly's voice as that of the "other," a Joycean "other," predicating origin not as a transcendent presence but, if at all, as material, physical, organic.

Indeed, Molly has an uncanny way of dislocating the meaning of logocentric icons.[4] The abbreviations IHS and INRI, both denoting Christ, the symbol of the logos, are rendered in Molly's speech as "I have suffered" and "Iron nails ran in" (v, 373, 374), thus fleshing out the letter of the sign denoting the spirit in terms of the physical effect of suffering. Similarly, the powerful presence of the masculine voice of Ben Dollard is reduced to a physical effect in referring to it as a "base barreltone voice" (VIII, 117–18). It is, of course, characteristic of Bloom, the least sexually chauvinistic of epic heroes, that he should lovingly explicate his wife's style: "He

---

[4]Freud's essay "The Uncanny," *Standard Edition,* vol. XVII, pp. 219–53, points to the element of repetition and recognition involved in the uncanny.

has legs like barrels and you'd think he was singing into a barrel. Now, isn't that wit. They used to call him big Ben. Not half as witty as calling him base barreltone. Appetite like an albatross. Get outside of a baron of beef. Powerful man he was at stowing away number one Bass. Barrel of Bass. See? It all works out" (VIII, 118– 23). Thus Bloom underlines Molly's understanding of voice as a "base" function of the physical, and the alcoholic spirit, and he confirms what our reading of "met him pike hoses" already suggested: Molly's native wit, her (m)othertongue, subverts the pretensions of presence and voice by pointing to their dependence on the physical, the material matrix.

In "Ithaca," the chapter of definition and of coming and bringing home, the peculiarity of Molly's language is related to a deficiency of mental development: "Unusual polysyllables of foreign origin she interpreted phonetically or by false analogy or by both: metempsychosis (met him pike hoses), alias (a mendacious person mentioned in sacred scripture)" (XVII, 685–87). From a conventional point of view Molly's style may, indeed, be considered uneducated (just as Joyce was considered underbred by Bloomsbury), but the point is that Molly's style rewrites polysyllables of foreign origin by decomposing them into simple, single words that have their own syntax and, in her rewriting, somehow still make sense, albeit a different kind of sense, a sense for which we might use the term *nounsense* provided by *Finnegans Wake*. The familiarity of Molly's "vulgar speech," however odd, cannily liberates "a sudden spiritual manifestation" of meaning "whether in the vulgarity of speech or of gesture or in a memorable phase of the mind itself"—to use the definition of epiphany in *Stephen Hero*)[5]—signifying by means of the subversion of conventional signification, affirming and denying the logos at once.

Thus Molly's style, even if the text presents it as a curiosity of the feminine mind, is important as the perhaps unwitting but more likely deliberate *mise en abîme* of Joyce's own "voicing" of *The Odyssey*, phonetically, by false analogy, and especially, by dislocation of syntax. It is Joyce who cries "O rocks" about homecom-

[5]*Stephen Hero*, ed. Theodore Spencer (New York: New Directions, 1959), p. 211.

ings and apocalyptic endings, who decomposes the unified voice of epic into eighteen distinct styles, most of them familiar from literary traditions or popular fiction but nevertheless uncannily new in the Joycean syntax. It is James Joyce who, like Molly Bloom, deflates the cultural prestige clinging to the idea of a transcendent signifier by pointing to the physical substrate of the idea of the spirit.

Molly's language is fascinating indeed, not only because it presents a highly suggestive portrait of a remarkable Irish housewife but also because it speaks of Joyce's notion of "feminine" language. I was tempted to extend this analysis of Mollyisms to "Penelope," but doing so would not have added much to the conclusion that Joyce's dislocation of the narrative tradition mirrors Molly's style, simultaneously weaving and unweaving, *Verneinend* and *Bejahend*. Indeed, this brief analysis of Molly's style should be sufficient to illustrate the three points I want to make: first, that "Penelope" and the other passages featuring Molly's style characterize her as an emblem of otherness; second, that the style of this otherness is a figure for the otherness of the text as a whole; third and most important, that this otherness is never absolute. It always remains and, to preserve intelligibility and meaning, must remain part of, enclosed within, conventional "educated" discourse. The discourse of the "other" is never truly other. It is always a variant of, and within, the dominant discourse. Thus Molly Bloom can never speak for herself as wholly other, not merely because she is Joyce's creature and the product of a masculine imagination but because a language of the essentially other, "alias" *écriture féminine,* is a logical impossibility. The original "other" (feminine) identity can *qua* identity not express itself in language, for language, after all, is the very instrument and constitution of the logos/logic of difference. Extending this conclusion to the otherness of *Ulysses,* one notes that just as Molly's voicing of Greek polysyllables is a dislocation within the bounds of signification, so *Ulysses* is a rewriting of the epic which, in deconstructing the tradition of narrative, remains within the boundaries of its genre. Just so the otherness of deconstructive readings, including this one, remains within the philosophical tradition of Western metaphysics.

Why is this important? What worries me is that *Ulysses* seems to suggest the futility and the logical impossibility of a discourse of the "other" and yet to depend for the coherence of its structure as fiction on the viability of the idea of making the "other" present in language. There is a clear suggestion in the text that Molly is indeed to be taken as the embodiment of essential otherness, a new view of original presence, not metaphysical but physical, flesh rather than spirit, womb rather than phallus, flow rather than logos. Instead of a long discussion to substantiate this conclusion, I shall just quote Frank Budgen, who said: "There is none of the coldness of an abstraction in Molly Bloom, but she is more symbolical than any other person in Ulysses. What she symbolises is evident: it is the teeming earth with her countless brood of created things."[6] But apart from the view of Molly as *Gea Tellus,* this suggestion is carried and underlined by the teleological structure of the fiction. Though *Ulysses* avoids the traditional happy ending of the circular quest and perverts the notion of a climactic *coniunctio oppositorum,* the fiction preserves a linear progression from episode to episode which implicitly lends pride of place to "Penelope." Popular prejudice holds that women must always have the last word, and "Penelope" is the overwhelming embodiment of that idea. "The last word (human, all too human) is left to Penelope" Joyce wrote to Frank Budgen in February of 1921, confirming the suggestion implied in the syntax of the text.[7] Thus, even if *Ulysses* subverts the epigenetic structure of knowledge and discovery which (re)constitutes original presence in classic plot, the syntax of the text nevertheless reveals the figure of Molly Bloom as an emblem of original presence. This suggestion of revelation is reinforced by Molly's language, which, as we have seen, is the fulfillment of the stylistic qualities of the Joycean text as a whole. Thus Molly's otherness functions at once as the end and the origin, the omega and alpha—in other words, the matrix—of *Ulysses.* And to the extent that it does, it violates the tenet that the "other" can never be known as self-present, as origin in and by itself. In fact,

---

[6] *James Joyce and the Making of "Ulysses"* (1934; rpt. Bloomington: Indiana Univ. Press, 1972), p. 262.

[7] *Selected Letters,* ed. Ellmann, p. 278.

Joyce seems to be shifting the locus of origin from a phallocentric logos to a hypostasis of the idea of the "other," the Word made Flesh, thus invertedly continuing the practice of Western metaphysics. *Ulysses* may be based not on the illusion of presence but on the dream of the realization of otherness through and within language.[8]

Indeed, Molly represents otherness as presence. It is because she herself embodies essential origin and truth that the fiction can characterize her as debunking received ideals and ideas of origin. Wondering about the word *arsenic,* she concludes that her husband would say "its from the Greek leave us as wise as we were before" (XVIII, 241–42). She is also beyond the need to postulate a point of absolute origin or beginning: "Who was the first person in the universe before there was anybody that made it all who ah they dont know neither do I so there you are" (XVIII, 1569–72). Thus her critique of the futility of the need to know and to have origins and hierarchies rests upon the understanding of Molly as already fully self-present, not in need of affirmation of identity. She can voice her charmingly ignorant feminine views because in the world of the fiction she is seen as *embodying* essential origin and truth, no longer the logos as spirit but the word become flesh.

Joyce's strategy of inverting the hypostasis of logocentrism into a seeming centrism of the female body, a "hysteracentrism," has unusual consequences for the image of woman in the text. *Bleak House* and *Tom Jones* were elaborate rhetorical structures for the expulsion and eradication of the qualities associated with womanhood: duplicity and irrationality in *Tom Jones* and subversion of the symbolic order in *Bleak House*. In contrast, *Ulysses* presents the feminine as the essence of presence, whose style and lack of ratio and logic are weapons to attack what the text depicts as mistaken illusions of patriarchal self-presence. Bloom's identification with Molly's witticisms, his secret glee at her lack of reverence, at-

---

[8]It is to be regretted that MacCabe does not detect the fallacy. Instead he reconfirms it by his own hypostasis of the "other" as the desire of the mother. His argument that *Ulysses* creates the "possibility of women's speech, the possibility of desire" (p. 56), proves to hinge on an allegorical personification of the opposition between classic realism (embodied in George Eliot, a woman writing like and as a man) and "writing" (represented by Joyce, a man writing the desire of woman).

tribute to her a power he lacks himself—the power and force to slay the suitors. Her final preference for her own impotent husband over the sexually and socially more powerful Blazes Boylan, vindicates Bloom as the new womanly hero.

At first sight, Joyce's celebration of this myth of womanhood would seem to make *Ulysses* the unique feminist vindication of the place of woman in the history of fiction. It redresses the fear and exclusion of the feminine in *Tom Jones* and *Bleak House* and lends to the idea of woman a power and function unprecedented in literary history. We might even consider that *Ulysses* inverts the structural roles of masculine and feminine in *Tom Jones*. If Allworthy is the unmoved mover of Fielding's novel, Molly Bloom, or the idea of womanhood in general, is the inert source of the action of *Ulysses,* its still point in a turning world. Foucault's analysis of Velazquez's painting *Las Meninas* comes to mind. Just as the king, though absent from the representation, is still its ordering principle, so Molly Bloom, representing the feminine principle, is the agent of action and attraction who moves the plot though she does not participate in it as major protagonist. Stephen's question "Was that then real? The only true thing in life? . . . *Amor matris:* subjective and objective genitive" (II, 143, 165) scintillates with meaning as the possible suggestion of the text as a whole—the feminine, the biological as true and ultimate "genitrix." The "hand that rocks the cradle" rules the world no less than it orders the structure of the fiction.

I have already intimated that this suggestion of the text is fallacious. The irony of human consciousness and human culture is that language cannot present a full and original identity. Either the suggestion of full presence and totality presented by a text rests upon a notion of totality outside the text which precedes and unconsciously informs it, or it is textually determined by means of the artful orchestration of logical opposites. Closer reading of the text shows that the image of Molly Bloom is, indeed, also mythic, because her character hinges on the ambivalent combination of contradictory qualities within the compass of one entity. If fairy tales are resolved and concluded by the timely and beneficent intervention of ambivalent "characters" who mediate between opposites, *Ulysses* is resolved by the presentation of a woman with phallic qualities, as Mark Shechner convincingly demonstrates in *Joyce in Nighttown*. As one of the incarnations of the Joycean stock figure of the "phallic mother," Molly Bloom, like ALP, Gretta Conroy, Bertha in *Exiles,* is what Stephen calls "an androgynous angel." She has the power of the word, which turns her into Joyce's—no less than Bloom's—agent of vengeance against masculine rivals and castrating females alike. Moreover, Shechner argues, the profusion of fetishes with which Joyce has fleshed out her character—shoes, stockings, drawers, gloves—serves as defense against the specter of femininity as token of castration. As I have implied, the point of my analysis is not the psychological constitution of the implied author of *Ulysses.* I am interested in Joyce's creation of the type of the "phallic mother" only to the extent that it helps us acquire insight into the general strategies of Western signification in the first decades of this century. What Shechner helps me see, then, is that Molly's sexual ambivalence allows her to function as the central agent of resolution of opposites in *Ulysses.* In her, as image and idea, the contradiction between male and female, fidelity and infidelity, nationalism and humanism, freedom and dependence, art and Ireland are resolved. Like "the grave, the womb, or the Freudian id," Molly contains no contradictions.[9] She is, indeed, the very symbol of reconciliation which stands, indifferent and neutral, above the limitations of masculinity or femininity as "sane full amoral fertilisable untrustworthy engaging limited prudent indifferent *Weib*. 'Ich bin das Fleisch das stets bejaht!' "[10]—where we notice that both nouns *Weib* and *Fleisch* are grammatically neuter.

What I especially appreciate in Shechner's psychoanalytic reading is that it does not succumb to the temptation to suspend rational insight, which the figure of Molly Bloom has represented for male and female critics alike. How easy it would be to conclude that Joyce redresses the exclusion of the idea of the feminine from the plot of patriarchy; to applaud Joyce as the true psychologist of woman, as Jung and many others have done; or more topically, to eulogize Joyce's liberation of the speech of female desire. To read

[9]See Shechner, p. 199.
[10]Budgen, p. 266.

Joyce in these ways, however, is to read through the lenses of desire. We can arrive at a more accurate definition of Joyce's signifying practice if we investigate Molly's ambivalent aspects a little more closely by taking another look at the function of the image of woman in the text.

One curious aspect of *Ulysses* is its continuous relation of woman to flowing water, especially the sea. In itself this metaphor is not unusual, but the ambivalence of Joyce's use of it certainly is. As Patrick Parrinder points out, *Ulysses* begins with the sea, "*Thalatta! Thalatta!* (I, 80), in relation to Stephen's mother, and concludes with "the sea the sea" (XVIII, 1598), as Molly's consciousness dissolves into dream.[11] Molly's thinking of the sea at the moment of surrender to sleep foreshadows the ending of *Finnegans Wake* where the river ALP flows into the ocean, the "cold mad feary father" (*FW* 628.2) at the moment of death. The peculiarity of *Ulysses* is that it combines two contradictory aspects that remain separated in *Finnegans Wake*. In *Ulysses* there is no distinction between water as fertile sea—"our great sweet mother (*la mer/la mère*)"—the source of life, and water as the cold and impersonal paternal ocean, the agency of death. For Stephen, his mother and the sea with which she is associated by symbolic identification stand for both the idea of nature as complex inexhaustible life and the threat of individual extinction through engulfment. The sea is at one and the same time Swinburne's "great sweet mother" (I, 78) and the "scrotumtightening" agent of castration. And if we try to reason this paradox away, ascribing it to the peculiarity of Stephen's psychological makeup, we find the constellation repeated in the consciousness of Leopold Bloom. For him, too, woman is at once the elusive Heraclitean *panta rhei* ("Woman. As easy stop the sea. Yes: all is lost" [XI, 641]) and *Lacus Mortis,* the Dead Sea in the Promised Land: "A dead sea in a dead land, grey and old. Old now. It bore the oldest, the first race. A bent hag crossed from Cassidy's, clutching a naggin bottle by the neck. The oldest people. Wandered far away over all the earth, captivity to captivity, multiplying, dying, being born everywhere. It lay there now.

---

11 "These Heavy Sands Are Language. . . . ," *James Joyce Broadsheet* 7 (February 1982), 1.

Now it could bear no more. Dead: an old woman's: the grey sunken cunt of the world." (IV, 222–27). Always woman is source of life *and* image of death. And the antidote to the horror of that final image is the paradoxical return to the vital, affirmative warmth of living female flesh. Thus the circularity of the structure of the text, which takes Molly's language as matrix and as final objective of signification, is mirrored in the ambivalent image of woman projected by the text.

Not only is she the source of both life and death, she also represents both the masculine and the feminine as locus of origin. This function is, perhaps, even clearer when we concentrate on the aspect of flowing. Rivers, seas, and oceans flow, and in *Finnegans Wake* ALP flows down from the mountain to the ocean—but not only ALP. Molly Bloom, too, is shown as a "flower." When her monthly period begins, she seems in the grip of a supernatural force flowing from her body: "O patience above its pouring out of me like the sea" (XVIII, 1122–23) or "O how the waters come down at Lahore" (XVIII, 1148). She recalls that her husband called her "flower of the mountain yes so we are flowers all a womans body yes" (XVIII, 1576). My conflation of the two possible pronunciations of *flower* is, of course, unorthodox. It is, however, not alien to Joyce's own punning sensibility, even if this pun is not upon the sound but upon the written symbol. My reading is suggested by the occurrence in the text of the words "Got your lett and flow" (XI, 861), which demand of the reader, who knows that the letter contains a flower, a conscious adjustment of his pronunciation. "Flow" in the sense of "stream" is also deliberately conflated with the first syllable of "flower" in: "Means something, language of flow" (XI, 297–98), while in an earlier chapter Bloom had identified language as flow in defining the essence of Shakespeare's blank verse: "The flow of language it is" (VIII, 65). At any rate, this conflation helps in understanding the semantic conflation of feminine and masculine qualities in the image of Molly Bloom. For Joyce, the notion of flow relates, on the one hand, to the flow of urine and to the nonerect penis—Bloom's "languid floating flower" (V, 571–72). On the other hand, it is associated with menstruation, the color crimson, and feminine fertility (the language of flowers is for Bloom the language of women). What we have, then, in Molly Bloom is not just the representation of a woman with masculine qualities. The complex of meanings related to *flower* suggests that Joyce is giving us a mythic or symbolic fusion of the notions of masculinity and feminity in the central, embracing image of the crimson flow of Molly's blood, the flow of fertility and life,[12] and that the supremacy of that image also affects the character of the male protagonists. If Molly is phallic, Bloom is Henry Flower, who identifies with his wife as the be all and end all: "My wife, I am" (xv, 777). Not only does *Ulysses* seem to shift the locus of the idea of origin from the paternal principle to the maternal principle; it simultaneously denies sexual difference. It banishes otherness in the *Darstellung* of the very idea of the "other." If Buck Mulligan lifts the chalice with the words "For this, O dearly beloved, is the genuine christine: body and soul and blood and ouns" (i, 21–22), his mockery of the saving blood of Christ seems to foreshadow Joyce's mythic celebration of the blood in the chamberpot as the transcendent annihilation of difference. Molly is the paternal and maternal instance of Joyce's fiction, or in another sense, she is Joyce's muse— the imaginary source of inspiration as well as its aim and end.

Thus Joyce's ambivalence, his struggle to unsettle the logos of difference, paradoxically proves in the final analysis to be inspired by a desire for totality and wholeness which, if not dependent on patriarchal repression, hinges on appropriation and assimilation as an oral incorporative strategy. Joyce can generate a deconstructive text like *Ulysses* because of his identification with the self-generated idea of woman as originally other, an idea that seems confirmed by the successful creation of the figure of Molly Bloom (forgetting that she is the product of language and imagination). The curious double echo of simultaneous affirmation and derision ringing in *Ulysses* may very well be due to the peculiar resonance of the uncanny place from and through which its author speaks. Is *Ulysses* ventriloquated through the womb of Molly Bloom? Is the idea of the mystery of the womb—the "incertitude of the void," of which both Bloom and Stephen, the masculine protagonists, are

[12]Shechner argues that *Ulysses* shows the displacement to language of the urinary and menstrual flow (p. 217). I find his explanation of Joyce's motivation as inspired by "menstruation envy" more convincing than Ellmann's symbolizing rapture in "Why Molly Bloom Menstruates," *Ulysses on the Liffey*, pp. 159–77.

acutely conscious (XVII, 1015, 1020) and which Molly need never acknowledge because she experiences the womb as fullness and flow—the mythic source of Joyce's fiction? Does Joyce, "a conscious reactor against the void of incertitude" (XVII, 2210–11), invade the womb to use it as a "portal . . . of discovery" (IX, 229)? However this may be, the fact is that the final episode of the novel, as well as the "last word (human, all too human)," is not just the "indispensable countersign to Bloom's passport to eternity," as Joyce argued,[13] it is at once the countersign, the affirmative repetition of the unique otherness of the text, which constitutes Joyce's passport to immortality as the author of *the* novel to deconstruct the logos of fiction. The idea of Molly Bloom is both effect and source of textuality. The word is with Molly and of Molly. The ambivalent phrase that preoccupies Stephen Dedalus, *amor matris,* may serve as catchword for the peculiarly incestuous quality of Joyce's authority, which conflates subject and object, self and other, masculine and feminine in *the idea* of the (m)other. As Marilyn French has written, Molly is "a symbol for the feminine principle as it exists in the mind of a feminate (androgynous) male."[14]

Thus, "Penelope," the "clou" of *Ulysses,* suggests that the denial of sexual difference is the rationale of difference of Joyce's text. In other words, the ultimate reality behind *Ulysses* may lie in a mythic vision of wholeness and totality transcending the common human reality of divisiveness, fragmentation, and incompletion. Indeed, the turn to androgyny, as Mircea Eliade points out in *Myths, Dreams, Mysteries,* is "an archaic and universal formula for the expression of *wholeness,* the co-existence of the contraries, or *coincidentia oppositorum.* More than a state of sexual completeness and autarchy, androgyny symbolizes perfection of a primordial non-conditioned state. . . . to say of a divinity that it is androgynous is as much as to say it is the ultimate being, the ultimate reality."[15] Since this vision of totality is imagined in terms of the

---

[13]Letter to Frank Budgen of February 28, 1921, *Selected Letters,* ed. Ellmann, p. 278.

[14]*The Book as World: James Joyce's "Ulysses"* (Cambridge: Harvard Univ. Press, 1976), p. 259.

[15]Eliade quoted in Angus Fletcher, *Allegory: The Theory of a Symbolic Mode* (Ithaca: Cornell Univ. Press, 1964), p. 356.

familiar figures of family romance, we cannot avoid the conclusion that *Ulysses,* for all its subversion of the classic plot of family romance, does not and cannot escape its determination. *Ulysses,* too, belongs to the category of family romance, but it no longer presents or stages the return to origin in the progressive development of the story. It enacts a version of family romance in its textual return to the idea of origin of its writing. I am referring not to the mimetic function of Molly as earth goddess but to the way the chapter embodying and staging her essence functions as be-all and end-all in the structure of Joyce's argument, as in W. Y. Tindall's words, "agent of reconciliation and its symbol."[16] The odyssey of *Ulysses* leads the reader to the vision of female viraginity as magical and original totality.[17]

In my discussion of *Tom Jones* I drafted a diagram to visualize the semantic configuration of the characters populating Fielding's family romance, noting that the opposition between Tom and Blifil was "resolved" by the expulsion of Blifil from Paradise Hall. The plot of *Ulysses* would not seem to lend itself to easy schematization. Yet there is the informative presence of two triangular configurations centering upon the two male protagonists in the fiction. The first triangle, consisting of two male rivals and a female figure to whom access is blocked, suggests itself in the first chapter, "Telemachus." Both Stephen Dedalus and Buck Mulligan want the favor of a maternal instance, a mother figure, variously embodied as the old milkwoman, Stephen's mother, and mother Ireland. The second triangle, which Joyce introduces in "Calypso," consists of Bloom, Boylan, and Molly.[18] And the

[16]*James Joyce: His Way of Interpreting the Modern World* (New York: Charles Scribner's, 1950), p. 37.

[17]This conclusion contradicts the findings of Robert Caserio in *Plot, Story and the Novel* and those of Frank Kermode, *The Sense of an Ending,* p. 113, that "*Ulysses* alone of these great works studies and develops the tension between paradigm and reality, asserts the resistance of fact to fiction, human freedom and unpredictability against plot. . . . We might ask whether one of the merits of the book is not its *lack* of mythologizing. . . . From Joyce you cannot even extract a myth of Negative Concord." Both Caserio and Kermode notice Joyce's refusal to continue the classic closure of family romance but fail to notice the subtler conceptual closure offered in the form of "Penelope."

[18]On triangulation in *Ulysses,* see, in addition to Ellmann's *Ulysses on the Liffey,* Jean-Michel Rabaté, "A Clown's Inquest into Paternity," in *The Fictional Father:*

interesting feature that emerges from a comparison of the two is that the two pairs of masculine figures show a similar semantic configuration. Each consists of a sensitive, artistic, and socially ineffective figure, ousted from his natural rights to female attention by a blatantly phallic, virile, vulgar, or blasphemous figure, who usurps his place. It is the old opposition between the man of action and the man of contemplation all over again, and it is possible to draft a semiotic square of the four male characters after all: two young ones, two mature ones; two men of the word, two men of action.

To do so, however, would be to go against the very gist of my argument in the previous chapter, in which I tried to show that Joyce escapes univocal semantic definition. The symmetry and rationality of *Tom Jones* seem to invite schematization to bring out the beautiful order of the fiction, but the simultaneous weaving and unweaving of *Ulysses* suggests that the very idea of stable structure is a falsifying simplification. *Ulysses,* as I read it, is a Modern text, and the application of a diagrammatic grid to it would be a reductive simplification of the text's ambivalence.

Still, *Ulysses* cannot and does not escape the determination of structure, though that structure is unusual. It is, predictably, the chapter titled "Penelope" that demonstrates this determination. There, the two triangles overlap in Molly Bloom's stream of consciousness and crystallize into the single triangle of Stephen, Bloom, and Molly, which Ellmann celebrates as a "human improvement upon the holy family as upon the divine trinity."[19] And indeed, the reader may feel disappointed to arrive at a seeming cliche after having scrutinized hundreds of difficult pages. Like John Eglinton in "Scylla and Charybdis" after hearing Stephen's abstruse interpretation of *Hamlet,* we might complain: "You are a delusion. . . . You have brought us all this way to show us a French triangle" (IX, 1064–65). But there is more to the connotation of the triangle. As James Maddox argues, "It may signify a pattern of relationships among characters (as in 'French triangle')

Lacanian Readings of the Text, ed. Robert Con Davis (Amherst: Univ. of Massachusetts Press, 1981), 89.

[19]*Ulysses on the Liffey,* p. 150.

or it may be a female symbol (as it is in the De Quincey pastiche in 'Oxen of the Sun')."[20] In the idea of Molly as symbol and "Penelope" as agent of resolution, both of these connotations fuse. Thus, a look at the semantic structure of the fiction confirms the conclusions of a deconstructive analysis: the final fusion of the two triangles is a symbolic resolution of the contradictions and oppositions presented in the fiction. It has its locus not in action and events but in imagination—Molly's (and, of course in this epic of mutuality, to a lesser extent also Bloom's) wishful thinking. What we notice, once again, is the use of the idea of the virago as a totalizing category subsuming all divisions and distinctions. Structurally, too, then, *Ulysses* can be understood as family romance, even if it shifts the locus of origin from a patriarchal to a seemingly matriarchal personification of the idea of origin. To use the words provided by *Finnegans Wake*, *Ulysses* as family romance, is the "primal made alter in the garden of Idem" (*FW* 263.20–25)— origin made other, but still within the compass of mythic self-identity, and predicated upon the imperialist invasion of the idea of the feminine.

As we saw in *Bleak House* and *Tom Jones*, the way a fiction structures and presents itself as family romance is inseparably related to or intertwined with the writers's conception of authority. Fielding explicitly derives justification for the extreme manipulation of his characters and events from the idea of a transcendent divine agency working toward the ultimate restoration of paradisal order; his act of writing imitates God's voicing of the book of nature. Dickens, too, enacts in his fiction the conceptualization of ultimate origin of the fiction as a mildly patriarchal restitution of order. His careful and patient detection of the hidden connections between events derives from the view that ultimate origin is temporarily obscured, though not beyond imaginative retrieval. The logical conclusion is that the peculiar incestuous nature of Joycean authority—always denying difference, conflating opposites, eroding logic—is likewise to be understood as the consequent enactment of the ambivalent idea of revisionary origin projected by the text.

---

[20] *Joyce's "Ulysses" and the Assault upon Character*, p. 194.

If we understand Joyce's curious authorial stance as collateral to the notion of origin in the text, our first gain is that Stephen's worries about gender and origin become significant. His desperate attempts to find an adequate conceptualization of his relationship to his father and mother becomes more than a single human being's coming to terms with the peculiarities of his family. Stephen Dedalus's struggles in "Proteus" and "Scylla and Charybdis" have a mythic dimension in that all by himself he is trying to solve the philosophical and religious problem of origin which has always beset Western consciousness: "Aristotle's experiment. One or two?" (IX, 297). Stephen's father and mother represent the paternal and maternal instance, and his stream of consciousness plays variations on the whole Western tradition of discourse relating to the conceptualization of origin and the problem of the One and the Two, in order to arrive at a satisfactory configuration.[21]

Stephen proves a child of his age, in that he no longer automatically identifies the paternal principle with ultimate origin. For him, paternity has become a "legal fiction," a "ghost" story to preserve the patriarchal law of order, or a mythic construction deriving authority from the legal documents or the institution of the law. To Stephen, truth appears related to evidence and sensual perception, and he calls the derivation from the mother the only certitude. Thus he tries to reverse the traditional position of Western metaphysics, which has always conceptualized ultimate origin as masculine. In the Christian story of origin, the creator is understood as a paternal agent. In the New Testament, the Holy Family may consist of Joseph, Mary, and Christ the Son, but the real, transcendent father is God, and Mary is no more than the vessel of transmission, a means of exchange. The rationale of this conceptualization is not difficult to understand. Our logos understands ultimate origin as a monistic singularity. If Mary, the means of material reproduction, were assigned autonomous presence, the self-identity of God would be threatened. Indeed, church history shows that even the shade of suggestion of nonspiritual presence

---

[21]See Mircea Eliade's discussion of the paradox implicit in mythological and religious views of origin in *The Two and the One,* trans. J. M. Cohen (New York: Harper and Row, 1969).

which the figure of Mary as mother of God entails was to be erased from consciousness when the triangle of father, mother, and child was overlaid with the articulation of the Trinity as Father, Son, and Holy Ghost, in which the role of material reproduction has been wholly suppressed. Thus origin is made wholly spiritual, self-identical, disembodied, and implicitly masculine.

Stephen's initial attempt to replace the orthodox myth of the father with a myth of the mother can be taken as a tribute to the importance of physical, material nature, but it constitutes an inversion of the locus of origin which does not solve the underlying logical problem: that the notion of origin will always break out of the corset of self-identity. The One is always made up of Two, or rather, of One plus Supplement. In fact, Stephen's version is probably even more reductive than the orthodox Christian one. If voice or spirit cannot be thought without embodiment, matter cannot be thought without mind.

Apparently, Stephen himself recognizes the reductiveness of his attempted revolution. To escape the deadlock, he invents a strategy that seems to me highly significant because it exemplifies Modern thinking (where I define *Modern* as understanding reality by analogy with the differential system of language) whether psychic, linguistic, or philosophical. I am thinking of Nietzsche, Peirce, Wilde, Freud, De Saussure, and more recently, Derrida and Lacan. Thus in "Oxen of the Sun," the chapter devoted to gestation, Stephen argues: "Mark me now. In woman's womb word is made flesh but in the spirit of the maker all flesh that passes becomes the word that shall not pass away. This is the postcreation" (XIV, 292–94). The unanswerable questions related to the conceptualization of origin are artfully dodged. The problem of relating a philosophical conceptualization of origin to biological difference is not resolved but shifts to a different level because ultimate reality is no longer understood as either transcendent or biological/physical but as textual and relative. Matter loses its substantiality to become sign. Flesh is a simple given, and is to be transformed into the word, or text. The author, not as physical being but as "spirit of the maker," fulfills a transformative or generative role similar to that of the womb and—this is very curious—embodies at one and the same time a newer version of the logos of Western tradition.

Instead of choosing between a paternal or a maternal instance as locus of origin—or wholly evading that choice—the mentalistic notion of a "postcreation" conflates logical opposites in assuming the maternal role for the spirit in a revisionary articulation of the logos as text.

As I said, Stephen's thinking about a "postcreation" is interesting because it seems to illustrate Joyce's own strategy perfectly. I have already argued that Joyce signs himself as at once spiritual father and mother of his text by identifying with the feminine function of transformation in the womb. This identification, too, is a usurpation and the denial of an autonomous role to the "other," though it is different from the strategy of total exclusion in church history, which replaced the triangle of the Holy Family with that of the Trinity. If all is spirit in the New Testament, in Stephen's Modernist gospel all creation—even material reproduction—is subsumed by the idea of an androgynous and dematerialized imagination. Indeed, the idea of the imagination as ultimate shaping spirit comes to replace the logocentric concept of a transcendent signifier. In Modern aesthetics the imagination is the ultimate reality and source of being, and imagination is styled androgynous. Thus Joyce "transcends" the dualistic polarity of masculine-feminine, patriarchy-matriarchy, matter-spirit by depriving them of essential status and suspending them in the medium of mind as spirit.

Ultimately, the Joycean configuration of the triangle of origin returns to the saving idea of spirit. His Mariolatry, his identification with the language of the "other," should not be understood as acceptance of the feminine as "other" and willingness to open up to the castrating threat of materialism. Joyce's experimentation with language and logos is not a tribute to a real womanhood of flesh and blood but has from its inception been rooted in the supremacy of the imagination over matter, language or text over physical presence. Like Pallas Athene, born of Zeus, Molly Bloom has sprung, full quivering flesh, from Joyce's imagination. If Molly is his muse, Joyce is simultaneously her creator and her son and heir. The circularity of Stephen's *amor matris* keeps offering itself as a metaphor for different aspects of Joyce's solipsism, and if we return to Stephen Dedalus and his obsession with the primal scene, we now notice that Joyce's strategy of dematerialization, of "refinement out of existence," to use the words of Stephen's theory of authority, has been preinscribed in the very terms that describe the primal scene in "Proteus": "Wombed in sin darkness I was too, made not begotten. By them, the man with my voice and my eyes and a ghostwoman with ashes on her breath" (III, 45–48). While acknowledging conception as the effect of sexual intercourse, Stephen disembodies his parents, refining them out of physical existence as "voice" and "ghost." In the final analysis, then, he does *not* take the biological tie with the mother as the principle of conceptualization. Stephen's theory of Shakespeare as "the ghost of his own father," his poetics in *A Portrait of the Artist,* is founded on the "mystical estate" of the idea of paternity. It is precisely because paternity does not offer concrete material evidence that Stephen can reverse the source of origin from transcendent to incarnate and can depict the artist's imagination, language, as the locus of the real. In sublimating sexual difference as text, Joyce "selfpens" his own origin. Unlike Dickens, who saw the pen as an instrument for ordering and clarifying an objectively existing reality outside the imagination and the psyche, Joyce uses the pen, still a phallic image, to squirt the text that *is* the real and the self.

Again, the analysis of the signifying practice of a single author provides insight into the implicit ideological motivation of an era in literary history. Joyce is the contemporary of Eliot, Pound, and Lawrence, the precursor of Beckett, O'Brien, Gaddis, Coover, Barth, Barthelme, Fowles (and even the poetics of Wallace Stevens and John Ashbery). Joyce was first and is still, perhaps, foremost in the attempt to use language not as medium of representation but as articulation or enunciation, as goal in itself; and it seems fair to take him as representative of Modern writing in general.

In an earlier chapter I argued that the symbolization of plot, its mediation of a radical opposition, created an illusion of wholeness and presence through partial reparation of the sense of loss of absolute presence inherent in human consciousness. This sense of loss, this desire for paradise characteristic of the conscious rational animal human being, can be characterized in biblical terms as the awareness of the Fall. Thus humanity's removal from the face of God is partially "redeemed" by the mediation of language and thought. Indeed, the circular quest of homecoming, the family romance, functions as psychological, sublimated restoration of what is felt as irrevocably lost. If *Ulysses* at first sight seems to deny and even mock that restorative or mediating function of plot, we are now in a position to realize that this fiction can only afford to do so because it has already displaced that function from plot to the very act of writing or signification. *Ulysses* celebrates the paradox of the Fortunate Fall no less than *Tom Jones,* but for Joyce it is not imitative action, mimesis, that restores the sense of presence; it is utterance, the Incarnation of the Word. Thus language, the token and consequence of the Fall, remains the unique remedy to suggest the symbolic healing of the breach between culture and nature, self and other, human being and God.

Conclusion

In writing *Ulysses,* Joyce revised the narrative tradition while uprooting the ground of mimetic fiction. In fact, his paradoxical strategy of writing, which unweaves the family romance, constitutes a practical deconstruction of the form long before French poststructuralist thought began to investigate the nature of narrative and its relationship to identity and culture. From within it, Joyce took up some threads and began to reweave the form to demonstrate its texture. The final result is that his web includes the doubleness or multiplicity that is normally hidden and should have remained repressed. After all, the exclusion from presence or consciousness of what is considered undesirable, or "other," had been the logos of the family romance. Family romance in its classic form is a structure, an instrument, to establish difference and hierarchy (as a secondary modeling of the oppositional structure of the logos). Joyce's writing, however, erodes the validity of both oppositional thought and hierarchical valorization. *Ulysses* demonstrates that difference and hierarchy are the effects of a relationship within and of the process of signification; the text steadily undoes the conventional severance between subject and object, model and copy, in returning the repressed. In short, Joyce's attitude toward plot and fiction is skeptical about the received understanding of narrative as *re*-presentation.

It is only recently that Joyce's implicit practice has found discursive articulation, suggesting that we may not have advanced much in our thinking beyond Joyce's ideas. T. S. Eliot said, "*Ulysses* is a book to which we are all indebted, and from which none of us can escape."[1] I might have concluded this investigation of the morphology of family romance on a similar note, but I want to do more than simply interpret a number of family romances. I am trying, however tentatively, to sketch the story of the functional relation of the genre to the Western individual's self-constitution as transcendent subject, arguing, moreover, that this story is itself a form of family romance. Though I have touched in previous chapters upon the context for Joyce's deconstructive mode, more needs to be said about it here. We cannot just conclude with Alan Friedman that the open-endedness of the novel is a "mutation in the form of the novel which corresponds to a mutation in the ends of culture."[2]

Over the cradle of the novel in Western Europe rises the shadow of *Don Quixote,* and most histories and theories of the genre begin with a discussion of Cervantes' fiction. Lukács, for example, in his *Theory of the Novel* relates the appearance of the novel to the historical loss of a quality he calls "unity of being," characteristic of the experience of life in epic times:

> Thus the first great novel of world literature stands at the beginning of the time when the Christian God began to forsake the world; when man became lonely and could find meaning and substance only in his own soul, whose home was nowhere; when the world, released from its paradoxical anchorage in a beyond that is truly present, was abandoned to its immanent meaninglessness; when the power of what is—reinforced by the utopian links, now degraded to mere existence—had grown to incredible magnitude and was waging a furious, apparently aimless struggle against the new forces which were as yet weak and incapable of revealing themselves or penetrating the world.[3]

Lukács describes a process of loss of presence and progressive alienation, a fall from a state of unity into divisiveness. After the

---

[1]Eliot, p. 268.

[2]*The Turn of the Novel* (New York: Oxford Univ. Press, 1966), p. xviii.

[3]Pp. 103–4. See also Erich Kahler, *The Inward Turn of Narrative,* trans. Richard and Clara Winston, Bollingen Series 83 (Princeton: Princeton Univ. Press, 1973), who points out the dependence of the genre on humanity's increasing interiorization of experience.

analysis of the structure and function of plot in these pages, it will not be difficult to see that Lukács has emplotted "the rise of the novel" as "the fall" of epic from full presence. Indeed, he has applied the epigenetic plot structure provided by Christian epic narrative to the history of the novel in order to account for its essence. Lukács's thinking in *The Theory of the Novel* clearly derives from the German idealist tradition of the nineteenth century, and we now see his strategy of emplotment as a fictional device of troping order which need not necessarily convey truth.

As I have said, the state of unity which Lukács needs to project into the past to explain the present seems to me the mythic construction of a *tempus aureus,* preserving the desire for magic fusion with Mother Nature, but his insights into the ontological motivation of the form have been confirmed by our readings. Each of these fictions not only projected a state of alienation, division, and fall; it also constituted a novel attempt at overcoming that situation through the exercise of the imagination. We should not discard idealist histories of the development of the novel, then, because we no longer "believe" in epigenetic structures of order. Though the general *figura* of emplotment may not receive our intellectual endorsement, Lukács's articulation of the strategy of fiction and the ontological condition it addresses may still be illuminating. Instead of picturing the history of the novel as a progressive falling off from Edenic unity, we may revise our conceptualization in accord with our modern sense that language, even in epic times, probably never embodied full presence. Thus we might conceptualize the general form and function of the novel as a series of repetitive reenactments of acts of articulation directed at overcoming a breach or lack in reality, the awareness of which is concomitant with consciousness itself. Hence our excursion through the past would not be a journey toward one great goal or the progressive estrangement from paradise and the father but a trek in the desert without known beginning or end.

With this conceptualization, we detach our account from the idea of progress or fall. We also loosen the specific bounds of the genre as idea. As a "secular scripture" (turning again to Northrop Frye's term for romance), the novel may now be seen to reenact for its era what the Bible or the religious epic accomplished in

earlier times. Thus the difference in function between secular and
sacred writing proves to be not absolute but a difference in social
denomination. The novel may not be the pathetic reflection of "a
world without God" as Lukács wished to see it. On the contrary,
its vital continuity is proof of the inherent human need to affirm,
to reaffirm, the desire for presence (even if presence seems to
manifest itself as absence) and testifies to endless human creativity
in imagining new forms, new images to embody this desire. The
novel has housed the Western notion of the self and its predication
upon contemporary ideas of presence, just as our temples and the
evolutions of architectural style have housed our ideas of God.

What I have tried to show is that the success, the credibility of
this embodiment in language of the human desire for presence has
rested upon a double strategy of representation. The division of
consciousness—the rift in the real (the Fall) which is itself the
occasion or impulse for speech—is projected upon the narrative
structure as a logical contradiction. In the course of the act of
narration, that contradiction is somehow resolved. In addition to
this embodiment of its own occasion, the novel has always given
the problem of dualism (or desire) a local habitation and a name,
very often by using sexual difference as a metaphor for the logical
opposition between presence and absence, order and disorder,
which is the basis of thought. The metaphor of woman (standing
for the undesirable "other," the threat to full self-identity) has
been the repressed center of the novel.

The novels I have discussed, novels epic in scope and intention,
are rewritings *sub specie temporis illi* of that most ancient and most
venerable story of all: the story of the origin of the cosmos, of
nature, of man, woman, and evil. And just as Genesis struggles to
account for the presence of dualism or evil in God's Paradise—
assigning the burden of otherness to Eve—the novel has exerted
itself to trace the way back to the full presence of Paradise Hall, to
return the two to the one, the "other" to the same, Eve to Adam's
rib.

From the vantage point of a Modern understanding, the different rewritings of the primal scene of Genesis reveal themselves as
paradoxical attempts to turn language against itself. Language is a
medium, a sign, and shares the characteristic quality of the sign: it

can be used to lie. In writing narrative to establish self-identity, to fix truth, and to repress the presence of the "other"—the patriarchal project—language was engaged in illusionary denial of its own mediating nature. Indeed, if there is a difference between Joyce (and us), on the one hand, and Fielding and Dickens, on the other, it may be that the latter two wrote in what is nowadays sometimes called "the epoch of presence," the period from Descartes to Nietzsche, which constituted self-presence by means of the split into conscious and unconscious, suppressing otherness. Their use of the family romance, therefore, may perhaps have carried powers of conviction which are no longer available to our ironic, Modern consciousness, which has devised the primal scene as the scene of writing.

As I noted in my reading of *Ulysses,* the twentieth century no longer seems to want to repress or exclude otherness. Instead the "other," as nature, woman, and language (the media for patriarchal self-presence), takes center stage. Duplicity, the connotation of woman and the sign, is no longer feared but celebrated as a new version of essential reality; in a dialectical reversal the vehicle has become the focus. Has this reversal occurred because Western imperialism has exhausted the possibilities of subjection? Have the ugly effects of industrialization suggested the ideal of pristine nature? Or has the drive to conquer nature led to the paradoxical overvaluation of human media? One may speculate about causes; all I dare say is that the inscription of woman as the image of immanent presence (however elusive) has become predominant in Modern discourse. We nowadays witness unprecedented genderization of the rhetoric of philosophy, literary criticism, and fiction—not to mention advertising or journalism. The metaphor of sexual difference (which, according to Modern theory, has no objective existence) seems to have become *the* explanatory principle. Indeed, the "other" is fallaciously used as image of the "Other." Thus the Modern contradicts itself.

It is a feature of contemporary discourse which is hailed by some feminist critics as a step forward in the struggle for social equality. Thus, Carolyn Heilbrun writes, "Poststructuralism, indeed, has taken over the feminine as one of its major metaphors, going beyond the impasse between feminism and structuralism, challenging what Derrida has called 'credulous man, who, in support of his testimony, offers truth and his phallus as his own proper credentials.'"[4] It should be clear by now that I do not share Heilbrun's optimism about the presence of woman in contemporary literature and philosophy. Though it assigns significance to the metaphor of woman as the ever-elusive "other," this embrace·of otherness remains an almost self-destructive act of defense on the part of patriarchy. It does not and cannot say anything about woman as nonsymbolic, historical being. She is disembodied, etherealized as text. Modernity, moreover, reduces the complexity of woman's being in the world as both *anthropos* (human being) and *gyne* (sexual creature) to a merely sexually determined identity.

The problem is compounded when female writers also resort to the metaphor of woman. Virginia Woolf's projection of Clarissa Dalloway and especially Mrs. Ramsay as symbols of unity transcending life and death (hostess, mother) does not use woman's body or her experience of the sexual act as vehicle but resorts to the idea of woman's social role. More recent writers, however, especially the French, explicitly feature the female body as ground of textuality. Thus Hélène Cixous celebrates the mother's voice, open-ended and flowing; Luce Irigaray uses the image of female genitalia as double and other in themselves and perpetuates the association with flow. Julia Kristeva, finally, sees Freud's archaic father as a pre-Oedipal, androgynous mother. While she does not resort to the image of the female body, she nevertheless employs the metaphor of gender. At first sight, a woman's use of the sexual metaphor may seem less exploitive than a man's, since it is used as vehicle for female authority, but this practice cannot escape implication with the denotative value femininity still has in our culture.

In other words, as the detailed analysis of *Ulysses* in an earlier chapter demonstrated, it would be simplistic to take the apparent celebration of feminine sexuality (groundless and indeterminate, as the myth goes) as expressing the demise of logocentrism, even in

---

[4]"Women, Men, Theories, and Literature," *Profession 81: Selected Articles from the Bulletin of the Association of Departments of English and the Association of Departments of Foreign Languages* (Spring 1985), 28.

texts produced by female authors. Instead of a surrender to the hegemony of flesh and matter, the sheer obsessiveness of the concern with gender and the body may also be taken as a magic gesture of self-defensive warding off. Out of fear of total calamity, human beings have invented the ritual of sacrifice—giving a little in order to keep or acquire more. Joyce's inscription of the "other" as flesh may be such a self-protective gesture, aimed at laying the specter of spiritual annihilation. In signing woman as flesh, Joyce still implicitly aims at signing himself spirit or *Geist*. The discourse of sexuality (and woman as the embodiment of nature) remains the invention or discovery of the patriarchal logos. It rests upon the spiritual creativity of the imagination and may even present itself, as in the case of Freud and Krafft-Ebing, as objective "science." An ironic proof is given by the latter. The *Psychopathia Sexualis* begins by citing Maudsley to provide a justification for its interest in deviant sexual practice. The gist of this reference is that the sexual instinct is important because without it all poetry and morality would vanish![5] Interest in the flesh is in the service of the spirit. One may conclude that Joyce's apparent celebration of female sexuality is not an acceptance of castration, as some critics hold, but a ritual gesture of self-protection, of salvaging the logos. This gesture relates to total catastrophe as circumcision relates to castration. Joyce's ambivalence is deconstructive but also magical, meant to preserve the idea of the spirit, and it shares this intention with Modern thought in general.

It should not be thought that the problems of origin, identity, and authority of *Tom Jones* and *Bleak House* have been overcome or eradicated in the course of the past two hundred years. There have been shifts and variations in embodiment and expression, but the problem of the logos—of the self-identity of the One and the conceptualization of origin—remains the underlying invariable. *Ulysses*, too, is a fiction written against the threat of meaninglessness, the annihilation of order and identity. This threat is not only evident in Bloom's castration fears—as his companions say, he cannot put it out of sight. Nor is it just Stephen Dedalus's fear of

[5](Stuttgart: Enke, 1894), p. 1.

water and drowning. *Ulysses* identifies womb with tomb, woman with death, and what this death, as specter, might entail is suggested at unexpected moments, for instance when Stephen Dedalus muses about (female) human lives that are aimless like seaweed: "Under the upswelling tide he saw the writing weeds lift languidly and sway reluctant arms, hising up their petticoats, in whispering water swaying and upturning silver fronds. Day by day: night by night: lifted, flooded and let fall. Lord, they are weary; and, whispered to, they sigh. Saint Ambrose heard it, sigh of leaves and waves, waiting, awaiting the fullness of their times, *diebus ac noctibus iniurias patiens ingemiscit.* To no end gathered; vainly then released, forthflowing, wending back: loom of the moon" (III, 461–68). Underlying the identification of woman with death is the fear of loss of pattern, order, and the meaning of human existence, of being "to no end gathered." It is the fear of the loss of plot and of the concurrent loss of the closure that institutes meaning. The feminine is identified with the endless, meaningless weavings of the "loom of the moon." Joyce's own signifying practice of open-endedness and deconstruction, then, can be seen as an act of magic imitation to defer the threat of total loss of pattern. For all its celebration of indeterminacy, Modernity remains ambivalent.

In a previous chapter I took the analogy between Derrida and Joyce as pretext. From a strictly historical point of view, Joyce's text should be seen in the context of Freud, Jung, Krafft-Ebing, and the other writers of the beginning of this century who used the metaphor of woman to propose a new model for understanding reality and the self. In fact, the aspect of *Ulysses* which received most public attention in the first decades of this century is its obscenity. In his revelation of the scandal of, especially, female sexuality, Joyce was representative of the epoch. Indeed, if we want to place *Ulysses* in a cultural-historical context, we should choose not Modern philosophy but the rise of the new *Sexualwissenschaft*. Freudian psychoanalysis, which takes sexual functioning as the reflection of psychic maturation, might also be a more appropriate context. At any rate, Jung's well-known comments that "the 40 pages of non stop run in the end is a string of veritable psychological peaches. I suppose the devil's grandmother knows so much about the real psychology of a woman, I didn't."[6] seem an emphatic confirmation that contemporary readers understood Joyce's creation of Molly as flesh as a revelation of truth. The information Ellmann gives about Joyce's comments about women lead one to suspect that for Joyce himself, too, the *Darstellung* of Molly was as an act of lifting the hem of truth.

And once we suspect that Joyce's invention of Molly in *Ulysses* may have been the expression of a Zeitgeist, perhaps not an English one but one deriving from Central Europe, we recognize that Joyce was not alone in turning to the figure of woman to embody and legitimize the inscription of an idea of ontological otherness— fleshing out what is and can never be more than a trace. The metaphor of woman as device for the inscription of otherness within the text is fairly common and occurs in Continental European literature, philosophy, and the visual arts of the second half of the nineteenth century and the early part of the twentieth. In philosophy Nietzsche used woman strategically as figure of groundlessness. (Earlier, Hegel had identified woman with the life of the family—a less developed, unconscious form, existing in contrast with the greater self-consciousness of civil society.)[7] Psychoanalysis presented itself as the science of the "other"—it began as the study of hysteria, the illness of the womb—and attempted to demonstrate the influence of the unconscious upon conscious behaviour. The question "What is the rhetorical function of the Irmas, Annas, and Doras in Freud's theory of the unconscious?" still needs full analysis, perhaps in the context of a wider study of how Freud's views on sexuality relate to the widespread practice of inscribing the "other" as woman in German and Austrian art and thought of the turn of the century. I am thinking of Weininger's insistence upon male and female as irreconcilable principles of being; Kokoschka's plays, which stage love as a battle between a higher, spiritual essence (Factor Man) and a lower, animal essence (Factor Woman); Schnitzler's female creations, for instance,

[6]Quoted in Ellmann, *James Joyce*, p. 629.
[7]See Lloyd, "Hegel: The Feminine Nether World," in *The Man of Reason*, pp. 80–86.

Fräulein Else. Is not her rhetorical function to lend reality to the idea of an unconscious? Did Freud not write to Schnitzler to acknowledge that literature had been prior in its discovery of the truth of the complexity of the human psyche? Even Klimt's femmes fatales or such of his images of heroic womanhood as the *Nuda Veritas* are, as recent scholarship argues, instrumental projections of otherness in the artistic inscription of the self-identity of the painter.[8] Indeed, it is not difficult to see a relationship between Joyce's depiction of Molly as both flower and flesh and Egon Schiele's drawings of woman as at once flower and human figure. The Art Nouveau heritage of using woman as symbol, which had come to Germany from England in Arthur Symons's study of women in the art of Aubrey Beardsley,[9] may well provide the best general cultural context for the practice of the inscription of otherness as nature in the figure of woman as flesh, as we have noticed it in Joyce.

As the Introduction pointed out, this is not a feminist book in the received sense of the word. From a Modern point of view classic feminism is the reverse imitation of phallogocentrism. This is not to say that one should desist from articulating the limitations of Modern thought, but such articulation can do very little toward changing the actual historical circumstances under which most women in this world live. Moreover, the personification of woman as the "other" in Modern discourse can be read as a reconfirmation of the social status quo, even though it is not intended as such. Thus Derrida's implicit personification of the "other" as woman in *La carte postale*—an "other" only once, I think, named "Bettina" but addressed as beloved and given such traditionally feminine attributes and functions as waiting at home with dinner—may be intelligible as a trope to the sophisticated reader. Others may fail to understand the double coding of this text, since its personification of the "other" revives the time-honored cliche of woman. Moreover, the reader may fairly wonder why Derrida must use the image of woman as metaphor. Is there no other symbol that might

[8]See Michael Pabst, *Wiener Grafik um 1900* (Munich: Schreiber, 1984), pp. 104–91.

[9]"Das Weib in der Darstellung Aubrey Beardsleys," *Ver Sacrum* 6 (1903), 117.

convey the mystery of transference, the mediated ek-stasis of the self? Is not the use of gender as metaphor still implicitly dependent on the patriarchal tradition of *using* woman as a medium for the constitution of subjectivity?

Indeed, there is a question about the use of woman as metaphor for the inscription of the "other" which must be asked but beyond which we cannot advance. If, as poststructuralist writing has taught us, the "other" can never be present in language except as trace, does not the essentially literary practice of personifying the "other" as woman, of sending picture postcards rather than letters, always entail a paradoxical denial of its own argumentation that language does not and cannot incarnate presence? Moreover, does this practice not rest upon a new idolatry, a mystique of sexual difference as ontological presence and ultimate truth? Finally, does it not continue the patriarchal project of making woman text? The Modern strategy of using woman as metaphor for the critical relationship to logocentrism may be more sophisticated than Rembrandt's use of Eve as image, but it seems very similar and suggestively reminiscent of the contemporary use of the figure of woman in advertisements.

It will not surprise the student of Joyce's text that even these questions are preinscribed in *Ulysses*. In an attempt to prove and establish his own identity, a false Ulysses presents a picture postcard in "Eumaeus." The "printed matter" on it reads: "*Choza de Indios. Beni. Bolivia*" (xvi, 475). The image, however, presents "a group of savage women in striped loincloths, squatted, blinking, suckling, frowning, sleeping amid a swarm of infants (there must have been quite a score of them) outside some primitive shanties of osier" (xvi, 475–79). Thus the signifier, the written text that defines and determines the meaning of the image, presents it as an "Indian hut" (*Choza de Indios*). But the message of the text seems to differ from the image, which foregrounds the savage women and children. Thus the letter, the signifier, does not (re)present the visual image in words but displaces it in presenting it as a product of human culture—a building. This subtle discrepancy between signifier and signified might be understood as suggesting that the signifier, the personification, can never coincide with the wild originality of the signified, which must always remain "other." It would be a very appropriate reading of a passage in a chapter that centers on the obliqueness of the relationship between language and reality, name and person. (Since the name of the addressee does not corroborate the identity of the owner, it is almost as if the text suggests not only that writing is used as the seal of identity but that this seal rests upon convention, not truth, since the text can also be the vehicle of the lie.)

But the function of the presence of the picture postcard in the drama of "Eumaeus" proves to be different. The men in the shelter who get to see it do not raise philosophical questions about identity and language as I have done here. To a man, "all focussed their attention at the scene exhibited" (xvi, 475). Even if the twentieth century has revised the primal scene and reimagined it as a scene of writing, that revision has done little to change the traditional identification of woman as object and mediator of desire—rationalized as instinctive and natural. The function of the image of woman as primitive source of life in "Eumaeus" is to lend "natural," immediate, and autonomous interest to the postcard, independent of philosophical problems of the inscription of identity. The power of attraction of the image of woman—woman as nature—subverts reflection by titillating.

We might interpret the presence of the postcard in *Ulysses* as one more of Joyce's many self-reflexive ironies. Even so, this oblique juxtaposition of word and image on a postcard held up by a false Ulysses, should warn us of the dangers of personifying the "other," whether as an old man with a beard or as the new Eve. The question Joyce's postcard asks in all but words is whether Modern thought, with its style of personifying the "other" as female and sprinkling the text with terminology and imagery relating to sexual difference, is not "always already" having "it" both ways.

Finally, have we not come face to face here with the question of the novel itself? Do we still expect to read fiction that attempts to incarnate the "other" in family romance? Now that we have grown so acutely aware of language as sign, what will be the future of the novel? Thus, inquiry into the function of the metaphor of woman leads us back to the more general theme of the function of plot in the generic identity of the novel and the future of the genre. First we noted that whereas the structure of the family romance seems to have undergone a development between 1750 and 1922, the use of the metaphor of woman as symbol of that which a cultural epoch imagines as "other" remains constant. Then we realized that within this continuity of the emblematic function of the feminine we should make a distinction between its use as the embodiment of an objective truth about nature or reality and its self-conscious use as trope. What these conclusions suggest is that the fate of plot seems to have been interwoven with a mystique of presence, a belief in the power of language to incarnate and embody the real. As long as the process of doubling and excommunication it practices was endorsed and supported by contemporary belief in the power of language to (re)present a reality, the family romance could be used un-self-consciously. Now that this belief seems lost, the process of differentiation of plot can no longer function as an ordering of the world, an act of separating black from white, good from evil, chaos from cosmos in imitation of the divine institution of order in Genesis. The differentiation of plot has now grown to portray the self-reflexive mirroring of the duplicity of the medium language. The closure of classic plot becomes the *mise en abîme* of the so-called naïve illusion that language can coincide with apotheosis; and as the power of language to suggest objective presence wanes, the metaphor of woman (as groundlessness, as source of duplicity and lie, which had always been identified with what Frye called the "daimonic") changes its negative connotation and grows to symbolize the mediating nature of language itself. As I have said, this development forces us to ask a question about the future of the novel. Can the genre survive as form after the realization that its embodiment of the "other" can never present truth, will always remain a provisional rewriting of origin, identity, or authority—a rhetorical configuration, never an incarnation of presence? Do we still have the desire to try and imagine ways of fleshing out and representing our world now we have come to feel that mimesis is "tootoological" (*FW* 468.5–9) and imitates its own logos of division into self and other?

Indeed, should the novel follow in the self-conscious footsteps of Joyce, whose *Work in Progress* seems the consequent enactment of the insights reached in the writing of *Ulysses?* Or are we witnessing the rise of a new form of fiction in the international, postmodern novel—a strategy of writing beyond the doubleness of representation, beyond mastery or questions of truth and epistemology? Will there be a novel of affirmation, based on the idea of reality itself as "text" or "postcreation," a literature that would be, in Wallace Stevens's words, "the cry of its occasion, / Part of the res itself and not about it," an enunciation without personification, a "Description without Place"?[10] In the terms provided by *Ulysses,* shall we begin to write "letters" rather than to send "picture postcards"?

If that is so, the novel will be carrying out an insight articulated by Derrida in his reading of Lévinas:

> I could not possibly speak of the Other, make of the Other a theme, pronounce the Other as object, in the accusative. I can only, I *must* only speak to the other; that is, I must call him in the vocative, which is not a category, a *case* of speech, but, rather the bursting forth, the very raising up of speech. Categories must be missing for the Other not to be overlooked; but for the Other not to be overlooked, He must present himself as absence, and must appear as nonphenomenal. Always behind its signs and its works, always within its secret interior, and forever discreet, interrupting all historical totalities through its freedom of speech, the face is not "of this world." It is the origin of the world. I can speak *of it* only by speaking *to it.*[11]

In other words, the "novel" of the future may well be the place of articulation of Derrida's "*reaffirmation* (yes, yes) of life, in which the *yes,* which says nothing, describes nothing but itself, the performance of its own event of affirmation."[12] In order to do so, however, it will have to suspend the personification of the "other" of family romance.

[10]"An Ordinary Evening in New Haven," in *The Palm at the End of the Mind: Selected Poems and a Play,* ed. Holly Stevens (New York: Vintage, 1972), p. 338. "Description without Place" is the title of a poem in the same volume, pp. 270–77.

[11]From "Violence and Metaphysics," in *Writing and Difference,* trans. Alan Bass (Chicago: Univ. of Chicago Press, 1978), p. 103.

[12]Derrida, "Living On: Border Lines," trans. James Hulbert, in *Deconstruction and Criticism,* ed. Harold Bloom et al. (New York: Continuum, 1979), p. 104.

Bibliography

Abrams, M. H. *Natural Supernaturalism: Tradition and Revolution in Romantic Literature.* New York: Norton, 1973.

Alter, Robert. *Fielding and the Nature of the Novel.* Cambridge, Mass.: Harvard Univ. Press, 1968.

Attridge, Derek, and Daniel Ferrer, eds. *Post-structuralist Joyce: Essays from the French.* Cambridge: Cambridge Univ. Press, 1984.

Auerbach, Erich. *Mimesis: The Representation of Reality in Western Literature.* 1946; rpt. Princeton: Princeton Univ. Press, 1973.

Bachelard, Gaston. *The Poetics of Space.* Trans. M. Jolas. Boston: Beacon Press, 1969.

Baker, Sheridan, ed. *Tom Jones: An Authoritative Text.* New York: Norton, 1973.

Bal, Mieke. "The Narrating and the Focalizing: A Theory of the Agents in Narrative." *Style* 17 (1983), 234–70.

——. *Narratology: Introduction to the Theory of Narrative.* Trans. Christine van Boheemen. Toronto: Univ. of Toronto Press, 1985.

Barthes, Roland. "Introduction à l'analyse structurale des récits." In *Poétique du récit.* Paris: Seuil, 1977, pp. 7–58.

——. *S/Z: An Essay.* Trans. Richard Miller. New York: Hill and Wang, 1974.

Battestin, Martin C. "Fielding's Definition of Wisdom: Some Functions of Ambiguity and Emblem in *Tom Jones.*" *ELH* 35 (1968), 188–217. Rpt. in *Tom Jones,* ed. Baker, pp. 817–44.

——. "Henry Fielding, Sarah Fielding, and 'the Dreadful Sin of Incest.'" *Novel* 13, 1 (1979), 6–19.

——. *The Moral Basis of Fielding's Art: A Study of "Joseph Andrews."* Middletown, Conn.: Wesleyan Univ. Press, 1959.

——. *The Providence of Wit: Aspects of Form in Augustan Literature and the Arts.* Oxford: Clarendon Press, 1974.

——. "*Tom Jones:* The Argument of Design." In *The Augustan Milieu: Essays*

Presented to Louis A. Landa, ed. Henry K. Miller et al. Oxford: Clarendon Press, 1970, pp. 289–320.

Beer, Gillian. *Darwin's Plots: Evolutionary Narrative in Darwin, George Eliot and Nineteenth-Century Fiction.* London: Routledge and Kegan Paul, 1983.

Blanchard, Frederic T. *Fielding the Novelist: A Study in Historical Criticism.* New York: Russell and Russell, 1966.

Boheemen-Saaf, Christine van. "The Semiotics of Plot: Towards a Typology of Fictions." *Poetics Today* 3, 4 (1982), 89–97.

Bonaparte, Marie. "The Murders in the Rue Morgue." *Psychoanalytic Quarterly* 4 (1935), 259–93.

Brontë, Charlotte. *Jane Eyre.* Ed. Q. D. Leavis. 1847; rpt. Harmondsworth, Eng.: Penguin, 1976.

Brooks, Peter. *Reading for the Plot: Design and Intention in Narrative.* New York: Knopf, 1984.

Brown, Homer Obed. "*Tom Jones:* The 'Bastard' of History." *Boundary 2* 7, 2 (1979), 201–33.

Budgen, Frank. *James Joyce and the Making of "Ulysses."* 1934; rpt. Bloomington: Indiana Univ. Press, 1973.

Burke, Kenneth. *The Rhetoric of Religion.* Boston: Beacon Press, 1961.

———. *Terms for Order.* Ed. Stanley Edgar Hyman. Bloomington: Indiana Univ. Press, 1964.

Caserio, Robert L. *Plot, Story, and the Novel: From Dickens and Poe to the Modern Period.* Princeton: Princeton Univ. Press, 1979.

Cassirer, Ernst. *The Philosophy of the Enlightenment.* Trans. Fritz C. A. Koelln and James P. Pettegrove. Princeton: Princeton Univ. Press, 1951.

Chase, Cynthia. "The Decomposition of the Elephants: Double-Reading *Daniel Deronda.*" *PMLA* 93 (1978), 215–28.

Cixous, Hélène. *The Exile of James Joyce.* Trans. Sally A. Purcell. 1968; London: Calder, 1976.

———. *La jeune née.* Paris: 10/18, 1975.

Coleridge, Samuel Taylor. *Unpublished Letters of Samuel Taylor Coleridge: Including Certain Letters Republished from Original Sources.* Vol. II. Ed. Earl Leslie Griggs. New Haven: Yale Univ. Press, 1933.

Coward, Rosalind, and John Ellis. *Language and Materialism: Developments in Semiology and the Theory of the Subject.* London: Routledge, 1977.

Crane, R. S. "The Plot of *Tom Jones.*" *Journal of General Education* (1950), 112–30. Rpt. in *Tom Jones,* ed. Baker, pp. 844–70.

Culler, Jonathan. *On Deconstruction: Theory and Criticism after Structuralism.* Ithaca: Cornell Univ. Press, 1982.

———. *The Pursuit of Signs: Semiotics, Literature, Deconstruction.* Ithaca: Cornell Univ. Press, 1981.

Danahy, Michael. "Le roman est-il chose femelle?" *Poétique* 25 (1976), 85–106.

Danielson, Dennis R. "*Imago Dei,* 'Filial Freedom,' and Miltonic Theodicy." *ELH* 47 (1980), 670–82.

Darwin, Charles. *The Origin of Species*. Ed. J. W. Burrow. Harmondsworth, Eng.: Penguin, 1979.

Deleuze, Gilles, and Félix Guattari. *Anti-Oedipus: Capitalism and Schizophrenia*. Trans. R. Hurley et al. New York: Viking Press, 1977.

Deming, Robert H., ed. *James Joyce: The Critical Heritage*. Vol. I: *1907–1927*. London: Routledge and Kegan Paul, 1970.

Derrida, Jacques. *La dissémination*. Paris: Seuil, 1972.

——. "Le facteur de la vérité." *Poétique* 21 (1975), 96–147.

——. "Living On: *Border* Lines." Trans. James Hulbert. In *Deconstruction and Criticism*, ed. Harold Bloom et al. New York: Continuum, 1979, pp. 75–177.

——. *Spurs: Nietzsche's Styles*. Trans. Barbara Harlow. Chicago: Univ. of Chicago Press, 1979.

——. "Two Words for Joyce." In *Post-structuralist Joyce: Essays from the French*, ed. Derek Attridge and Daniel Ferrer. Cambridge: Cambridge Univ. Press, 1984, pp. 145–60.

——. *Writing and Difference*. Trans. Alan Bass. Chicago: Univ. of Chicago Press, 1978.

Descartes, René. *Philosophical Writings*. Trans. N. K. Smith. New York: Modern Library, 1958.

Dessner, Lawrence Jay. "*Great Expectations:* 'The Ghost of a Man's Own Father.'" *PMLA* 91 (1978), 436–49.

Dewey, John. *The Influence of Darwin on Philosophy*. New York: Holt, 1910.

Dickens, Charles. *Bleak House*. Ed. Duane DeVries. Crowell Critical Library. New York: Thomas Y. Crowell, 1971.

Eagleton, Terry. *The Rape of Clarissa: Writing, Sexuality and Class Struggle in Samuel Richardson*. Oxford: Blackwell, 1982.

Eco, Umberto. *Semiotics and the Philosophy of Language*. Bloomington: Indiana Univ. Press, 1984.

——. *A Theory of Semiotics*. Bloomington: Indiana Univ. Press, 1976.

Eddins, Dwight. "*Ulysses:* The Search for the Logos." *ELH* 47 (1980), 804–19.

Eliade, Mircea. *The Sacred and the Profane: The Nature of Religion*. Trans. Willard R. Trask. New York: Harcourt, Brace and World, 1959.

——. *The Two and the One*. Trans. J. M. Cohen. New York: Harper and Row, 1969.

Eliot, Thomas Stearns. "*Ulysses,* Order and Myth." *Dial* 75 (1923), 480–83. Rpt. in *James Joyce,* ed. Robert H. Deming, pp. 268–72.

Ellmann, Mary. *Thinking about Women*. New York: Harcourt Brace Jovanovich, 1968.

Ellmann, Richard. *James Joyce*. New and rev. ed. New York: Oxford Univ. Press, 1982.

——. *Ulysses on the Liffey*. New York: Oxford Univ. Press, 1972.

——, ed. *Selected Letters of James Joyce*. New York: Viking Press, 1975.

Else, Gerard F. *Aristotle's Poetics: The Argument*. Cambridge, Mass.: Harvard Univ. Press, 1963.

Engell, James. *The Creative Imagination: Enlightenment to Romanticism*. Cambridge, Mass.: Harvard Univ. Press, 1981.

Engler, Rudolf H. *Die Sonne als Symbol: Der Schlüssel zu den Mysterien*. Zürich: Melanthius, 1962.

Ermarth, Elizabeth. "Realism, Perspective and the Novel." *Critical Inquiry* 7 (1981), 499–521.

Felman, Shoshana. "On Reading Poetry: Reflections on the Limits and Possibilities of Psychoanalytic Approaches." In *The Literary Freud: Mechanisms of Defense and the Poetic Will,* ed. J. H. Smith. Psychiatry and the Humanities 4. New Haven: Yale Univ. Press, 1980, pp. 119–49.

Fielding, Henry. *Amelia*. Ed. Martin Battestin. The Wesleyan Edition of the Works of Henry Fielding. Oxford: Clarendon Press, 1983.

——. *The History of Tom Jones, A Foundling*. 2 vols. Ed. Martin Battestin and Fredson Bowers. The Wesleyan Edition of the Works of Henry Fielding. Oxford: Clarendon Press, 1974.

Fletcher, Angus. *Allegory: The Theory of a Symbolic Mode*. Ithaca: Cornell Univ. Press, 1964.

Foucault, Michel. *The Order of Things: An Archaeology of the Human Sciences*. Trans. anon. New York: Random House, 1973.

Fradin, Joseph I. "Will and Society in *Bleak House*." *PMLA* 81 (1966), 95–109.

French, Marilyn. *The Book as World: James Joyce's "Ulysses."* Cambridge, Mass.: Harvard Univ. Press, 1976.

Freud, Sigmund. *Moses and Monotheism*. Trans. Katherine Jones. 1939; rpt. New York: Vintage, 1967.

——. *Standard Edition of the Complete Psychological Works of Sigmund Freud*. Ed. James Strachey. London: Hogarth, 1953–72.

Friedman, Alan. *The Turn of the Novel*. New York: Oxford Univ. Press, 1966.

Froula, Christine. "When Eve Reads Milton: Undoing the Canonical Economy." *Critical Inquiry* 10 (1983), 321–48.

Frye, Northrop. *Anatomy of Criticism: Four Essays*. Princeton: Princeton Univ. Press, 1973.

——. *The Secular Scripture: A Study of the Structure of Romance*. Cambridge, Mass.: Harvard Univ. Press, 1976.

Fussell, Paul. *The Rhetorical World of Augustan Humanism: Ethics and Imagery from Swift to Burke*. Oxford: Clarendon Press, 1965.

Garrett, Peter K. "Double Plots and Dialogical Form in Victorian Fiction." *Nineteenth-Century Fiction* 32, 1 (1977), 1–18.

Gilbert, Sandra M., and Susan Gubar. *The Madwoman in the Attic: The Woman Writer and the Nineteenth-Century Literary Imagination*. New Haven: Yale Univ. Press, 1979.

Gilbert, Stuart. *James Joyce's "Ulysses."* 1930; rpt. New York: Vintage, 1955.

——, ed. *Letters of James Joyce*. London: Faber and Faber, 1957.

Girard, René. *Violence and the Sacred*. Trans. Patrick Gregory. Baltimore: Johns Hopkins Univ. Press, 1977.

Goux, Jean-Joseph. *Economie et symbolique*. Paris: Seuil, 1973.

——. *Les iconoclastes*. Paris: Seuil, 1978.

Graff, Gerald. *Literature against Itself: Literary Ideas in Modern Society*. Chicago: Univ. of Chicago Press, 1979.

Greimas, A. J. "Les actants, les acteurs, et les figures." In *Sémiotique narrative et textuelle*, ed. C. Chabrol. Paris: Larousse, 1973.

Guthrie, W. K. C. "Flux and *Logos* in Heraclitus." In *The Pre-Socratics*, ed. A. P. D. Mourelatus. New York: Anchor/Doubleday, 1974, pp. 197–213.

Hamon, Philippe. "Pour un statut sémiologique du personnage." In *Poétique du récit*, pp. 117–63.

Hart, Clive, and David Hayman, eds. *James Joyce's "Ulysses": Critical Essays*. Berkeley: Univ. of California Press, 1974.

Hartman, Geoffrey. *The Fate of Reading*. Chicago: Univ. of Chicago Press, 1975.

Harvey, W. J. *Character and the Novel*. Ithaca: Cornell Univ. Press, 1965.

Hayman, David. *"Ulysses": The Mechanics of Meaning*. Englewood Cliffs, N.J.: Prentice-Hall, 1970.

Heath, Stephen. *The Nouveau Roman: A Study in the Practice of Writing*. London: Elek Books, 1972.

Hegel, G. W. F. *Hegel's Logic*. Trans. William Wallace. Oxford: Clarendon Press, 1975.

——. *The Phenomenology of Mind*. Trans. J. B. Baillie. New York: Harper and Row, 1967.

Heidegger, Martin. *Identity and Difference*. Trans. Joan Stambaugh. New York: Harper and Row. 1969.

——. *An Introduction to Metaphysics*. Trans. Ralph Manheim. New Haven: Yale Univ. Press, 1980.

——. *Poetry, Language, Thought*. Trans. Albert Hofstadter. New York: Harper and Row. 1971.

Heilbrun, Carolyn G. "Women, Men, Theories, and Literature." *Profession 81: Selected Articles from the Bulletin of the Association of Departments of English and the Association of Departments of Foreign Languages* (Spring 1985), 25–30.

Horkheimer, Max, and Theodor W. Adorno. *Dialectic of Enlightenment*. Trans. J. Cumming. 1944; rpt. New York: Seabury Press, 1972.

Hume, David. *Dialogues concerning Natural Religion*. Ed. Norman Kemp Smith. Oxford: Oxford Univ. Press, 1935.

Hunter, J. Paul. *Occasional Form: Henry Fielding and the Chains of Circumstance*. Baltimore: Johns Hopkins Univ. Press, 1975.

Irigaray, Luce. *Ce sexe qui n'est pas un*. Paris: Minuit, 1977. In English: *This Sex Which Is Not One*. Ithaca: Cornell Univ. Press, 1985.

——. *Speculum de l'autre femme*. Paris: Minuit. 1974. In English: *Speculum of the Other Woman*. Ithaca: Cornell Univ. Press, 1985.

Irwin, John T. *Doubling and Incest/Repetition and Revenge: A Speculative Reading of Faulkner*. Baltimore: Johns Hopkins Univ. Press, 1975.

Iser, Wolfgang. *The Implied Reader: Patterns of Communication in Prose Fiction from Bunyan to Beckett*. Baltimore: Johns Hopkins Univ. Press, 1974.

Jameson, Fredric. "Magical Narrative: Romance as Genre." *NLH* 7, 1 (1975), 135–63.

Jardine, Alice A. *Gynesis: Configurations of Woman and Modernity*. Ithaca: Cornell Univ. Press, 1985.

Jehlen, Myra. "Archimedes and the Paradox of Feminist Criticism." *Signs* 6 (1981), 575–601.

Johnson, Edgar. *Charles Dickens: His Tragedy and Triumph*. New York: Viking Press, 1977.

Jones, Ernest. *Hamlet and Oedipus*. New York: Norton, 1976.

Joyce, James. *Dubliners*. London: Jonathan Cape, 1927.

———. *Finnegans Wake*. New York: Viking Press, 1974.

———. *A Portrait of the Artist as a Young Man*. London: Granada, 1977.

———. *Stephen Hero*. Ed. Theodore Spencer. New York: New Directions, 1959.

———. *Ulysses: A Critical and Synoptic Edition*. Ed. Hans W. Gabler. New York: Garland, 1984.

Jung, C. G. *Symbols of Transformation: An Analysis of the Prelude to a Case of Schizophrenia*. Vol. I. Trans. R. F. C. Hull. New York: Harper and Brothers, 1962.

Kahler, Erich. *The Inward Turn of Narrative*. Trans. Richard and Clara Winston. Bollingen Series 83. Princeton: Princeton Univ. Press, 1973.

Kain, Richard M. "The Significance of Stephen's Meeting Bloom: A Survey of Interpretations." In *Fifty Years: "Ulysses,"* ed. Thomas F. Staley. Bloomington: Indiana Univ. Press, 1974, pp. 147–60.

Keener, Frederick M. *The Chain of Becoming: The Philosophical Tale, the Novel, and a Neglected Realism of the Enlightenment: Swift, Montesquieu, Voltaire, Johnson, and Austen*. New York: Columbia Univ. Press, 1983.

Kenner, Hugh. "Circe." In *James Joyce's "Ulysses,"* ed. Hart and Hayman, pp. 341–63.

———. *Joyce's Voices*. London: Faber and Faber, 1978.

Kermode, Frank. *The Sense of an Ending: Studies in the Theory of Fiction*. 1966; rpt. New York: Oxford Univ. Press, 1973.

Kimball, Jean. "Family Romance and Hero Myth: A Psychoanalytic Context for the Paternity Theme in *Ulysses*." *James Joyce Quarterly* 20 (1983), 161–74.

Krafft-Ebing, Richard von. *Psychopathia Sexualis*. Stuttgart: Enke, 1894.

Kristeva, Julia. *Desire in Language: A Semiotic Approach to Literature and Art*. Ed. Leon S. Roudiez. New York: Columbia Univ. Press, 1980.

Lacan, Jacques. *Ecrits: A Selection*. Trans. Alan Sheridan. New York: Norton, 1977.

——. "The Seminar on 'The Purloined Letter.'" Trans. Jeffrey Mehlman. In *French Freud*. *Yale French Studies* 48 (1972), 38–72.

——. "Le sinthome: Bouts-de-réel." *Le séminaire de Jacques Lacan*. Text established by J. A. Miller. *Ornicar* 9 (1982), 32–40.

Laplanche, Jean, and J.-B. Pontalis. "Fantasmes originaires, fantasmes des origines, origines du fantasme." *Les Temps Modernes* (April 1964), 1833–68.

——. *Life and Death in Psychoanalysis*. Trans. Jeffrey Mehlman. Baltimore: Johns Hopkins Univ. Press, 1976.

Lasch, Christopher. *The Culture of Narcissism: American Life in an Age of Diminishing Expectations*. New York: Norton, 1978.

Lawrence, Karen. *The Odyssey of Style in "Ulysses."* Princeton: Princeton Univ. Press, 1981.

Leach, Edmund. *Genesis as Myth and Other Essays*. London: Jonathan Cape, 1969.

Lévinas, Emmanuel. *Totality and Infinity*. Trans. Alphonso Lingis. Pittsburgh: Duquesne Univ. Press, 1969.

Lévi-Strauss, Claude. *The Elementary Structures of Kinship*. Trans. J. H. Bell and J. R. von Sturmer. Boston: Beacon Press, 1969.

——. *Structural Anthropology*. Trans. Claire Jacobson and Brooke Grundfest-Schoepf. Harmondsworth, Eng.: Penguin, 1972.

Lewis, Percy Wyndham. *Time and Western Man*. London: Chatto and Windus, 1927.

Litz, A. Walton. *The Art of James Joyce: Method and Design in "Ulysses" and "Finnegans Wake"*. London: Oxford Univ. Press, 1961.

——. "Ithaca." In *James Joyce's "Ulysses,"* ed. Hart and Hayman, pp. 385–407.

Lloyd, Genevieve. *The Man of Reason: "Male" and "Female" in Western Philosophy*. London: Methuen, 1984.

Lotman, Jury M. "The Origin of Plot in the Light of Typology." *Poetics Today* 1, 1/2 (1979), 161–85.

——. *Die Struktur literarischer Texte*. Munich: Wilhelm Fink, 1972.

Lukács, Georg. *The Theory of the Novel: A Historico-Philosophical Essay on the Forms of Great Epic Literature*. Trans. Anna Bostock. 1920; rpt. Cambridge, Mass.: MIT Press, 1975.

MacCabe, Colin. *James Joyce and the Revolution of the Word*. London: Macmillan, 1978.

Macherey, Pierre. *Pour une théorie de la production littéraire*. Paris: Maspéro, 1966.

McKillop, Alan Dugald. *The Early Masters of English Fiction*. Lawrence: Univ. of Kansas Press, 1956.

Maddox, James H., Jr. *Joyce's "Ulysses" and the Assault upon Character*. New Brunswick, N.J.: Rutgers Univ. Press, 1978.

Maranda, Elli Köngäs, and Pierre Maranda. "Strukturelle Modelle in der

Folklore." In *Literaturwissenchaft und Linguistik,* ed. Jens Ihwe. Vol. II. Frankfurt: Athenäum Fischer Taschenbuch, 1973, pp. 127–215.

Miller, Henry Knight. *Henry Fielding's "Tom Jones" and the Romance Tradition. ELS* Monograph Series 6. Victoria, B.C.: Univ. of Victoria Press, 1976.

Miller, J. Hillis. *Charles Dickens: The World of His Novels.* Cambridge, Mass.: Harvard Univ. Press, 1958.

——. *Fiction and Repetition.* Cambridge, Mass.: Harvard Univ. Press, 1982.

——. *The Form of Victorian Fiction: Thackeray, Dickens, Trollope, George Eliot, Meredith, and Hardy.* Notre Dame: Univ. of Notre Dame Press, 1968.

Miller, Nancy K. "The Exquisite Cadavers: Women in Eighteenth-Century Fiction." *Diacritics* 5, 4 (1975), 37–43.

Milton, John. *Poetical Works.* Ed. Douglas Bush. London: Oxford Univ. Press, 1966.

Morris, Humphrey. "The Need to Connect: Representations of Freud's Psychical Apparatus." In *The Literary Freud: Mechanisms of Defense and the Poetic Will,* ed. Joseph H. Smith. Psychiatry and the Humanities 4. New Haven: Yale Univ. Press, 1980, pp. 309–45.

Munster, Arno. "Psycho-analysis and Schizo-analysis: An Interview with Félix Guattari." *Sémiotext(e)* 2, 3 (1977), 77–86.

New, Melvyn. "'The Grease of God': The Form of Eighteenth-Century Fiction." *PMLA* 91 (1976), 235–44.

Newsom, Robert. *Dickens on the Romantic Side of Familiar Things: "Bleak House" and the Novel Tradition.* New York: Columbia Univ. Press, 1977.

Norris, Margot. *The Decentered Universe of "Finnegans Wake": A Structuralist Analysis.* Baltimore: Johns Hopkins Univ. Press, 1976.

Pabst, Michael. *Wiener Grafik um 1900.* Munich: Schreiber, 1984.

Panofsky, Erwin. *Meaning in the Visual Arts.* Garden City, N.Y.: Doubleday, 1955.

Parrinder, Patrick. "These Heavy Sands Are Language. . . .", *James Joyce Broadsheet* 7 (February 1982), 1.

Paulson, Ronald. *Emblem and Expression: Meaning in English Art of the Eighteenth Century.* London: Thames and Hudson, 1975.

Pederson-Krag, Geraldine. "Detective Stories and the Primal Scene." *Psychoanalytic Quarterly* 18 (1949), 207–14.

Poétique du récit. Paris: Seuil, 1977.

Poovey, Mary. "Journeys from This World to the Next: The Providential Promise in *Clarissa* and *Tom Jones." ELH* 43 (1976), 300–15.

Pope, Alexander. *Collected Poems.* Ed. Bonamy Dobrée. London: Dent, 1963.

Pound, Ezra. "Pound on Ulysses and Flaubert." In *James Joyce,* ed. Robert H. Deming, pp. 263–68.

Rabaté, Jean-Michel. "A Clown's Inquest into Paternity." In *The Fictional Father: Lacanian Readings of the Text,* ed. Robert Con Davis. Amherst: Univ. of Massachusetts Press, 1981, pp. 73–115.

Rank, Otto. *Beyond Psychology.* New York: Dover, 1958.

———. *The Double: A Psychoanalytic Study*. Trans. Harry Tucker, Jr. 1925; rpt. Chapel Hill: Univ. of North Carolina Press, 1971.

Rawson, C. J. *Henry Fielding and the Augustan Ideal under Stress*. London: Routledge, 1972.

Richardson, Samuel Taylor. Letter to Mrs. Donellan, February 22, 1752. In *Novel and Romance, 1700–1800: A Documentary Record*, ed. Ioan Williams. London: Routledge and Kegan Paul, 1970, p. 174.

Robert, Marthe. *Roman des origines et origines du roman*. Paris: Bernard Grasset, 1972.

Rycroft, Charles. *Imagination and Reality: Psychoanalytical Essays, 1951–61* London: Hogarth, 1968.

Said, Edward W. *Beginnings: Intention and Method*. New York: Basic Books, 1975.

Segre, Cesare. *Structures and Time: Narration, Poetry, Models*. Trans. John Meddemmen. Chicago: Univ. of Chicago Press, 1979.

Senn, Fritz. *Joyce's Dislocutions: Essays on Reading as Translation*. Ed. J. P. Riquelme. Baltimore: Johns Hopkins Univ. Press, 1984.

Shapiro, Barbara J. "Latitudinarianism and Science in Seventeenth-Century England." In *The Intellectual Revolution of the Seventeenth Century*, ed. Charles Webster. London: Routledge, 1974, pp. 286–317.

Shechner, Mark. *Joyce in Nighttown: A Psychoanalytic Inquiry into "Ulysses."* Berkeley: Univ. of California Press, 1974.

Sklovskij, Viktor. "The Mystery Novel: Dickens' *Little Dorrit*." In *Readings in Russian Poetics: Formalist and Structuralist Views*, ed. Ladislaw Matejka and Krystyna Pomorska. Ann Arbor: Michigan Slavic Publications, 1978, pp. 220–27.

Spacks, Patricia Meyer. *The Female Imagination: A Literary and Psychological Investigation of Women's Writing*. London: Allen and Unwin, 1976.

Spilka, Mark. *Dickens and Kafka: A Mutual Interpretation*. Bloomington: Indiana Univ. Press, 1963.

Spivak, Gayatri Chakravorty. "Displacement and the Discourse of Woman." In *Displacement: Derrida and After*, ed. Mark Krupnick. Bloomington: Indiana Univ. Press, 1983, pp. 169–96.

———. "Translator's Preface." Jacques Derrida, *Of Grammatology*. Baltimore: Johns Hopkins Univ. Press, 1976, pp. ix–lxxxix.

Stanford, W. B. *The Ulysses Theme: A Study in the Adaptability of a Traditional Hero*. New York: Barnes and Noble, 1964.

Stevens, Wallace. *The Palm at the End of the Mind: Selected Poems and a Play*. Ed. Holly Stevens. New York: Vintage, 1972.

Stoehr, Taylor. *Dickens: The Dreamer's Stance*. Ithaca: Cornell Univ. Press, 1965.

Stoll, E. E. *Art and Artifice in Shakespeare: A Study in Dramatic Contrast and Illusion*. 1933; rpt. New York: Barnes and Noble, 1963.

Symons, Arthur. "Das Weib in der Darstellung Aubrey Beardsleys." *Ver Sacrum* 6 (1903), 117.

Taylor, Mark C. *Journeys to Selfhood: Hegel and Kierkegaard.* Berkeley: Univ. of California Press, 1980.

Thomas, Brook. *James Joyce's "Ulysses": A Book of Many Happy Returns.* Baton Rouge: Louisiana State Univ. Press, 1982.

Tillyard, E. M. W. *The Epic Strain in the English Novel.* Fair Lawn, N.J.: Essential Books, 1958.

Tindall, W. Y. *James Joyce: His Way of Interpreting the Modern World.* New York: Charles Scribner's Sons, 1950.

Van Ghent, Dorothy. "The Dickens World: A View from Todgers's." In *Dickens: A Collection of Critical Essays,* ed. M. Price. Englewood Cliffs, N.J.: Prentice-Hall, 1967, pp. 24–38.

Weeks, Jeffery. *Sex, Politics and Society: The Regulation of Sexuality since 1800.* London: Longman, 1981.

Weinstein, Arnold. *Fictions of the Self, 1550–1800.* Princeton: Princeton Univ. Press, 1984.

Wilden, Anthony. "Lacan and the Discourse of the Other." In Jacques Lacan, *The Language of the Self: The Function of Language in Psychoanalysis.* Trans. Anthony Wilden. New York: Dell, 1968, pp. 159–312.

——. *System and Structure: Essays in Communication and Exchange.* 2d ed. London: Tavistock, 1980.

Winnicott, D. W. *Playing and Reality.* Harmondsworth, Eng.: Penguin, 1980.

Wright, Andrew. *Henry Fielding: Mask and Feast.* Berkeley: Univ. of California Press, 1965.

Zwerdling, Alex. "Esther Summerson Rehabilitated." *PMLA* 88 (1973), 429–39.

Index

Library of Congress Cataloging-in-Publication Data

Boheemen, Christine van.
    The novel as family romance.

    Bibliography: p.
    Includes index.
    1. English fiction—History and criticism. 2. Family in
literature. 3. Psychoanalysis and literature. 4. Fielding, Henry, 1707–
1754. History of Tom Jones. 5. Dickens, Charles, 1812–1870. Bleak
house. 6. Joyce, James, 1882–1941. Ulysses. I. Title.
PR830.F29B64 1987   828'.009'353   87-47553
ISBN 0-8014-1928-X (alk. paper)